Slipstream:
The Autobiography
Of An Air Craftsman

by

Eugene E. Wilson

Slipstream:
The Autobiography
Of An Air Craftsman
by Eugene E. Wilson

ISBN: 978-93-58592-94-8

Published by

DOUBLE 9 BOOKS

2/13-B, Ansari Road
Daryaganj, New Delhi – 110002
info@double9books.com
www.double9books.com
Tel. 011-40042856

ABOUT THE AUTHOR

Eugene E. Wilson, the son of Mr. and Mrs. Eugene Tallmadge Wilson, was born on August 21, 1887, in Dayton, Washington. In Helena, Montana, from 1897 to 1902, his father, a well-known banker in the Tacoma, Washington, region, served as receiver for insolvent banks. Young Eugene attended schools in Helena at that time. He earned his degree from the U.S. Naval Academy in 1908, and in 1911 he married Genevieve Speer. He graduated with a master's in engineering from Columbia University in 1915.Eugene fought in the USS Arkansas during World War I and left the service in 1930. He pursued a career in civil aviation, holding executive positions at Chance Vought Corporation, Sikorsky Aviation Corporation, and Hamilton-Standard Propeller Corporation. Wilson came to be known for important technological advancements such the first carrier task force, long-range fighter bombers, controllable pitch propellers, and radial air-cooled engines. He published books as well. He was still interested in his early Montana links, and he and his father, Eugene T. Wilson, co-wrote an article about the Nez Perce War. Wilson passed away in July 1974.

CONTENTS

PREFACE

To the world at large, Berlin Airlift headlines only highlighted another crisis in the "cold war." Yet behind those headlines lay an epochal event: commercial air transports—not combat aircraft—had become the spearhead of United States foreign policy.

This dramatic incident brought renewed hope to air craftsmen who, nearly a half century earlier, had embarked on a starry-eyed crusade to utilize the airplane for the benefit of mankind. In World War I, they had helped smash the German Kaiser, only to find Hitler rising phoenixlike in his boots. Two decades later, they had strafed Hitler to earth, only to discover a colossal portrait of Joseph Stalin looming beyond a smoke curtain. Still later, as atomic bombs and lethal bacteria became weapons, they were asking themselves, "what next?" when the Berlin Airlift came up with the answer: air cargo, air commerce, air industry, air finance—air power for peace!

In December, 1943, we air craftsmen had our frustrations dramatized at a banquet staged in honor of the Wright brothers on the fortieth anniversary of Kittyhawk. Orville Wright, mouselike in a dinner jacket and obviously uncomfortable, had sat through a barrage of clichés microphoned by air power advocates. When finally called on to respond, he refused point-blank. Later, in an anteroom off the banquet hall, he gave vent to intense bitterness: evil men had seized upon the airplane to make it the most lethal weapon in history; he hated everything about the airplane; he rued the day he and his brother had invented the thing.

We manufacturers, who had engineered their fantastic contraption into a decisive instrument of World War II, echoed Orville Wright's concern. Our lives had been a kaleidoscopic drama of "the five Ms": men, management, money, materials, machines. Across our stage had walked the big names of a bloody quarter century involving two world wars. The setting had been fogged by haze from smoke-filled Washington hotel rooms and highlighted by klieg lights in Congressional investigating committees. Sucked by our own slipstream into the maelstrom of politics, we had all but lost sight of the dim off-stage shape of One World being remorselessly forged by air transport. Whether this should be a world of peace in our time, or whether it must wait on centuries of slavery, would depend on what we Americans did with the airplanes we had created.

Following the 1918 Armistice, we had carelessly taken a wrong turning. After the Italian General Douhet in his book *Command of the Air* had extolled the virtues of the air bombardment of civil populations, Brig. Gen. William Mitchell raised the air power banner at home. Later Alexander P. de Seversky, a former Russian combat pilot, spread the Douhet gospel in a best seller, *Victory Through Airpower*. When the American press followed this lead, air force in war became the major role of the airplane.

This Douhet doctrine is, of course, the negation of the philosophy expressed in the great body of international law which developed following the Dark Ages. Chivalry, a concept devised by Christendom to protect civilization from destruction by the Four Horsemen, had introduced the era in which differences were resolved through conflicts between military forces, rather than the destruction of civil populations. Behind the morality of the principle lay the practical consideration that it spared the conqueror the expense of rebuilding establishments which he himself might otherwise have battered down.

If Douhet, in our time, mistook air force for the foundation of air power, our British cousins, in the Elizabethan Era, had not failed to look at sea power through the correct end of the telescope. After fifteenth-century geographic discoveries had placed Britain at the crossroads of maritime commerce to America, Asia, and Africa, her merchants and mariners recognized freedom to trade as the guarantee of prosperity. The basic requirement for freedom to trade was a superior fleet, utilized to guarantee, hopefully through measures short of war, the right of all and sundry to proceed upon their lawful occasions. Having seen the vision, the English mustered the courage and enterprise to seize control of the sea and employ it to build Pax Britannica, a period of spiritual as well as material progress, motivated by the Christian ideal, such as the world had not hitherto known.

In the early 1930's, after American commercial air transport had revealed its potentialities, we Americans likewise stood at a crossroads. Had we but recognized our opportunity and displayed the courage and enterprise to foster a forward-looking air policy, we might have so directed our superior technology in the air as to match Pax Britannica with Pax Aeronautica. History discloses that the peaceful progress of civilization has always been paced by discoveries in transport. Had we recognized the revolutionary character of air transport, we might have removed enough of the causes of war to have avoided World War II. Instead, we hamstrung our own air power and provided our enemies with a favorable opportunity to seize control of the air.

The performance of air transport in the war revealed that the air is like an ocean that affords uninterrupted access to any spot on land or sea. Experience proves that the airplane, contrary to widespread belief, is inherently an economical vehicle. It demands no costly investment in fixed rights of way; its right of way is the air, which is free and infinitely flexible. Since the speed of the airplane permits it to transport goods a maximum of ton-miles for a minimum of initial investment, airline ownership of property of any kind is at a minimum. During the thirty-year life of air-mail service, the United States Post Office Department has recovered through sales of air-mail stamps alone more than it has paid out to the airlines for carrying the mails. While segments of the airline transport system have been subsidized in the interests of national security, the system as a whole has proved self-sustaining. The Postmaster General regards air mail not as an expense but as an investment. He recently stated publicly, "Probably no investment made by this government ever returned greater national benefits in commercial and cultural progress, and national security."

It therefore seems a pity that, at the moment when providence has placed in American hands the instrument with which to speed world recovery, we should lack the wit to recognize the opportunity, and the initiative, courage, and enterprise to exploit it. Where the mission of the Air Force is to enforce the peace, the major role of the airplane is in air commerce, the key to world recovery. Responsibility for utilizing air power for peace resides with the people of the United States.

To air craftsmen, Orville Wright's reaction served to emphasize the fact that all of us had been sucked up by the slipstream of our own propellers and whirled about like withered leaves or bits of waste paper. Yet underneath we knew that this apparently confused and wasteful process had accelerated progress. As engineers, we realized that when an airplane is earthbound with its engine revving up, the engine's power is all wasted in noise and heat. In free flight, on the other hand, an airscrew converts upward of 80 per cent of its power into "effective forward thrust," leaving but 20 per cent as "slip." Our slipstream is therefore an efficient machine measured by any standard. To permit aviation to soar to new heights we must cast off its shackles. To this end we must needs understand its fundamental import.

My own thinking along this line began one November day in 1918, while watching the vaunted German High Seas Fleet surrender to the famed British Grand Fleet. At that time I was chief engineer of the battleship *Arkansas*, one of five American vessels that comprised Adm. Hugh Rodman's Sixth Battle Squadron of Sir David Beatty's Grand Fleet. Beatty had a secret weapon, a force of aircraft carriers. Some observers ascribed the German surrender to knowledge of this fact, yet Beatty himself realized that victory had been won, not by the ironclads which, since Jutland had not come into decisive action, but by the battered nine-knot tramps, the doughty drifters and trawlers, the troop-carrying liners and the wallowing tankers—merchantmen that had been keeping the life blood coursing through the Empire's veins. Watching this triumph of sea power, even as the shadow of an airplane flitted across the gun turrets of the Grand Fleet, I had sought to draw an analogy between sea power and air power but had dismissed the idea because there had been no such thing then as commercial air transport.

The war over, Rear Adm. William Adger Moffett, founder and first Chief of the Navy Bureau of Aeronautics, called me in from general service to specialize in aircraft engine production and, incidentally, to lend him a hand in his fight with Brig. Gen. William Mitchell, Assistant Chief, U.S. Army Air Service. This conflict between belligerent giants was more than a revival of the old Army-Navy Game. To the admiral, an inspiring leader and astute politician, the task was to prevent Mitchell, a brilliant pilot and ardent air enthusiast, from monopolizing all aviation—commercial, naval, and military—under an administrative setup resembling the new British Air Ministry. This separate and independent department, in the opinion of the admiral, had already begun to wreck British naval aviation and thus undermine British sea power.

Amid the rough and tumble of interdepartmental politics, I discovered the fundamental precepts of aeronautic technology: the power plant was the heart of the airplane; progress in its development could be measured in terms of "pounds per horsepower"; the key to technological progress was competition within the private manufacturing and transport industries; under pressure of free competition, the "impossible" got done today—the fantastic took a little longer. It was no accident that the airplane had been invented in America or that it had here attained its maximum development. Technological leadership stemmed directly from the concept under which our government had been created, the creative idea of the dignity of the individual and his innate right to liberty under just law.

In Washington, the struggle over the separate air force climaxed in the summer of 1925. The big Navy rigid airship *Shenandoah*, barnstorming over western country fairs, was destroyed in Ohio by a line squall. General Mitchell, previously exiled to San Antonio, Texas, seized upon the crash as a favorable moment for hurling charges at both the Army and the Navy of their treasonable neglect of aviation. President Calvin Coolidge, in order to sift the charges, convened a public inquiry by a board of distinguished citizens under the chairmanship of Dwight W. Morrow. Testifying before the Board, Admiral Moffett took sharp issue with Mitchell on the question of the independent air force, but took advantage of the opportunity to outline the basis of a constructive national air policy.

The Morrow Board, while disapproving the Mitchell proposal for the time being, did recommend a separate air corps status in the Army for military aviation. It took strong exception to the idea of including air transport in any military establishment and urged instead its orderly development under civil authority and preferably by competitive private industry. The Board's recommendations were approved by the President and transmitted to Congress where they were quickly implemented by the Air Corps Act of 1926 and the Air Commerce Act of the same year. These acts fixed responsibility for aeronautic development upon the several government agencies concerned.

General Mitchell was convicted by an Army court-martial of "conduct unbecoming," but was permitted to resign. He died ten years later, having become firmly established in the public mind as a man of vision martyred by reactionaries. Admiral Moffett followed up the Morrow Board findings with a recommendation for legislation establishing a five-year development program for naval aviation. The Army followed suit. The Post Office inaugurated contract air mail. In the favorable climate induced by the Morrow Board policy, American aviation attained the world leadership which it held until after the air-mail contracts were canceled in the middle 1930's.

Having become interested in naval aviation as a career, I qualified as a naval aviator and later became Chief of Staff to Rear Adm. Joseph M. Reeves, Commander, Aircraft Squadrons, Battle Fleet. There I helped commission the new aircraft carriers *Saratoga* and *Lexington*, equipping their air squadrons with the new aircraft we had created in the Bureau of Aeronautics. During fleet maneuvers we developed the new tactical concept of the carrier task force, and in January, 1929, by delivering a successful attack on the Panama Canal from a point 150 miles at sea, we demonstrated the revolutionary strategy of a mobile-based, long-range, naval air striking force, the first American strategic air force. Yet while we succeeded in our demonstration, we failed to impress upon the high command the revolutionary character of the idea. Twelve years later at Pearl Harbor, the Japanese did a better job of selling. Paradoxically enough, Admiral Reeves, as a member of the Roberts Board, went out to Honolulu to investigate the wartime effectiveness of his peacetime concept.

Meanwhile, in January, 1930, I resigned from the Navy to accept a position as chief executive of a subsidiary of the United Aircraft and Transport Corporation, the Hamilton-Standard Propeller Corporation. Within a year I found myself responsible for two additional subsidiaries, Sikorsky and Chance Vought, the one a builder of large flying boats, the other a producer of shipboard aircraft. In private industry, I enlarged my experience in the so-called "aviation game."

When in the middle 1930's the air-mail contracts were suddenly canceled, American aviation received a body blow. Repercussions from the punitive Congressional investigations sponsored by Senators Gerald P. Nye and Hugo Black—now Mr. Justice Black of the United States Supreme Court—interfered with both military and commercial development and halted progress. While American aviation was being kicked around as a political football, Messrs. Hitler, Mussolini, Hirohito, and Stalin seized the favorable opportunity, so unexpectedly handed them, to inaugurate their bids for world dominion under the Douhet doctrine of victory through air force.

The American aircraft manufacturing industry, its domestic market impaired by the abandonment of the Morrow Board policy, was forced to fall back on foreign sales. For a while we existed by selling our superior commercial air transports abroad, and in our frantic struggle to survive, each manufacturer risked everything to develop improved types of possible interest to our government. Early in 1939, when many companies were all but out on their feet, orders from France and England arrived in the nick of time. It was thanks to those orders that when the American aircraft-expansion program was finally undertaken we were able to expand swiftly.

However, this shot in the arm was all but neutralized by the workings of our own Arms Embargo Act. In order to deny France or England access to American arms, Hitler had only to make them belligerents—in other words declare war on them. After he had done so, we repealed the act, and still later President Roosevelt called for 50,000 airplanes. The first news we aircraft manufacturers had of this decision came by way of a radio fireside chat. This released a flood of production, the magic of which surprised us as much as anyone else—a flood on which American air power reversed the tide from sure defeat to certain victory.

Upon our entry into the war, I found myself president of United Aircraft Corporation. In the razzle-dazzle of the wartime Washington merry-go-round, I watched the expansion of air transport until it became a decisive factor in the war. Hurdling the Himalayan Hump and leapfrogging submarine-infested sea lanes, it delivered important persons and critical cargoes to decisive points inaccessible to other forms of transportation. Believing that this performance presaged the advent of expanding air commerce, we manufacturers began investing our earnings in bigger and better transports.

One day Navy Secretary James V. Forrestal sent for me. At the time when some critics were still harping their cry, "too little and too late," he gave me private instructions to cut back production. His problem had become "too much and too soon." The cutback brought us face to face with the nightmare that had haunted our dreams since the outbreak of war. Following the Armistice of 1918, our government had so ruthlessly canceled war contracts that the aircraft industry had been all but destroyed. When I pointed out this danger, the secretary suggested the only possible solution: the aircraft industry must take its story to the public. He advised that I undertake to lead the industry in our campaign for survival.

This made it necessary for me to relinquish the presidency of my company and accept the chairmanship of the board of governors of our trade association. The first step was to decide on an industry policy and obtain agreement on a program. Out of the history of aviation I drew the analogy between sea power and air power and formulated a program of peace through air power. We took for our objective the appointment of a new Presidential advisory commission to hear testimony in public and recommend a new air policy revised to conform with technological developments. As the basis for our operations we covenanted to cooperate with one another in the public interest in matters pertaining to policy but to continue to compete vigorously in our business operations.

In an effort to crystallize aeronautic opinion, I published a book called *Air Power for Peace*. This study, an objective technical treatise, patterned on Adm. A. T. Mahan's *The Influence of Sea Power upon History*, disclosed that, despite spectacular war performances by Army and Navy air forces, the Mahan doctrine still prevailed: victory had again rested with those who had secured to themselves—and denied to their enemies—freedom of communication by sea. No overseas assault could have been mounted nor could our own supply lines have been secured without first subduing German submarines in the Atlantic and sweeping Japanese sea power from the Pacific. Yet in both actions an important new strategic factor had developed: command of the air over the sea had become vital to command of the sea itself. It was the carrier task forces that had proved to be the decisive instruments in both oceans. Furthermore, brilliant, though limited, success by military air transports had disclosed that air power was an integration of air force, air transport, aircraft production, and in fact all that went to make us strong in the air. Yet, until air transport could assume the full burden of overseas trade, victory in war and prosperity in peace must still rest with him who is strong enough—and wise enough—to retain command of the sea. Russia's submarine fleet later gave added strength to this conclusion.

Meanwhile, as spokesman for the aircraft manufacturers, I addressed organizations of all kinds, seeking to interest the molders of public opinion in the air power problem. Our association and our members participated in a nationwide program of public information. The key to our effort was our endeavor to promote the public interest as the means of serving our own enlightened self-interest.

Yet for all our effort, we were unable to get full cooperation from the two other elements of integrated air power, air transport and the armed forces. The Army Air Force, fighting for its autonomy, tangled with naval aviation in a jurisdictional dispute. The airline transport operators, jockeying for individual advantage under the policy of so-called "reasonable regulation," split wide open on such questions as "the chosen instrument." Government agencies, fearful of the possible loss of their prerogatives, gave less than enthusiastic support to our plea for a public policy-forming board. The appointment of the commission therefore lagged, while both airline transport and aircraft manufacturing suffered crippling losses. Convinced that this situation called for a new book on aviation, a sort of bible of air-power, or at least its gospel, I decided to write *Slipstream*. In December, 1946, in order to gain freedom to express my personal points of view without compromising my company, I resigned from United Aircraft.

While it was Mahan, the historian, who first revealed to the world the decisive influence of sea power upon history, it was Richard Hakluyt, author of *The English Voyages*, who inspired Englishmen to exploit sea power to their commercial advantage. By collecting the journals of the world's leading merchants and the adventure narratives of its greatest navigators, and by editing them so as both to entertain his readers and stimulate them to seek their fortunes on the high seas, he influenced the course of history. There are no such journals and narratives of contemporary aviation. Although the whole record is comprised in the lifetimes of a single generation of still-active men so that no protracted research is needed to reveal the intimate background, much of it already tends to become dim, even in the minds of men who wrote the record. Unless it be set down now it may be forever lost, and that would be a pity, for the fantastic story holds lessons that apply equally well to other technological developments such as atomic energy. In undertaking to set forth the intimate narrative of events which, in the last quarter century, have helped shape the destiny of American aviation, I am impelled to proceed partly because of deep convictions and partly because my unusually varied experience gives me a somewhat broader point of view from which to judge the impact of events.

While engaged on this task, I was disturbed to note that matters were going from bad to worse. In the summer of 1948, however, help came from an unexpected source. The Russians imposed their blockade on Berlin. The American public, aroused now to the need for preserving American air power, clamored for action. The Republican Congress voted a Congressional Aviation Policy Board; President Truman countered with his own Air Policy Commission. Before this latter organization, known as the "Finletter Board," the aircraft manufacturers presented a well-prepared case. The airline transport operators, having suffered disastrous losses, were demoralized almost to the point where they were willing to accept a subsidy such as that long paid to the merchant marine. The Air Force, having earlier won its autonomy, made a vigorous plea for funds to provide a strong strategic air force.

Under the circumstances, the Finletter Board, whose report was published under the title, "Survival in the Air Age," naturally gave priority to the military aspects of aviation. The Congressional Aviation Policy Board supported a long list of recommendations made by the Finletter Board and recommended legislative action, little of which has been forthcoming. But military appropriations, easily the immediate answer to the air power problem, were passed largely because the public had been convinced that this country must maintain a technically superior aircraft-manufacturing establishment under private management. Thanks to these appropriations, the aircraft industry has survived the ordeal of reconversion.

Meanwhile, bureaucratic muddling had all but wrecked the airline transport industry when, in the summer of 1949, Senator Edwin C. Johnson of Colorado, chairman of the Senate Interstate and Foreign Commerce Committee, commenced hearings to inquire into its ills. Out of the welter of testimony before this committee—evidence replete with inconsistencies and strongly flavored by self-interest—someone familiar with the intimate history of aviation could crystallize his convictions as to what must be done to make American air power a force for peace. Believing that these convictions should be expressed, even though they might prove distasteful to some of the customers of the aircraft manufacturers, and desiring to avoid embarrassment to my former associates, I resigned the chairmanship of the board of governors of the Aircraft Industries Association and severed my last connection with the industry. Now, I should at least be able to view the whole subject of air power objectively.

Out of the twisting and turning of our slipstream, air policy is revealed, not as so many believe, as a code book of detailed administrative procedures, but as a course of public conduct. It is no technical complexity of materials, money, management, or machines, but rather a simple expression of the spirit of men, one that can be stated in words of one syllable, "Air Power For Peace."

CHAPTER ONE
IT'S ANYBODY'S FIGHT

It was a day in March of 1924 when I first stepped across the threshold of the anteroom to the office of Rear Adm. William Adger Moffett, Chief of the new Bureau of Aeronautics in the Navy Department at Washington. The anteroom lay at the center of the extreme after end of the top deck of the third wing of the temporary frame structure which then housed, and in fact still houses, the Navy Department. Through the windows I could see the greening lawns of the Mall and the budding cherry blossoms along the rim of the Tidal Basin. Directly below, the Reflecting Pool, a square-cut sapphire, mirrored the tip of the Washington Monument and the cottony clouds of a blustery day. I handed my orders to the admiral's secretary and, as she disappeared through a door to the left, I glanced around.

To the right of the secretary's desk, a latticed, swinging half door of the type once common to saloons of the preprohibition era bore a gilt-lettered sign reading "Assistant Chief of Bureau." To the left, on a similar door, the letters spelled "Chief of Bureau." As it swung open, the secretary waved me toward a stiff-backed chair and said, "The admiral will see you in a few minutes, sir."

Lifting my sword off its hook, I stripped the white lisle gloves from my hands, dusted a bit of lint off my two and a half gilt stripes, and sat down in the chair. Most young officers bearing such orders as mine would have thrilled at the thought of duty in Washington, but I was vaguely uneasy. That sword, standing on the tip of its scabbard between my knees, seemed, in a way, to point up my doubts. Forged into its blade was a quotation from one of Teddy Roosevelt's slogans, "The only shots that count are the shots that hit." Judged by that standard, I had not scored too well since graduation from Annapolis in 1908. Having set out on a career in gunnery, I had let myself be diverted from it.

I had been appointed to the Naval Academy from the state of Washington and had been admitted at the age of sixteen. Having grown up in the Pacific Northwest, where I enjoyed the great outdoors, hunting and fishing with my father, I had drifted onto the Naval Academy rifle team, where I found fun in competition that made a sport out of a branch of my profession. Rifle shooting had intensified my interest in gunnery and had helped me to win my sword. The opposite side of its blade carried the words, "Class of 1871 prize for excellence in practical and theoretical ordnance and gunnery." It was out of this background that I had determined to specialize in gunnery, but circumstances had deflected me into engineering.

After the close of the national rifle matches at Camp Perry in 1909, during which the Navy rifle team had won the military championship, I had been assigned to duty on a four-piper, a coal-burning torpedo-boat destroyer, the *Hull*, then attached to the Pacific Torpedo Flotilla based on San Diego, California. Just before I had reported to the ship, there had been an accident to one of the boilers; and since, up to that time, it had not been customary to assign officers to the engine room of destroyers, the subsequent court of inquiry had not been able to hang an officer for the explosion. Until the case could be reported as completed, the Navy Department could find no way to close its file, thus leaving an annoying piece of unfinished business. To guard against future lapses of this kind, someone had to be made Chief Engineer, and since I, a passed midshipman, was the junior officer aboard the *Hull*, I was handed the accolade.

Early in 1911, my Annapolis June Week Girl, Genevieve Speer, and I had been married at her home in Joliet, Illinois. We had later commuted between the Hotel del Coronado and less commodious accommodations in the Navy Yard town of Vallejo, California, until the summer of 1913, when we had been ordered back to our beloved Annapolis for duty, in compliance with my request for instruction in the new postgraduate engineering school, which had just been opened. The course included a year at Annapolis and another in New York at Columbia University, and was directed by Dr. Charles Edward Lucke, Dean of Mechanical Engineering and a pioneer in his profession.

Dr. Lucke, who had just published his monumental work *Engineering Thermodynamics*, found his Navy charges none too susceptible to his teaching techniques. Finally one day he discovered the reason; we were, to use his expression, "an aggregation of photographic memorizers." And so far as I was concerned he was probably right—to win my sword I had memorized all the textbooks on ordnance and gunnery. The doctor had now to start from scratch to teach us "to reason from a set of facts to a logical solution."

This was an era in which college professors made a mystery of science; it gave them a feeling of superiority over the practical man. The latter similarly looked down their noses at the theorists. The term "engineer" was used to designate the driver of a railway locomotive or, in New York City, the superintendent of an apartment house. Dr. Lucke was of the opinion that, if the time ever came when the practical man and the theorist combined their talents as professional engineers, they would set the world on fire.

"As engineers," he stated for the opening gun of his new approach, "we deal with the application of combustion to industrial purposes."

And having thus stated the role of the engineer he went on to develop the fundamental requirements for combustion:

"The fuel and oxygen," he advised, "must be present in the proportions necessary to chemical combination; they must be intimately mixed; they must be brought to the ignition temperature and retained there until combustion is complete."

And having expounded this truth he went on into one of his excursions into philosophy:

"That," he said, "might be taken as a prescription for life. And remember," he warned, "that whereas material things respond always in the same way to the same stimuli, that is not true of the human spirit. As engineers you will deal quite as frequently with the spiritual as with the material and must understand both."

The doctor, who exercised a strong influence on some of us, inspired us to do creative work. My first opportunity came shortly after graduation from Columbia in 1915, with my assignment as Chief Engineer of the battleship *Arkansas*. The *"Old Ark"* had been commissioned three years earlier with Comdr. William Adger Moffett as her Executive Officer, and still retained the marks of his leadership. In fleet athletics and in the gunnery competitions she had won honors. In engineering, however, she had, like other ships with the new turbines then replacing reciprocating engines, earned a reputation as a "coal hog." To overcome this, I had worked out a scheme for using the waste heat of auxiliary exhaust steam for distilling sea water, thus saving about one-third of the daily port consumption. For this development I had narrowly escaped being disciplined because I had not previously obtained permission from the Bureau of Engineering.

After our entry into World War I, the *Arkansas* was assigned to the Sixth Battle Squadron of the British Grand Fleet and had been present at the surrender of the German High Seas Fleet. It was there, on the afternoon of November 21, 1918, that the shadow of the airplane had first fallen across my path.

The Sixth Battle Squadron had returned to its anchorage east of the great Forth Bridge. Adm. Sir David Beatty, Commander in Chief of the Grand Fleet, on his flagship *Queen Elizabeth*, had swept through the

American Squadron. And as the "Q.E." passed us, so close aboard that one could have heaved a spud onto her decks, Beatty had stood on his bridge, gold-visored cap cocked over his right eye, bulldog chin jutting out over the bridge screen, hand raised to his visor in acknowledgment of our cheers. As these died away, Q.E.'s searchlights had begun flashing a bridge signal that burned itself on my memory:

FROM: COMMANDER IN CHIEF GRAND FLEET
TO: BRITISH EMPIRE
BRITAIN HAS THIS DAY WITNESSED A
DEMONSTRATION OF SEA POWER WHICH SHE WILL
FORGET AT HER PERIL

Then as the flagship had slid by, her turrets topped by fighter aircraft poised for take-off, she had uncovered to our view the loom of a hulk lying down toward May Island. It was the aircraft carrier *Argus*, latest addition to the world's one and only carrier force. And I had thought that, even as British sea power had triumphed, the shadow of air power was darkening the fleet.

I had learned details of the *Argus* from an enthusiastic naval aviator, Godfrey de Courcelles de Chevalier, class of 1909, one of our big boat pilots from the Northern Bombing Base, who, detailed to observe carrier operations, had been billeted on the *Ark*. The British Admiralty, fearful lest the Hun decoy Beatty into the Skagerrak and hit him below the armor belt with torpedoes carried by shore-based aircraft, had mounted fighters on every available ship, and had augmented this defense with aircraft carriers. Most of these had been converted from old battle cruisers and, like other vessels, could only launch aircraft. Their fighting planes were expected to return to prepared air fields on shore, such as the Grand Fleet base at Turnhouse, whence they would be lightered off to their vessels.

But the *Argus*, originally built for the Italian Line as the *Conte de Savoia*, had been the first flattop capable of receiving aircraft aboard as well as launching them. And she had carried torpedoplanes with which to hit the Hun below his own belt. This force had been Beatty's "secret weapon," and, some thought, had helped persuade the Hun to surrender without firing a shot.

After the German surrender, the *Ark* had been ordered home, and I had been assigned to the Naval Training Station, Great Lakes, Illinois, as Officer in Charge, Aviation Mechanics Schools. Here again I was to encounter Dr. Lucke and Capt. William Adger Moffett. During the war, Captain Moffett had commanded the training station and used it to show the Navy's colors to the Middle West. One of those rare personalities, a naval officer with a flair for public relations, he had made many friends on the North Shore, but after the Armistice, was sent to the Pacific in command of the *Mississippi*, one of the few battleships with an airplane catapult aboard. Dr. Lucke had offered his services to the Navy upon the outbreak of the war and had established a chain of aviation mechanics schools, operated on the new principle of line production in education. One of these had been located at Great Lakes and, at the end of the war, Captain Moffett had succeeded in consolidating them all there.

When, after the Armistice, Dr. Lucke had sought a regular officer as his relief, he had recommended me to the Navy Department. I had accepted the appointment with enthusiasm because the station was near my wife's former home in Joliet. After we had been there on duty a year or so, Captain Moffett had returned for a visit with his friends and had surprised me one morning by calling on me in my office.

He had completed his tour of duty at sea and was headed for Washington on a new project. As Captain of the *Mississippi*, he had been hampered in his catapult work by the lack of direction in Washington. Aviation activities were scattered all over the Department: engines in the Bureau of Engineering; airplanes in the Bureau of Construction and Repair; guns in the Bureau of Ordnance; and Operations in a branch of the Office of Naval Operations. Moffett had decided to go before Congress with a proposal to create a new Bureau of Aeronautics in the Navy Department and expected to be made its first Chief.

And that morning at Great Lakes he had asked me point-blank if I would accept duty in his new bureau in charge of the Engine Section. I had first shied away from the idea, but he brushed my objection aside. He would have me ordered to sea duty in aviation, he said, and then bring me ashore to his bureau. Accordingly, in 1921 I was ordered to New York to put the seaplane tender and kite-balloon ship *Wright* into commission, with duty as Chief Engineer, a job which had turned out to be that of wet nurse for a lot of dizzy, heavier-than-air and lighter-than-air pilots. As a "Kiwi," the current name for a nonflying officer, I had found my young charges willing to concede me all the responsibilities of the organization, provided no one interfered with their authorities.

Our first "cruise," nominally to Guantánamo Bay, Cuba, strewed aircraft all along the Atlantic Coast after forced landings, with dense concentrations at Palm Beach. All failures in this outfit were classified as "mechanical"; the term "cockpit failure" had not yet been created. On analysis, I had discovered that practically all forced landings and delayed starts were chargeable to a few pilots. But when I posted the figures on the wardroom bulletin board, this act had been considered hardly cricket. Fed up with the vagaries of this school of aviation thought, I had looked around for a change of duty, and found it during the summer of 1922.

That year, the National Rifle Association of America had decided to enter a team in the international free rifle matches at Milan, Italy, and extended me an invitation to compete for the squad. Here was an opportunity to escape the razzle-dazzle of naval aviation into something I knew about. Better still, it afforded an opportunity for my wife and me to make a joint European tour. At Milan, our team won the championship of the world. By that time, my wife had obtained tickets to the last performance of the Passion Play at Oberammergau, an event destined to shape my outlook.

We had been billeted in the home of Antone Lang, the Christus of the play, and had been stirred by the devout spirit shining in the faces of the villagers. The play, too, had moved us deeply as a revelation of the fundamental tenets of our Christian faith. Though spoken wholly in German it had remained for us a vital religious experience.

During the evening following the performance we had talked with Antone Lang in his parlor and obtained his autograph on a photograph of himself in his role. And when we had come to settle with Frau Lang for our lodgings, we had been astonished to find them so absurdly cheap. Upon our offer to contribute to a local charity—this at a time when inflation had put the exchange rate up to several thousand marks to the dollar—Frau Lang had set a limit of twenty-five marks. At my exclamation of surprise she had hurried to explain, "We need honest work, not charity. Today there is nothing that money can buy!" I had left with a deep impression of the disaster of inflation and the folly of war.

Upon our return from Europe, I had avoided the Bureau of Aeronautics and obtained an assignment as Executive Officer of the destroyer tender *Bridgeport*, a converted former German merchantman. Under command of Capt. R. Drace White, I had enjoyed a year and a half of pleasant duty, trying to make a yacht out of a floating machine shop, and had just begun to feel at ease, when Adm. William Adger Moffett reached down into the Caribbean to pluck me off my happy home and install me in his bureau.

Thus it had been that, thanks to Dr. Lucke and the admiral, I was diverted from gunnery into engineering and then into aviation. Now as a buzzer sounded, and the admiral's secretary smiled her signal to enter the sanctum, I hooked on my sword and pushed open the door, not with the enthusiasm of an aviator but with the reservations of the professional seaman.

Inside his sunny corner office, Admiral Moffett leaned against the old-fashioned high desk at which he stood when signing out papers. That desk, I thought, was a relic of the days of high stools and celluloid eyeshades, and must have been dragged out from some old storeroom by the admiral for the sake of sentiment. He was like that, a curious mixture of sentimental attachment to the days of sail and nervous enthusiasm for the airplane. Over his shoulder draped the silk cord of a pince-nez, poised on the bridge of his nose. His double-breasted blue-serge civilian suit, cut to look like the new uniforms, bespoke revolt against the executive order which had instructed officers on duty in Washington to stow their regimentals away with moth balls in sea chests.

This order was a manifestation of the "return to normalcy," under which slogan, Senator Warren G. Harding and Calvin Coolidge were to be sledded into the White House and the Vice-Presidency later the same year. For the American people, disillusioned after their recent crusade to make the world safe for democracy, had now turned their backs on Europe to devote themselves to something they knew more about—how to make money fast. During the existing reaction against all things military, the Administration deemed it wise to keep uniforms out of sight as far as possible. They were only permitted to be worn by officers reporting for duty, as I was at that moment.

The admiral turned to shake hands with me and hand me my signed orders. His was the aristocratic bearing of the Southern cavalier.

"Glad to see you aboard," he greeted me warmly. "You are to relieve Lt. Comdr. B. G. Leighton as Chief of the Engine Section—an important department. I'm sure you'll do well at it." His was the accent of Charleston, South Carolina, but without the drawl. He clipped his words like a nervous Yankee.

"Aye, aye, sir," I replied, acknowledging the order in the conventional manner, "but what I don't know about aircraft engines," I added, "would overflow the library of Congress."

"Well," grinned the admiral, "you have one advantage—you know you don't know anything, which is more than I can say for some people in this Department." He reached for his pipe and struck a match. (I was to learn that he smoked more matches than tobacco.) As the pipe went out he glanced at me.

"Leighton tells me you are not too happy about coming here for duty."

"It breaks my sea cruise," I explained, "and I don't like to give the Selection Board an excuse to pass me over."

"The last Board picked you up," he said.

"Yes, sir."

"And a year ahead of time," he went on.

"Yes, sir."

"I am not supposed to discuss the proceedings of the Board," he continued, "but I was a member of it and, confidentially, I served notice on them that I would not approve a list that failed to reach down through you."

"Thank you, sir."

"I needed you here, and you can depend on me to look out for you in the future." He fumbled with his pipe.

"There's a lot going on around Washington," he volunteered. "That fellow Billy Mitchell over in the Army Air Service makes a lot of trouble for me. But back in 'twenty-two at the Limitation of Arms Conference I set him back on his heels. He tried to take over the chairmanship of the session on aviation, and the first subject on the agenda was reparations. This country was scheduled to get one of the latest German Zeppelins, converted to a merchantman, and I didn't intend to let the Army beat me to that punch." He paused to glance at a silvery model of a rigid airship, standing on top of his cluttered desk.

"And so," he went on, "when Mitchell breezed in with a secretary, all ready to take the chair, I inquired by what authority he pretended to assume the chairmanship. He mumbled something about rank. 'Since when,' I demanded, 'does a one-star brigadier rate a two-star admiral?' That stopped him, and the Navy got the *Los Angeles*."

He moved close to me, tapping me on the forearm with his pipestem. "It isn't just the old Army-Navy dogfight, though of course there is a lot of that in it. But these overzealous knights of the air actually believe that the airplane has already obsoleted the Navy. It isn't their own idea but the nonsense preached by that Italian General Douhet in a book called *Command of the Air*. And on his say-so, these wild-eyed enthusiasts want to scrap the Army and Navy, on no other grounds than their personal opinions, unsupported by experience or fact." He paused.

"And the old fogies over in Operations are no help to me, either," he added. "They lay themselves wide open to Mitchell. If they had let me handle the publicity on the bombing off the Virginia Capes, I could have made a monkey out of him." He began pacing the room.

"If the Navy doesn't hurry and build up its own air force," he rattled on, "it *will* be obsolete, just as Mitchell claims. Without an air force, the fleet would be a sitting duck. Mitchell knows that, and his game is to concentrate all aviation in a separate and independent air force under his command. With that setup he can emasculate naval aviation just like the British Air Ministry is doing in England. Meanwhile I am taking advantage of that to catch up with our own carriers. Give me a little time and we'll leave them in the ruck." A flush had crept up around his ears.

"So that's why I had to create this Bureau—and why I had you ordered here. We've got a fight on our hands to keep Mitchell from sinking the Navy, and the country along with it." He paused to cock his eye at me.

"Of course," he said, "if you don't like a nice knockdown, drag-out fight, I can send you back to General Service."

My thoughts flashed back to my last night aboard the old *Bridgeport*, a Caribbean night beneath the stars when the crew had given me a farewell "happy hour." Floodlights had glowed on the boxing ring, rigged on Number Three hatch. Brown-faced, white-shirted sailormen had looked up at the two gloved lads in boxing trunks whom the referee had called to the center of the ring for final instructions. And then as he had sent them back to their corners with a slap on each back he called after them, "Remember, now: break clean and come up fightin'. It's anybody's fight."

CHAPTER TWO
THE POWER PLANT,
THE HEART OF AN AIRPLANE

Down on the second deck of the third wing, I looked through the doorway into a long room that housed my new billet, the Engine Section. Three flat-topped desks stood deployed as a line of skirmishers; two typewriter desks closed the blank files. At these desks secretaries had begun to tap out their daily stints of paper work. Around three of the peeled walls, battered tables sagged under a load of assorted aircraft-engine parts—dusty, oily, and, for the most part, heat-blackened examples of unfortunate mechanical failures, some of which, no doubt, had led to loss of life.

Across the near side of the room, on either side of two doors, stood three engines on wooden horses. The bigger one was a Liberty, the smaller a Hispano-Suiza, and the third a new star-shaped contraption on which hung a label, "Lawrance J-1, single-row, air-cooled radial." The first two I recognized as war surplus, but the third I suspected to be the pride and joy, the hope and fear, of the Engine Section of BUAERO. Here was the Navy's first promising postwar development, a project destined to exercise a controlling influence on the future of aviation.

Around the room, marred woodwork and grease-spotted floors joined with a musty smell to give the room the down-at-the-heel appearance of all those temporary wartime structures, themselves so expressive of the popular hope that war itself is but temporary. Drab enough at best, the old tenements had deteriorated swiftly with the slashing of appropriations for defense. Now as I stood in the doorway, someone slapped me on the back and I turned to find Lt. Comdr. B. G. Leighton, retiring Chief of the Section, greeting me like a long-lost brother.

"Am I glad to see you," he whooped, saluting me with an exaggerated flourish. Under his enthusiasm the drabness faded out like a morning fog under a warm sun. Waving an airy hand at each of his secretaries, Leighton introduced me to them with, "Ladies, meet your new boss."

Tossing an armful of homework on the right-hand desk, and waving me to a battered chair, he slid into a swivel-seated one behind it. There he sat grinning like an ape, peering at me around three mountains of paper work heaped up in trays marked, "Incoming," "Outgoing," and "Hold." Though still in his early thirties, Leighton had gray splashes around his temples with laugh wrinkles twinkling at the corners of his eyes—those early-bird aviators tended toward premature grayness. Now, clasping his hands behind his head and hoisting long legs so as to rest his feet on the battered old desk, he grinned his pleasure.

"Nobody knows the trouble I've seen," he quoted, "but now that I've finally got you here, I hardly know where to begin."

"Begin at the beginning," I countered. "It's all Greek to me."

"Well, in the beginning of power-driven flight," he commenced, "before the Wrights could take the hurdle from the glider to the airplane, they had first to find an engine whose weight was light enough, in proportion to its power, to get the contraption into the air. And since nothing suitable existed, they had to design and build their own. Thus from the beginning," he went on, "the power plant has been the heart of the airplane. Subsequent progress has been almost entirely a matter of getting more horsepower for less weight. When you want to lift yourself up by the bootstraps," he added with a grin, "you start reducing, and begin exercising your muscles. The history of aviation can be measured by that ratio, pounds per horsepower."

At the turn of the century, Leighton pointed out, gasoline engines were just coming into use. The Wrights, in designing their little 20-hp 4-cylinder model, had naturally followed the current automotive practice. They had arranged the cylinders in line and had cooled the engine with circulating water.

"It is only now," Leighton explained, waving a hand in the direction of the Lawrance air-cooled radial near the door, "that we are spreading our cylinders like the petals of a daisy and cooling them directly by air. And this section," he added with obvious pride, "is the foster parent of an innovation but recently classified by the engineering intelligentsia as 'impossible.' As for that obsolete term," he went on, "we have a saying in the Section that goes like this: 'The impossible we do today; the fantastic may take a little longer.'" He grinned as he watched me for the effect of another one of his phrases.

Leighton went on to point out, however, that back in 1914, the year the war broke out in Europe, this country had practically no military aircraft engines. The Wrights had not thought of the airplane as a weapon carrier. Over in Europe, however, where men had long been accustomed to look at things through military binoculars, the Germans, the French, the Italians, and the British had concentrated on military power plants. In the commercial field, the United States had a fair-to-middling engine in the Curtiss OXX, rated at less than 90 horsepower. This one later went into wide war use in the Curtiss Jenny training planes. But when, in April, 1917, the war had engulfed the United States, it caught us with our britches down around our ankles. We had no high-powered military engines of any kind, nor had we any designs for them. And even had we had the designs, there were no production facilities in this country nor the know-how for using them.

Quite undismayed by this, we had indulged in our usual penchant for adopting slogans as substitutes for elementary strategy. Our politicians boldly declared their intent to "darken the skies over Germany with clouds of aircraft." The headline figure had been 25,000 planes. But if anyone had any idea what we expected to do with them, other than darkening the skies, such information had been kept secret. There was a suspicion in some quarters that our bold brag had been designed to screen the simple citizens from the unhappy fact that we had no power plants with which to fly those clouds into the air.

That had been a period of childlike faith in the magic of mass production. Then the government, in a frantic effort to buy time, had called in the automotive industry. A handful of citizens, whose heads contained all that was known in this country about high-powered engines of any kind, had been locked in a smoke-filled room of the Willard Hotel in Washington, and there held incommunicado, until they gave birth to the Liberty engine.

The Liberty, conceived in a crisis, and literally bulldozed into production, had proved surprisingly effective in postwar flying, especially after the usual bugs had been engineered out of it. Actually, few if any engines had been used in front-line combat. Yet, keeping in mind the fact that we had only remained in the war twenty months, and that it usually takes at least two years to construct and test an experimental model, the production of several thousand engines had been little less than magic.

The Liberty had been rated at 400 horsepower on a dry weight of some 835 pounds, or at the rate of a little over 2 pounds per horsepower, a striking advance over contemporary practice. And although under the interallied agreement, we had been denied the right to build front-line planes of our own design, we had installed the Liberty in the British de Havilland observation plane and made quite a job out of it. Dubbed "flying coffins" until after correction of the bugs, these had passed through the initial stage of unpopularity, to become "the good old DH," and pretty much the standard for "cross-country" airplanes.

But during the war, failure by the automotive industry to meet the fantastic goals set by politicians had aroused a storm of criticism in the

United States. Hardly had the ink dried on the Armistice before the government, convinced that "munitions racketeers" had profited out of the war, had turned its wrath upon "malefactors of great wealth" by ruthlessly canceling war contracts, with little regard for its contractural obligations. Having now made the world safe for democracy, it felt at liberty to destroy its expensive and unnecessary war industry, venting its spite meanwhile on the industrialists.

Manufacturers, who before final accounting had anticipated profits, now found themselves facing losses instead. Some, the less well-financed, had gone into bankruptcy; others had reorganized and kept in business. Overall, it was estimated that representative suppliers of war goods had taken a write-down of nearly a billion dollars, or about one-half their "apparent" net worth. The automotive industry, licking its wounds, had gone back to do private business with its individual customers, resolved to leave future government business to the naïve.

Judged in retrospect, the venture had proved a fiasco. It would have been bad enough had industry earned its reputation for profiteering, but to have gained the reputation after losing its shirt must be counted a public-relations failure of the first magnitude.

Meanwhile, the giant aircraft industry had just withered on the vine. A handful of the hardier "old-line" aircraft manufacturers, pioneers still obsessed by undiminished zeal for aviation, still held on. Among such engine builders had been the Curtiss Airplane and Motor Company, of Buffalo, New York, and the Wright Martin Aircraft Corporation, of New Brunswick, New Jersey, now reorganized as the Wright Aeronautical Corporation, of Paterson, New Jersey. Of the automotive industry, Packard alone kept a finger in the pie.

During the war, Wright Martin had followed the other alternative to engine construction; they had bought a license to manufacture the famed French Hispano-Suiza engine. And although this procedure had been advanced as promising quicker returns, wartime experience had developed the complexities of putting foreign models into production. Designed around the European idea of handwork by skilled craftsmen, they had to be redesigned to conform to the American technique of machine-tool production. And so experience had demonstrated the necessity for having domestic types in production and ready for expansion.

After the Armistice, the new Wright Aeronautical Corporation continued to develop the Hispano type, under the aegis of the Navy Department. Using the method of "run'em, bust'em, fix'em, and run'em again," financed by the Engine Section, Wright had developed its temperamental wartime Hispano into a rugged, 200-hp Model E-4. Wright had also developed a 300-and later a 500-hp-model Hispano, but since Congress had appropriated limited funds, and on a hand-to-mouth basis rather than for a long-term program, they had found the going rough. As long as the surplus of wartime Liberties and Hispanos hung over the market, manufacture bogged down.

And to add a further complication, Leighton had shown a lively interest in the new air-cooled engine developed by Charles Lanier Lawrance. Charlie, while a student in Paris, had discovered the new 3-cylinder 60-hp Clerget, a fixed radial engine designed to overcome the deficiencies of the old Gnome-Rhone types with their rotating cylinders and gyroscopic effects. The Navy had at that time a demand for 180- to 200-hp engines, and suggested that Lawrance consolidate three of the 3-cylinder engines into a single 9-cylinder type.

Lawrance, with no production facilities of his own, had enlisted those of the de la Verne Machine Company, in New Jersey, and had begun his own development under the "run'em and bust'em" technique. In this he had looked for guidance to Capt. A. K. Atkins and Lt. Comdr. S. M. Kraus, of the Bureau of Engineering. When, later, Admiral Moffett created BUAERO, he placed Kraus in charge of Procurement and assigned Leighton as Chief of the Engine Section.

Meanwhile, Chance Vought, a clever airplane manufacturer in Long Island City, had built a smart little, two-seater, catapult-observation plane around the new engine, a craft that carried as much load as the Army DH using the Liberty engine, yet took up half as much space. And space was a critical factor within the narrow confines of a battleship or a cruiser's decks.

With this increased demand, the Bureau was confronted with the need for bringing in an experienced aircraft manufacturer to fabricate the Lawrance engines, and had selected Wright. But since the new Lawrance was a direct competitor with Wright's own Hispano E-4, Leighton had been obliged to bring pressure to bear and had finally forced consolidation of what he deemed the best design with what he considered the ablest manufacturer. Wright's purchase of Lawrance had but recently taken place and I was to have the job of making the marriage productive. This, according to Leighton, was the big project of the Engine Section, if not, indeed, of BUAERO.

Meanwhile, he discussed other assorted possibilities, like the Aeromarine Airplane and Motor Corporation, of Keyport, New Jersey, and the Kinney Manufacturing Company, in Boston. Of the automotive people, only Packard retained an interest in aero engines. Leighton admitted that mine was a slender reed on which to lean. "The heart of the airplane," he summed up, "has damaged muscles and leaky valves." I concluded that it would have ceased beating entirely save for the grim courage of B. G. Leighton and his Engine Section.

"The air-cooled engine," Leighton asserted, "is the Navy's white hope. There is less sense in liquid-cooling an aircraft engine than in air-cooling a submarine. The weight of the Liberty radiator, water pump, plumbing, and water runs about three-quarters of a pound per horsepower, or say 300 pounds. Now there's an old design adage that says 'it takes a pound to carry a pound.' In other words, each of those plumbing pounds takes another pound of wings and tail to lug it around. But with the air-cooled engine we can throw away the plumbing and convert that dead weight into pay load, with a smaller airplane. On board ship, you've got to keep 'em small or leave 'em off."

By the end of my first day in the Engine Section, I was a bit groggy. Leighton had tossed engineering terms around with complete abandon, terms that I must pause to translate, even as he moved on into new flights of technical verbiage. Yet from that first day's talk I gleaned the fact that the power plant is the heart of an airplane, that aeronautical progress is paced by an engine's "pounds per horsepower," and that the air-cooled engine, as yet quite undeveloped, offered the greatest promise of usefulness to the Navy. Meanwhile, with the Engine Section as the focus of that development, no dull moments loomed on the horizon.

CHAPTER THREE
ITS VITAL SPARK

Next morning we resumed my indoctrination, as we did on subsequent mornings. Leighton began by expounding the advantages of air-cooled over liquid-cooled engines, especially from the viewpoint of naval aviation. The Army could, of course, spread out all over the prairies, but the Navy must ride on the "backs of the fleet."

"If," I interposed, "it is as clear-cut as that, what has been retarding the development?" Leighton heaved a sigh.

"Inertia and politics," he replied. "If you have gained an impression that engine development is all engineering, you are in for a shock. All the engineers in the industry insist that, theoretically, it is impossible to build an air-cooled engine to compete with liquid-cooled, and their politicians keep busy making the prediction come true."

"Politicians?" I inquired.

"Some of them," Leighton replied, "are right here in the Bureau, but they are influenced by the liquid-cooled engine builders, and it is easy to understand the position of these fellows. They've already got a big stake in liquid-cooling: production facilities, engineering, and know-how — especially know-how. Naturally they aren't scrambling to obsolete their own designs." Leighton paused.

"Before you finish your shore cruise," he added, "you'll get a bellyful of engineering politics."

It developed that when Admiral Moffett had first created the Bureau, he expected to bring under his wing all aviation functions such as personnel, matériel, and operations, but vested interests had thwarted him. The Bureau of Navigation ("BUNAV," it was called) charged with responsibility for personnel had hung on for grim death to its prerogatives with respect to naval aviators. While conceding to BUAERO the privilege of recommending assignments, it reserved to itself the authority to turn BUAERO down whenever Admiral Moffett seemed to be getting a little too big for his britches. Again, Naval Operations (OPNAV) had held strict control of all aviation operations. As a concession, they had detailed naval aviators to liaison jobs in BUNAV, OPNAV, and on flag duty in the fleet—where they had carefully preserved the functions of these young specialists in the formaldehyde of an "advisory" capacity.

But Admiral Moffett had proved a match for most of them. The only high-ranking officer in the Navy Department with a flair for public relations, and the one man trained from boyhood in a school of practical politics, Admiral Moffett had shown a knack for getting aviation appropriations from Congress. Not too long on logic, the admiral had demonstrated a native intelligence and a knack with phrases that had netted him dividends. "Of course the country needs an air force," he had said before a naval affairs committee, "but let's make it a naval air force, one that isn't anchored to a land base but can go to sea—on the backs of the fleet." And that expression "on the backs of the fleet" had become a byword in BUAERO.

From Leighton's thumbnail sketch of BUAERO I noted that there was little system or organization to it. Leighton conceded as much.

"We have no organization chart, let alone a bureau manual. Somebody is supposed to be working on one but somehow it never gets beyond the admiral's desk. His organization is personal rather than functional—based on loyalties. Every man or woman in this Bureau," he asserted with emphasis, "would go to hell and back for good old Billy Moffett. And loyalty works both ways; the admiral's most striking quality is his loyalty to his subordinates. Sometimes I'm not so sure about it to his seniors; he loves to needle the old whales on topside." Leighton smiled as if in recollection of specific instances.

"No," he went on, "there is never a dull moment in BUAERO. It reminds me of that old adage handed down from the days of iron men and wooden ships, 'When in trouble or in doubt, run in circles, yell, and shout.' And that, my dear successor," he concluded, "is BUAERO in a nutshell—or should I say bombshell?"

The Bureau had set up as its number-one project, the job of "selling aviation to the fleet," and a fleet full of sales resistance at that. The Bureau had designed catapults—big compressed-air guns, for launching airplanes from the decks of battle wagons at sea. It had designed or procured new seaplanes to be launched by these catapults. It had trained aviators to man these planes, and incidentally, to try to sell them to the ships.

In this they had met hard sledding because those unwieldy catapults had cluttered up the decks, destroyed the symmetry of the ships' silhouettes, and shed grease all over the precious teak decks. However, the aviators had penetrated the cold front by learning how to spot the fall of shot in long-range battle practice, and how to signal the ship the correction that would put a salvo on a target. Ships with planes had thus gained an advantage in the gunnery competition over those that had none, and besides, their pilots had been trained for deck duty and could share watches at sea or in port.

Meanwhile, BUAERO had pushed on with its plans to match the British in carrier aircraft. Under the leadership of Kenneth Whiting, who as Commander of the Northern Bombing Group at Killingholm, Scotland, during the war had sent Godfrey de Chevalier down to the Grand Fleet to observe carrier operations, the old electric-drive collier *Jupiter* had been converted to the experimental carrier *Langley*, and pilots had been trained in deck landings, to gain experience from which to design new carrier aircraft. Here, too, the air-cooled engine offered important advantages, provided it could be made dependable. That job was to become the first order of business for the new chief of the Engine Section.

As a further extension of this carrier development, Admiral Moffett had put over a master stroke at the Washington Limitation of Arms Conference. At a time when the United States was making the fatal gesture of scrapping all its latest vessels, to bring "peace through disarmament," the admiral had salvaged from the scrap heap the giant battle cruisers *Saratoga* and *Lexington*, and was now supervising their conversion into the largest aircraft carriers in the world. In this he had been greatly aided by Capt. Henry C. Mustin, who had since died. Mustin, a wise man with a clear understanding of the principles of war as they might be affected by aviation, had drawn up a complete plan for the complements of the carriers. They would have single-seat fighters to gain command of the air, long-range scouts to obtain information of the enemy, torpedo bombers for attacking enemy vessels, and rescue craft for recovering pilots that might be forced down at sea. The larger craft would demand high-powered engines and since, as yet, we had no air-cooled engines above 200 horsepower, we must needs speed our high-powered liquid-cooled development to the limit.

Leighton gave me his own quick estimate of the personalities in the Bureau other than the admiral. The Assistant Chief was Capt. Alfred W. Johnson, an old Queenstown destroyer skipper. Brought up in the old school, he had been my skipper on the notorious Caribbean cruise of the seaplane tender and kite-balloon ship *Wright*, and I loved and admired him. We had both fought a losing battle against aviation extravagance. The skipper, hoping to cut down useless paper work by refusing to have a yeoman, had answered all his own correspondence in longhand, expecting thus to shame his correspondents into doing likewise, but only he had been shamed.

The Chief of the Matériel Division was Capt. Emory S. Land, of the Corps of Constructors. Unlike so many constructors, Jerry was no theorist but a thoroughly practical and competent leader. He had played football at the Academy and still refereed college games. Able to see both sides of an argument, forthright, and honest, he was an ideal head for a division like Matériel that contained both naval constructors and line officers. The old line-staff controversy was likely to burst out at any moment, and it took a sense of humor to break it up.

The Design Section of the Matériel Division, under which the Engine Section was set up, was headed by a grand old man of aviation, Capt. H. C. Richardson. "Captain Dick," one of the early pilots, a member of the crew of one of the NC boats of 1919 transatlantic fame, and a skilled engineer, had inherited Design from "Jerry" Hunsaker, a classmate of mine, when Jerry resigned from the Construction Corps to go to Massachusetts Institute of Technology as a professor. Jerry had founded the Design Group, and had built up a large drafting room and staff with which to carry on naval aviation design. His designs were to be built experimentally at the Naval Aircraft Factory at Philadelphia and then farmed out to the factory, or perhaps to some willing private manufacturer.

It was right at this point that Leighton stressed a difference between the Engine Section and the Design Section. There were but a handful of people all told in the Engine Section: Leighton himself; his assistant, Lt. Frank Maile, who had once served with me on the *Old Ark*; Lt. Ricco Botta, a former Reserve officer and a skilled engineer; Lt. (jg) Ralph M. Parsons, a former student under Dr. Lucke and my assistant at the Aviation Mechanics Schools at Great Lakes; and two secretaries. The senior secretary was Miss Alma Quisenberry, a quiet, soft-spoken young woman from Nashville, Tennessee. And this handful of people not only had no desire to design or build its own engines but had a clear conviction that the hope for the future lay in the Bureau's placing its dependence for design, development, and production entirely upon private industry.

In this respect, the Engine Section now stood quite alone. After the Armistice, the Army Air Service had devised a plan for setting up a great government production center at McCook Field, near Dayton, Ohio. Army aircraft were to be designed by brain trusters in government employ. The institution would be surrounded by a complex of interested private manufacturers who would produce aircraft to Army design and specification. The plan had fallen through, largely because ambitious young men had preferred to risk their futures in chancey private industry rather than rest secure in the dead end of a government establishment. But the idea still persisted, and many in both Army and Navy were still sold on nationalization for the aircraft industry.

I could tell from Leighton's development of this knotty problem that he was still uncertain as to where I stood. Conceivably I might be one who would want to build up a great engine-design group in BUAERO and another big production group at the Philadelphia Aircraft Factory and thus establish for myself quite a respectable empire. However, I had developed a few positive ideas of my own on the subject, and, curiously enough they had come out of the old rifle shooting competitions. I now relieved Leighton on this subject, obviously so close to his heart.

Under the rules for the national rifle matches, it was mandatory for military competitors to use government-issue cartridges, which, at the time, were produced solely by the government at Frankfort Arsenal. In quality this ammunition was reminiscent of Chinese firecrackers—many were complete duds, and of those that finally went off, many more were just "fizzlers." As to accuracy, there were so many "droppers" in each bandoleer that the element of skill was largely neutralized by the element of chance, thus undermining the foundation of competition. And worse still, there seemed to be nothing we could do about it. Army Ordnance, entrenched in its monopoly, turned a deaf ear to all complaints.

Meanwhile the quality of the ammunition provided by competing commercial companies for civilian matches had improved to the point where Frankfort Arsenal had become a public scandal among the shooting fraternity. At this point the National Rifle Association had raised such a furor that the Ordnance Department was forced down off its lofty perch and obliged to bring Frankfort into direct competition with the private trade. Improvement at Frankfort was immediate, but more important still, seeds were planted for a new government-industry cooperation in ordnance that has since paid off in two wars.

And so, having acquired my convictions at an early age and out of the hard school of experience, I now set Leighton right on my position as to the place of government in production. His relief was immediate, though he felt that the situation in aviation was less critical.

"We have the saving grace," he said, "of having strong competition within the government. As long as the rivalry between BUAERO and the Army Air Service continues keen, both of us will keep on our toes to press development."

My thoughts drifted back to the interview with Admiral Moffett earlier in the day.

"But," I countered, "suppose your friend Billy Mitchell should sell his independent-air-force idea to the Congress and take over the whole shebang, then what would become of your interservice rivalry?"

Leighton tossed both hands in the air in a gesture of helplessness. "Do you know the gentleman?" he asked.

I had met the general at Great Lakes back in 1920 when he had come up on a flying tour of inspection of the Aviation Mechanics' Schools. He arrived at the wheel of a roaring Stutz Bearcat touring car, with the top down, the cutouts open, and a white-faced sergeant hanging onto the seat beside him. He'd broken all records on the run up from Chicago. Later the sergeant informed one of our CPOs that he had long ago exceeded his life expectancy and was now on borrowed time.

At that time, our schools, organized as they had been by Dr. Lucke, were going like a house afire, while the nearby Army schools, at Rantoul, Illinois, were dragging bottom. At the close of the inspection, the general had remarked, without the quiver of an eyelid, "Keep working, Commander, and some day you may catch up with the Army."

As I opened my mouth to retort, he blimped the throttle and jammed the words down my throat, with the roar of his exhaust. The last I saw of him was a cloud of dust as he whirled away in the direction of the main gate, his sergeant hanging on with both hands.

Subsequently, Mitchell had kept up a running fire against the Navy until he finally badgered the Department into anchoring some obsolete vessels in Chesapeake Bay, close to the Army air base at Langley Field, Virginia. In a masterly display of showmanship for the benefit of the newsmen, Mitchell had delivered a mast-high attack on the undefended targets at short range. One phosphorous bomb dropped on the fighting top of the old *Alabama*, where an alert photographer snapped a dramatic picture of pyrotechnics that made the front page with a convincing smash.

All this had come along with the drive for reduction in armaments that had already set the Navy back on its haunches. Navy top brass, fighting hard for survival, had recognized in Billy Mitchell another Brutus, and some had even suspected Billy Moffett of a lean and hungry look. An old walrus over in Naval Operations had been heard to remark that Moffett was probably jealous of Mitchell for having first thought of the separate air force. In any event, the Old Navy had come to hate its own aviation almost as much at it hated Mitchell and the Army.

"Mitchell," I remarked, "is able, impetuous, and dynamic. He has an attractive personality and is long on the qualities that keep men willing to ride with him, hell for leather."

Leighton shook his head. "He takes a lot for granted. The time may come when airplanes will do the things he foresees, but first some of us slaves will have to solve a lot of the impossible technical problems that he now brushes off as unimportant. And one thing is sure," he added, "under the sort of department Mitchell advocates, they just won't get solved. Give him his autocratic control, and he'll set up an airtight government monopoly of research, development, and production that will lay the dead hand of bureaucracy on our new art and paralyze its glowing young spirit." All the smile had gone out of Leighton's voice and deadly earnestness replaced the half-banter with which he had discussed his job.

"Well," he sighed, "there's just one man standing between Mitchell and the attainment of his personal ambition for power." He paused. "And that man," he concluded, "is William Adger Moffett."

"Do you think he's got what it takes?" I asked. Leighton nodded. "He's got a mind like a steel trap. And believe me, he's no counter-puncher—he bores in like Old Battling Burroughs, the fleet champion, and keeps leading all the time, though never with his chin..."

"He's our catalyst," Leighton continued, "the mysterious reagent that keeps all our atoms and molecules in a state of constant, frenzied excitement. He's the ignition system of BUAERO. We chiefs of section are the explosive mixtures and when the admiral sparks us, we give the pistons a wallop and they start the connecting rods oscillating. That rotates the cranks, of which I am one," he added with a grin, "and the whole thing turns over like an aircraft engine—high-strung parts whipping back and forth, between clearances the width of a gnat's eyebrow. And, to complete our power-plant picture," he concluded, "the whole thing would burn out except for the admiral's other function; he's the lubricant, a high-grade product of some refinery that created him and then threw away the formula. It all looks a bit hectic and confused but, amazingly enough, it produces results."

"But," I asked, "what if the Congress is more impressed by the dynamic leader with all the right answers?"

"Then," Leighton replied with finality, "the country will be lost. Lost," he repeated, quoting the punch line of an old Navy yarn about the sailor man weaving his way back to the boat landing through a line of telephone poles, "lost in an impenetrable forest."

After returning to our hotel that evening, I reviewed the day's disclosures with my wife. We had both found that this was beneficial, on general principles, and besides, since a Navy wife is nearly as much subject to Navy Regulations as her husband, it seemed no more than fair.

Apparently this Army-Navy dogfight absorbed every waking hour of the combatants. Since the power plant is clearly the heart of the airplane, then it followed that the Engine Section was a decisive front in a major campaign. The technical issue of air-cooled versus liquid-cooled involved the ancient conflict of government monopoly versus private industry. And there was no question where Admiral Moffett might stand on that. Though armed with authority, he showed the wisdom to use it sparingly. With faith in the processes of nature, he had the guts to let nature take her course. In this respect he was the direct opposite of General Mitchell. Their conflict went right down to bedrock.

As my job in the struggle, the admiral had assigned me the task of creating a new line of engines. This I would do through fair competition and in private industry. The problem was tough because the industry was flat on its back. On the other hand, it was exciting because the admiral's convictions were my convictions, and well worth fighting for. Maybe that was the reason he had reached down into the Caribbean for me.

CHAPTER FOUR
A BACKWARD ART

By the time the Japanese cherry blossoms had come and gone around the Tidal Basin, my wife and I had settled in our apartment at 2301 Connecticut Avenue, and joined the social whirl—cocktail parties on bathtub gin, formal dinners at home or abroad, evenings of bridge, or just plain conversation. And wherever friends gathered, their one and only topic of conversation was "shop." While this was true of all Navy parties, it was especially so in aviation circles. The burning zeal these young pilots displayed for their profession was a constant source of wonderment to us. In what they affectionately characterized as their "old crates"—a description often all too accurate—they found the beginning and end of everything. And if the airplane itself was the object of their veneration, the "Aviation Game," as they fondly called it, was their religion. This seemed the more remarkable, for the airplane was ever a jealous mistress, one that brooked no liberties, a fact well known to the aviators who had solemnly escorted all too many friends off to their last resting place, across the river in Arlington.

Take young Hersey Conant, for one example out of many. Hersey, a delightfully gay young bachelor, had gained the distinction of coining a popular phrase, so to speak. At an afternoon cocktail party, where the gin had just been lifted almost steaming off the kitchen stove, Hersey had mixed it solemnly with orange juice and ice and then held his glass aloft for a toast. Pausing before tossing it off, he had said quite simply, "Let it age a second!" Here, it seemed, was a suggestion the whole Aviation Game might take to heart; but it didn't.

For the very next day, Hersey had blithely taken off in one of the fast Schneider-Cup seaplane racers for a short practice spin, and had hedgehopped his way toward Norfolk, flying right down on the water. Somewhere along the way, he stubbed his toe on one of the many fish traps and pitched headlong into shallow water. When a crane salvaged the wreck it was all wrapped up in a ball.

Old Navy families looked with jaundiced eyes upon the heedless carryings on of the aviators. At a dinner party one night my wife sat next to Capt. Claude C. Bloch, then Chief of the Bureau of Ordnance, and one of the most promising of the younger captains. The day would come when, as Commandant of the Naval District at Pearl Harbor on December 7, 1941, he would receive a visit from the little yellow men, but back there in the middle 'twenties, his promising career still lay before him. Then, addressing my wife earnestly, he gave her the benefit of his advice.

"Tell that husband of yours," he said, "to keep out of the side shows and get back under the main tent." Well, I'd tried to become a gunnery officer but fate had made a Kiwi of me.

And down in BUAERO, Leighton continued day by day to unfold to me the fantastic story of naval aviation.

"Now that you are well fouled up in the slipstream of BUAERO," he remarked one June morning, "it is about time you looked over the trade. If," he went on, "you are going to risk your future on the creative capacity of competition, then you ought to look over your new tools. Frankly," he added, "they aren't too hot." So Leighton asked Captain Johnson, Assistant Chief, for permission to make the trip in a cross-country DH, but the captain turned him down. Later on he advised me in confidence that engineers were too scarce to be risked unnecessarily in those flying coffins. And so we took off by train.

At Paterson, New Jersey, we sought out the multistoried loft building that housed Wright Aeronautical Corporation. President Frederick B. Rentschler received us in his office, sitting solemnly behind his desk. He looked to be a cool customer, a man of great singleness of purpose. Facing him across the table, Bruce Leighton exuded buoyant enthusiasm against a background of equal determination. Not having previously learned from Leighton the sharp differences in opinion between these two, I was unprepared for the sparring match that followed.

Leighton led off with an inquiry as to progress with the new J-3 model of the Lawrance air-cooled radial, which Rentschler fended off with a report on the splendid dependability shown by the liquid-cooled Hispano E-4 in its endurance tests. He had in mind that if Leighton would recommend another production order of Hispanos, Wright could use the time to get the Lawrance ready for the next production order. A flush spread up around Leighton's ears as he rather testily replied that the Bureau was already definitely committed to air-cooled engines in the 200-horsepower size, and that it was Wright's job to speed developments to meet Bureau requirements. Rentschler seemed to have a quiet knack of automatically tuning out any wave length he did not care to listen in on. Now he passed up the Hispano-Lawrance issue momentarily to develop the basic difference of opinion. He clearly felt that with all Wright's accumulated experience in liquid-cooled, they could expect to make more rapid progress with them than with Lawrance air-cooled.

Leighton let a smile flicker across his lips and redirected the discussion toward air-cooling. On the way up to Paterson, he had told me about a contract Wright had with the Navy for the development of a new 400-hp air-cooled radial called "P-1." Intended as an out and out replacement for the Liberty, the engine promised to save a lot of weight although it was just an overgrown Lawrance as to design. Now he asked Rentschler for a report on its progress.

Rentschler shrugged his shoulders in a gesture of hopelessness and reported that George Mead and Andy Willgoos, the Wright engineers, had encountered serious difficulties with piston scuffing. They were struggling with the usual cut-and-try "fixes" but so far with little positive success. Leighton thought that under the criticism of the liquid-cooled partisans he might have specified too small a diameter for the engine and suggested that if I agreed I might modify the requirements if absolutely necessary. Meanwhile, however, he was determined to push the new engine to the limit.

Rentschler shook his head in disagreement. He thought the problem went deeper than Leighton had indicated. He had a tendency to probe for fundamentals and it was his considered opinion that, for Wright at least, liquid-cooling offered the better course of engine development. Air-cooling, even though it might have inherent advantages in weight saving, suffered a handicap from the point of view of timing, and he doubted if these could be overcome. He preferred undertaking a completely new design by Wright to trying to get the bugs out of the Lawrance.

Leighton twisted in his chair as the flush spread up his neck and flooded through the gray at his temples. He had detected a note of arrogance in Rentschler's suave statement—an inference of sure judgment on the part of the civilian as opposed to the immaturity of the naval officer. I made a note of this fundamental conflict as Leighton set his jaw.

The Navy didn't propose to let anything stand in its way in realizing on the inherent superiority of air-cooling. Aside from the potential weight saving there was the vital factor of dependability. One-third of all Navy power-plant failures could be charged to liquid-cooled plumbing—leaky water jackets, leaky hose connections, and what have you.

"In other words," he summed up, "in addition to saving the weight of the plumbing we can eliminate the majority of engine failures by going to air-cooled engines. We're your customers," he added, "and that's our position."

Rentschler's face was a mask. The muscles of his jaw flexed as he faced Leighton. The latter broke the tension.

"What do you say," he queried, "to our taking a look at the new air-cooled engines?"

We took a slow-running freight elevator that dropped us to the basement, where George Mead waited for us in the experimental department. A solidly built fellow in his early thirties, with dark bushy eyebrows, George had the serious mein of the well-trained engineer but he combined this with unusual force and driving power. No one in the aircraft industry could drive a project to completion with such remorseless energy. Now he pointed to a large radial engine mounted on a teardown stand with its ignition wiring partly stripped.

"There she is," he remarked. The big engine was being torn down after a full-throttle run. She was up to rated horsepower but still scuffed her pistons. They were trying one more "fix" and if this one worked, they intended to go back on an endurance run. No suggestion of doubt entered Mead's cheerful voice.

Rentschler stood noncommittal. An engineer must needs be an optimist; his job is a creative one. Day after day he has to bow his head against an avalanche of grief, from failures either in his own shop or the field, yet still press on to correct the faults. There were no margins for error in this aircraft-engine business; the machinery was stressed right up to the limit. The trick was to keep it from going beyond, and the penalty for failure might be somebody's life. Management had plenty of worries, too; Rentschler, there, must wangle the financial problems and try to reconcile the conflicting interests of the several departments of a complex organization.

Now while Leighton and Mead discussed the teething troubles of their new baby with all the intense interest of a couple of young mothers, I tried to pick out the fundamental factors of the situation at Wright Aeronautical. BUAERO had taken the decision to stake its future on the trade. Wright Aero was our best bet. We were committed to air-cooled radials and the management of Wright was still committed, subconsciously at least, to liquid-cooled in-line. It wasn't a matter of sentiment with them; they had a big investment in their prior art. The big job from the point of view of the Engine Section was to instill some of our own enthusiasm into Wright Aero, and this would take some doing. As we left the factory to go to a hotel for lunch, I realized I had my job cut out for me.

Next day we ran down to Keyport, New Jersey, for a look at the Aeromarine Airplane and Motor Corporation plant. It was a discouraging picture, acres of idle machine shops and a powerhouse smokestack that gave out no smoke. The one bright spot there proved to be Roland Chilton, the chief engineer, a keen Englishman whom I mentally clothed in a costume for the *Midsummer Night's Dream*. He had the inventor's talent for innovation, with the engineer's knack for making ingenious mechanical contrivances work and he had created for Leighton the new Aeromarine Inertia Starter. This device, which utilized energy stored in a fast-running flywheel to crank over obstinate engines, had proved an outstanding success in the limited quantities Leighton had bought. Leighton had tried to keep Aeromarine alive in the hope that times might change for the better, but the air-cooled radials would obsolete the Aeromarine liquid-cooled in-line engines, just as they had set aside the Wright Hispano E-4.

A train ride to Boston took us to the plant of the Kinney Manufacturing Company. Their main product was heavy-duty pumps, a far cry from aircraft engines, but the management had shown a willingness to gamble on the remarkable ingenuity of its aircraft engineer, Warren Noble. His forte, like Chilton's, was a unique capacity for accomplishing the impossible through little-used mechanical devices and principles. If anything, he was even more ingenious than Chilton, but by the same token a little less productive; once he had made some contraption work, experimentally, he lost interest in it. Production for profit seemed to bore him. But at Leighton's request, he had undertaken to build a tiny, five-cylinder, air-cooled radial engine for a miniature airplane—one intended to be folded up and parked in a steel cylinder mounted on the deck of a submarine. The job, which imposed every known restriction on the already complicated airplane-design problem, intrigued Noble no end. His engine, with its oil-operated valve gear, incorporated every other unconventional device Noble's fertile brain could conceive, and it ran. Beyond that point, Noble's interest faded.

We left Boston stimulated by talking far into the night with Noble, exploring the realms of engineering fancy, but down in our hearts we knew the little engine would never get anywhere. After all the airplane itself was highly experimental and might never fly; the outlook for quantity production of air scouts for submarines was not encouraging. But it was worth the trip just to listen to the conversation of one of the most facile engineering minds in the business.

From Boston we moved out to the Army Engineering Division, then at McCook Field, Dayton, Ohio, one of those government arsenal-type establishments and about as far apart from Warren Noble as it was possible to get while still remaining on the same planet. The chief of the Engine

Branch out there was Ed Jones, a former Air Service major, now in civilian clothes, and a good solid citizen. He displayed none of the usual Air Service antagonism to naval aviation, and received us warmly.

His assistant, Sam Herron, was, like Chilton, a clever Englishman, one who had done highly useful research in air-cooled cylinders under Professor Gibson, in England, then the outstanding man in his field. Sam Herron was probably better informed on this important subject than anyone in this country and had done some good work even under the handicaps of a government establishment like McCook Field. Among other things "The Field," as it was called by the Air Service, had designed a 300-hp air-cooled radial engine which it had turned over to the Curtiss Airplane and Motor Company, of Buffalo, after competitive bidding, for construction of the first experimental model.

Leighton expressed lack of confidence in this procedure, which had carried over from the war. When disorderly reconversion had forced the automotive people out of aircraft production, "The Field" had determined to establish a great engineering division at Dayton, and to undertake its own design. After the government wizards had dreamed up their pet projects, a manufacturer would do the rest. Leighton argued that this procedure just divided the responsibility for a development between the government and the industry.

"The government," he remarked, "will claim all the credit for everything that turns out well, and will hang the contractor for all mistakes, especially its own." That, he insisted, was not the road to success.

"The only way to get progress," he added, "is to put a good engineer in a tight place where he will have to fight to survive. When it's 'root, hog, or die,'" he concluded, "they always do the impossible."

A run over to Detroit brought us to the Packard Motor Car Company, and another kind of setup. Here was one of the few remaining automotive companies with a continuing interest in aviation. This had probably resulted from the fact that Col. Jesse G. Vincent, a Packard vice-president, had been one of the designers of the original Liberty, and Capt. Lionel Woolson, Packard experimental engineer, still retained his interest in aircraft. The company felt that much of the aviation experimental work could be used in the automotive engines and was willing to continue to participate as a public service. In another emergency, in which the automotive industry must again convert to aircraft production, they could do a better job at it, against a background of continuing experience with aviation. The one drawback to this picture was the air-cooled engine; Packard could hardly be expected to show much enthusiasm for this.

Meanwhile, there was another consideration involved in continuing the automotive industry on a stand-by basis with respect to aircraft.

"Automobile prices," Leighton explained, "demand low-cost volume production, a requirement that is just incompatible with the high-quality, high-precision production required in aircraft. When your automobile breaks down," he added, quoting the old darky of the ancient wheeze, "why there yo' is. But when yo' airplane engine quits, where is yo'?"

And now as we moved on to Buffalo, Leighton gave me a quick preview of the Curtiss Airplane and Motor Company. Here was one of the "old-line" aircraft organizations. Though it had bid in the Army air-cooled radial project, now called the "Curtiss Radial 1454," its heart lay in the liquid-cooled development. The Curtiss D-12 was now one of the best in the world; both the Army and the Navy were using it in fair quantities. Curtiss, he thought, was one of the smartest engine builders in the country—sometimes he had wondered if they weren't a little too smart for their own good.

When we saw the R-1454, we were impressed. Herron's cylinder was an advance over anything we had seen at Wright. The valve-gear rocker boxes enclosed the valves and provided forced lubrication for them in place of the old Alemite fittings of our P-1. And the Curtiss had a single carburetor in place of the triple type on the Wright, an improvement made possible partly by the use of a gear-driven blower that sucked the mixture from the carburetor and pushed it up to the cylinders. This was geared low for rotary induction, and gave fine distribution; someday it could be geared high for supercharging.

That evening we were dinner guests of the company at a hotel overlooking Niagara Falls. Afterward, Arthur Nutt, chief engineer, gave us a sales talk on the D-12. Roy Keyes, president of the company, expressed no fear of competition from the air-cooled radials. Curtiss, he confided in us, had bid in the Army 1454 just to keep it under their control. He considered it unlikely that any radial rock crusher could replace the D-12; in fact, he had no intention of letting it.

That night, Leighton and I sat on the edges of our twin beds in the hotel room and, smoking a last cigarette together, sized up the situation. Curtiss, a good manufacturer, had a fine engine but was keeping it under wraps. Wright, also a competent producer, had an inferior engine and no enthusiasm for air-cooling as such. The problem was to get the best features of the Herron-designed 1454 into the second engine of our P-series at Wright. If we could sell them on that and build up their enthusiasm, we might put a new set of valves in the heart of the airplane and even build up its muscles. That called for another visit to Paterson.

But when we returned to Wright Aero we found that a change had taken place. Fred Rentschler had resigned from the presidency, leaving Charles Lanier Lawrance, the daddy of the American air-cooled radial, in his place. There was nothing left to worry about on the score of air-cooled enthusiasm, though the company had lost an able executive. Guy Vaughan, a dynamic and personable fellow, had moved up from quality manager to factory manager. A former automobile racing driver, Guy had plenty of zing. With George Mead to do a finished engineering job, we could release the P-2 engine with all the latest wrinkles in it.

Back at BUAERO, Bruce Leighton wound up his affairs in the Engine Section. For three and a half years he had fought and bled there, stacking up brief moments of triumph against hours of grief. As a matter of fact, aircraft engines were one big pain in the neck. Reports of poor performance in service streamed in under the heading "Trouble Report." If by some chance they performed well, that was only as it should be and certainly not a subject for comment. The art was still young, and even the best equipment could hardly be classified as safe to fly. In the face of disheartening problems, Bruce Leighton had never let his enthusiasm slacken; his heart and soul were all wrapped up in what he himself characterized as "these funny damned airplanes." He had pioneered air-cooled engines in the face of universal resistance; he had stood by private industry when everyone else had plumped for government ownership. Now he was "off to sea."

CHAPTER FIVE
TOIL AND TROUBLE

The summer of 1925, like most summers in the nation's capital, was almost unbearably hot and sultry. Even after one of those violent electrical storms had whirled up the Potomac and deluged the blistered asphalt with a tropical downpour, its passing left the whole town sweltering in a steaming heat, even more prostrating than before the storm. It was sticky enough in the permanent buildings, but in our temporary shack on Constitution Avenue, work became quite impossible, and we often sent the Bureau staff home in the early afternoons. And before that fateful summer could pass, lightning struck twice in the same place—BUAERO.

When Bruce Leighton had passed out to sea, most of his small staff went with him, having already overstayed their allotted period of duty on shore. Luckily, Ricco Botta, a lieutenant who had come in by way of the Naval Reserve, held over with me. A pilot, an engineer, and a skilled mechanic he had now become the practical wheelhorse of the Engine Section. Later on, Henry Mullinix joined up, bringing just the right qualities to balance out our little organization. Henry had been honor man in his class at Annapolis, had later led his flight class at Pensacola, and had finally completed the aviation postgraduate course at Massachusetts Institute of Technology with top honors. And along with his intellect, Henry had a fine personality and an admirable character. Our organization was rounded out by young Lt. (jg) Ralph Parsons, who now handled the highly technical liaison with the Aero Engine Laboratory at the Naval Aircraft Factory, Philadelphia, while Henry, Ricco, and I concentrated on the task of cleaning up the bugs in the engines and accessories under our cognizance.

Take, for instance, the Lawrance J-1 air-cooled radial engine, that coffee grinder on which all our hopes were based. It was so rickety that Lt. C. C. Champion, a rising young West Coast pilot, formally reported to BUAERO that, when embarking on a fifteen-mile cross-country flight from the Naval Air Station at North Island, near San Diego, to an emergency airport at Ream Field, down near the Mexican border, his squadron always carried a whole "quiverful" of spare push rods to replace those sure to be sprayed along the beach of the Coronado Silver Strand. Our treatment for this sort of trouble was to call in Charlie Lawrance or Guy Vaughan of Wright Aero and give them a session of plain and fancy kidding, with just the right amount of sting in it.

The magnetos for our air-cooled engines were something to write home about. Here was the instrument that provided the vital spark so essential to keep the engine ticking over, yet it had proved the least dependable of the parts of the high-strung mechanism behind which pilots risked their lives. And when we looked around for more promising sources of supply, none was to be found. The Delco Company, producers of the wartime Liberty battery-generator ignition systems, could not be interested in a new development; the volume to be expected was too small. The manufacturer of cheap truck magnetos, to whom we now looked, was willing to brighten up the outside finish but was unwilling to go further for the same reason— no volume. The board of directors of the great General Electric Company had, we were advised, studied the problem with ponderous care and finally concluded there was more money in electric light bulbs. A small privately owned company was willing to help, but lacked know-how. It looked like a stalemate until the Army Engineering Division at McCook Field discovered Scintilla.

Scintilla magnetos proved to be the answer to a maiden's prayer. Made in Soleure, Switzerland, they could be bought through Tom Fagan, of New York, and at a reasonable price. However, since we could not place full dependence on a foreign source that might be cut off in time of war, we investigated the possibility of creating an American source. The Swiss company had an excess of machinery and personnel and was willing to export them, but the red tape surrounding such a transaction, even back there in the days when the United States government had faith in private enterprise, tied us hand and foot. To cut through the tangle involved so many risks that we should have been completely discouraged save that the other alternative was to accept responsibility for the deaths of youngsters who daily risked their lives in the air.

In dilemmas of this kind, resort might be had to what was politely called "memoranda for file" but known privately as "the cover-up." A letter was prepared for the file covering the details of the proposed transaction and carried through the whole system to be finally approved by the Secretary of the Navy himself. Then, after the Great Seal of the Navy Department had been attached, and the author had privately retained a copy for his own use, the document was carefully filed away against the day when some Congressional investigation might be looking for a noteworthy scalp. When the spirit of cover-up gets into a business organization, the evil finally shows up in the financial results; in government it is just absorbed by the taxpayer.

It was through such a time-consuming process that we finally succeeded in transporting a part of the Swiss company bodily to the town of Sidney, New York, where it continued to be this country's source of dependable magnetos. And the time even came when I had to flash the Great Seal of the Navy Department to keep from being crucified for bringing it here. Later, when Charles A. Lindbergh arrived in London, after having flown the Atlantic behind a Scintilla magneto, it turned out that the General Electric Company had all along had the license to manufacture the British Thompson Houston Company's magneto, but no one in Schenectady had recalled the fact.

Meanwhile, in addition to concentrating on the job of keeping engines running, we had not neglected the other task of getting them started. The Aeromarine Inertia Starter, created by Chilton under Leighton's initiative, though employing a quite novel principle—the utilization of energy stored in a flywheel—had developed into the most dependable and efficient device in our gear locker. When, therefore, Messrs. Charles Marcus and Raymond P. Lansing of the Eclipse Machine Company called on us with a view to interesting us in a line of electric starters they had developed for the Army, we presented them with an affable but none the less impenetrable front. Things electric not only involved heavy lead storage batteries, heavy copper motors, and everything else designed around "base metals," but they always proved undependable and difficult to maintain. My years as engineer officer on a man-of-war had generated in me a sales resistance of many ohms.

On the day when we were honored with the visit from Charles Marcus and Ray Lansing, I bolstered my disinterest with a glowing and somewhat detailed account of the virtues of the Chilton starter and was somewhat taken aback by Charles Marcus's suave remark that Aeromarine had infringed an Eclipse patent involving the fundamentals of the Bendix drive. Marcus doubted that Eclipse could let Aeromarine live at all, and his inference was that I should shift my enthusiasm over to the Army-type starter.

Patents, I now pointed out, were outside the jurisdiction of the Engine Section. If Eclipse elected to make trouble for us, that was their privilege. If, however, they wanted to make our kind of starters, that was also their privilege. The patent matter could be left to the courts. I noticed an intent expression on Charley Marcus's face.

"Commander," he said quietly, "your approach is new to us and we may find it difficult to conform at first, but from the point of view of development and the public interest, it looks so sound to us, we'll play the game your way."

The Eclipse Machine Company did play the game our way. They developed a new starter for the Lawrance radial, and when, on its first installation down at Pensacola, it developed the usual bugs, the company moved most of its shopmen down to the air station and campaigned the trouble so enthusiastically that they made more character out of their defects than Aeromarine gained out of its satisfactory equipment.

When, after several years, the patent matter finally came to trial, the examiner for the court remarked that he could not recall a similar case but thought everyone's interests had been well served, as a result of the Bureau policy, and especially so the interests of the public.

Another perennial problem was spark plugs. It was almost incredible how sensitive such little things could be. One might think that the manufacturers should long ago have discovered all the secrets of such a simple device, and reduced the product to some degree of standardization. But everything in aviation was so high-strung, every device so sensitive, it seemed that just changing one minor dimension of a standard nut or bolt set in motion a whole chain reaction of troubles. Pressing always for higher power on lower weight, we created more and more troubles for ourselves. In this field we came to lean on the BG plug, and on Roy Hurley, its salesman, who was responsive to our suggestions and worked hard to improve his product. Mr. Goldsmith, the proprietor of the company, and a jewelry manufacturer, had turned to making spark plugs during World War I and now subordinated his other interests to doing a good job for aviation.

And so we fired away, searching for better accessories of every kind—a new fuel pump here, imported from France perhaps by Jimmy Diamond—a new carburetor there, produced by Stromberg under the wise direction of Leonard S. Hobbs—a new fuel developed by competing oil companies and fortified by Ethyl under the direction of Dr. Graham Edgar, of the Ethyl Corporation, and so on to cover the whole field. And in the process we began collecting a little group of sales engineers like Roy Hurley, Luke Hobbs, Tom Fagan, Ray Lansing, and others, men to whom we passed on the demands of the operating squadrons and with whom we connived to beat Old Man Trouble. To facilitate operations, we urged these key technicians to visit the flying units and get the word at first hand. We brought them into close contact with George Mead, of Wright, Arthur Nutt, of Curtiss, and Lionel Woolson, of Packard; and we keyed them in with our competitors out at McCook Field, so that we finally had a team of competitive yet cooperative agents, all working for the cause of dependable and durable power plants.

And behind our day-to-day jobs of trouble shooting on the accessory front, we had the major problem of engine development. Wright Aero, in order to earn the money with which to carry on their own experimental and development work, must first generate a reasonable volume of steady profitable business. This meant that we, and others, must buy enough airplanes to create the demand for new engines. But before we could do this, the airplanes must have been conceived, created, and tested. A number of aircraft had already been built around the air-cooled radial, among them the Chance Vought UO and the Curtiss TS, but the total was hardly impressive. Then Wright got a real break when it found a new home in Reuben Fleet's Consolidated Army training plane.

Fleet, a former major in the Army Air Service, had created a new company up in Buffalo which he called Consolidated Aircraft, and had designed and built a new type of training plane. Using the welded-steel tubular construction introduced to the United States by Anthony Fokker, the Dutch manufacturer, Fleet had created an airplane that was easy to build, easy to maintain and, more important, extraordinarily safe. His welded-steel fuselages, unlike the old stick-and-wire type of the Army Jenny or its Navy counterpart, the N-9, wouldn't splinter all to pieces in a crack-up nor punch holes in the ribs of hapless student aviators. The Army had tested the plane extensively and with such outstanding success that Fleet felt impelled to try to sell it to the Navy with obvious advantages to all parties.

This decision in itself was perhaps indicative of the audacity of one of aviation's immortal enterprisers, for none knew better than Reuben Fleet what the handicaps were; as a former procurement officer at McCook Field, Fleet had played the old Army-Navy game hard. And it took a swashbuckler like Fleet to dare intimate that anything designed for the Army could be worth hell-room to the Navy. And he probably would not have got to first base either, save that he had been smart enough to use the air-cooled radial Wright instead of the war-surplus Hispano engine. The Engine Section, at least, could be expected to favor the adoption of the Army PT, in order to increase the use of the air-cooled engines. And Reuben Fleet was right on that score.

But there were formidable obstacles. Naval air training was centered at the Air Station, Pensacola, Florida, where the N-9 seaplane was well established as a local favorite. Nearly every pilot in the Navy had qualified on it and now cherished for it the affection of a kid for his first pony. In order to keep the ancient aircraft flying, the station had built up an assembly and repair department manned entirely by civilians from the town of Pensacola—skilled carpenters, riggers, and fabric workers, fully competent to overhaul the stick-and-wire N-9's. As a matter of fact, they could build them new from the ground up, and this was where the rub lay. After an airplane had been washed out in a crack-up, it was supposed to be stricken from the list, an action that in due course would have absorbed all the war surplus and led to new construction. But at Pensacola, there were no washouts. In the local jargon, they just "jacked up the number plate and built a new airplane under it."

And so in addition to the natural reluctance of the old-timers to make a change in type, there was the powerful vested interest of the Pensacola workmen. This fact, however, was never brought into the open. It appeared rather that the Consolidated NY had a nasty flying characteristic, probably inherited from its Army ancestry: it possessed an "abnormal spin" as compared with the N-9. If the "good old N-9" lost flying speed and stalled, it whipped suddenly into a spinning nose dive that would lead to a crash if the pilot did what came naturally and opened his throttle. If, however, he "cut the gun" and dived to regain flying speed, he could recover control. The object of much of the student's early training was to get him to disobey that impulse and cut the gun in a spin. This, to our old-timers, was a "normal spin."

The trouble with the Consolidated NY was that it was difficult to make it spin at all, and equally difficult to get it out of a true spin. The old-timers, passing over the obvious advantage of reluctance to spin at all, and the priceless benefit of a fuselage that could not splinter and poke holes in a pilot, now stressed the disadvantages of the new plane; how could you teach a pilot to get out of a spin if you couldn't get him into one? To combat this argument and get the plane adopted so as to increase production of new Wright air-cooled engines was the task of the Engine Section. And the cockpit for the final contest was Admiral Moffett's corner office and a meeting of what was called officially a "Bureau conference." In the course of several contests here, I had begun to learn some of the ins and outs.

As the heads of divisions and chiefs of sections of BUAERO flocked into the admiral's office that morning, each one took up his position more or less according to rank; that is, with captains and commanders on the admiral's right. This suited me because I had come to learn that the discussion worked downward according to rank and that sometimes the last fellow to speak might turn the tide, especially if he could present some reasonable compromise. I knew, of course, that every man in the room had previously buttonholed the Old Man in an effort to sell his own bill of goods in advance, but that the admiral, who knew nothing about engineering and wanted to know even less, would now stimulate acrimonious discussion and draw his own conclusions from the discomfiture he saw on one man's face or the triumph he observed on another.

And as the contest raged this particular morning, everyone knew the real issue, including the admiral, but no one mentioned it. Argument and discussion raged about every irrelevant aspect, but everyone ducked the matter of Pensacola's vested interest. After a long while the admiral turned to me.

"Hasn't the Engine Section anything to offer?" he asked, well knowing that of course it had.

"Well, sir," I replied, "I'm afraid we're too much an interested party to bear weight here. We think that the adoption of the Consolidated would lead to faster engine development and that this fact alone would justify a favorable decision." The admiral didn't bat an eye.

"If you've got a suggestion," he said, "don't be afraid to let us have it."

"Well, sir," I went on, "it seems to me that what this conference must decide is this: what do we really want to do—train pilots, or kill them?" There wasn't a sound in the room. The admiral glanced from face to face and then stood up.

"Well, gentlemen," he said, "if that's your decision, it's agreeable to me. But remember now," he added, "I'll expect every officer in the Bureau to pitch in and make this Consolidated airplane a success."

As the conferees filed out through the door, I noticed the admiral watching me and detected the quick jerk of his head that signaled me to lag behind. He struck a match and took two puffs at his pipe.

"There's a lot going on around here," he remarked, using the very words with which he had received me the morning I reported to him. "I can't keep track of all of it," he added, and then with a grin that drew down the tight corners of his mouth, "keep your eyes open. If you see anything you think needs handling, take care of it, whether or not it comes under your department."

As we moved toward the door the admiral caught my elbow.

"That fellow Mitchell is on the rampage again," he said. "The Army has decided to order him to Texas to get him out of Washington. But he'll break out at the worst time, wherever he is." He struck another match and took two reflective puffs on his pipe.

"Keep your eye on him," he concluded, "and be ready to lend a hand with the counterpublicity."

CHAPTER SIX
WHAT THE DOCTOR ORDERED

The "Affair Fleet," as the celebrated episode of the Consolidated training plane came to be called in BUAERO, not only marked the advancement of the Engine Section from the limited environment of trouble-shooting into the more intricate realms of Bureau politics, but it also forecast our early graduation into the more creative field of aircraft engine development. And this important transition dated from a visit to the Engine Section by an aircraft manufacturer, Chance Milton Vought, president of the Chance Vought Corporation, of Long Island City, New York, a man with a waxed moustache and a fertile brain from which sprang the idea that touched off a chain reaction destined to alter the whole course of aviation.

Chance Vought was perhaps the most colorful of the unique personalities who made up the "airplane trade" as differentiated from the "engine trade." Unlike Glenn L. Martin, whose tastes then inclined to rather dressy suits, Chance favored the tweedy look. With dark hair and eyebrows and his blond moustache, he was our example of sartorial perfection—except upon certain occasions.

After he had about completed one contract and had begun to feel the pressing need for another, he would make his appearance in the Bureau in a dilapidated tweed suit, under a moth-eaten coonskin coat, wearing a lean and hungry look, and talking very poor. At least he tried to make his look lean and hungry, but behind the façade still shone the dapper first-nighter of Keith's Palace Theatre. Of course everyone was wise to the act, and since Chance himself was one of the wisest, he knew they were, and the recurrence of the cycle of poverty had become a source of amusement tending to soften up whatever sales resistance might develop.

This was a period of one-man organizations, when a Don Douglas, a Dutch Kindleberger, a Tony Fokker, or an Igor Sikorsky carried under the crown of his hat all there was to know about aircraft engineering. Most of these men dealt with the Design Section, located in larger quarters up the corridor from the Engine Section, but as time passed, and especially after the "Affair Fleet," others like Claire Egtvedt, of the Boeing Company, out in Seattle, and Chance Vought began filtering into the Engine Section. And now as Chance slid through our door, rigged out in his tramp regalia, the Section gathered around my desk for a little plain and fancy kidding. Although the room was warm, Chance was too much the showman to offer to take off the coat. Instead, he posed his question.

"What's cooking?" he inquired, biting his waxed moustache.

"Nothing's cooking," I countered. "In fact, I can report 'eight o'clock lights and galley fires out' like any other good sailor."

Chance grinned. "I'm running out of work," he said, "and if I can't get a new contract soon I'll have to close up shop."

Henry Mullinix shook his head as he put in his oar. "Mr. Vought," he said, "you must know that your little UO, once the sweetest little job in the air, has now become so overloaded it can hardly stagger off a catapult. Surely you don't expect the Bureau to buy any more trucks like that?"

Chance bristled with indignation. "It's the Bureau's own fault," he snorted. "They've added everything to it from automatic toilets to hot and cold running radios."

Ricco Botta added his salt to the wound. "It's still a kluck," he said, "no matter how you alibi it."

As Chance opened his mouth to retort, I gave him the *coup de grâce*. "Fact is, you've come to the end of your rope. If you want to do more business with this Bureau," I concluded, "you may as well make up your mind to create something new."

Chance sat silent, fingering his moustache. "Do you really mean that?" he inquired.

"We're your friends," I replied. Chance sat quietly as if debating his next course, and then, having made up his mind, he sprang a bombshell.

"All right, my friends," he said with a smile, "I've got a new airplane on the boards—one that will set the world on fire. But the new airplane calls for a new engine; I want three hundred and fifty real horsepower but on an engine weight of not over 650 pounds. If the Engine Section will give me that, I'll give the Bureau the world's best airplane."

The room became very still; all kidding had fled right out the window. Chance had passed the buck right back to the Engine Section; he'd written the prescription for a new power plant. And furthermore we realized he was absolutely right in his choice of size; the Wright 200 air-cooled, which by now was being called the "Whirlwind," was only a zephyr. The Wright 400-hp P-2, later named the "Cyclone," was overweight for Chance.

Something about halfway between seemed to be the answer, and Chance had called the turn. The catapults on the battleships and cruisers, together with their hoisting gear and other equipment, had been designed to handle a limited weight, and this, in turn, controlled the size of our new airplane. The weight of the engine determined the final all-up weight of the aircraft, and the power output was dictated by the necessity for getting the plane up to flying speed before it reached the end of the catapult. And while there was no such limitation on aircraft carriers, like the new *Lexington* and *Saratoga*, then building in the shipyards, the over-all size of the airplanes would determine the number each carrier might line up on her flight deck. The Vought prescription would also lead to a new type of fighter, smaller than anything around the P-2 but with higher performance.

Better still, Chance Vought's new engine seemed to lie within the realm of possibility. The 200-hp Whirlwind had a cylinder volume of some 800 cubic inches; the bigger Cyclone, at 450 hp, had about 1,650 cubic inches. A Wright engine just between these two might displace about 1,200 cubic inches, and conceivably be made to develop 350 horsepower. Chance had put the job up to us and we would put it up to Wright.

"All right, Chance," I said soberly enough, "you go on back to Long Island and start work; we'll get your engine for you." Chance Vought relaxed and grinned back at me.

"Meanwhile," he inquired, "what will I do to keep the shop open?"

"Go call on Commander Kraus, over in Procurement," I replied. "Tell him about this discussion. Maybe he can scrape up an order for enough UO's to keep you ticking."

As soon as Chance had left the room, I telephoned Charlie Lawrance and Guy Vaughan, of Wright Aero, and asked them to take the midnight train down for a conference the next day. They were not too enthusiastic at first, fearing that a completely new engine on top of their already heavy load might break them down. But we compromised on a proposal to scale the P-2 model down to about 1,200 inches displacement, without undertaking a completely new design. This was not so crazy as it might sound, for while you couldn't scale an engine up with any hope of success, you could scale it down if you were willing to accept a few compromises on weight. We were willing and Wright was agreeable. Thus was born the Wright R-1200, or Simoon, an engine that, though it never went into production, still had its impact on naval aviation.

The reason why it never got into production appeared nearly a year later in the person of Mr. Frederick B. Rentschler, former president of Wright Aeronautical Corporation, who walked in on us one morning carrying a dilapidated cowhide brief case and looking even thinner than when I had first met him on that visit with Bruce Leighton, a year earlier. I recalled that in his argument with Leighton over air-cooled versus liquid-cooled he had shown dogged singleness of purpose and ability to reason logically. He had resigned from the presidency of Wright Aero shortly afterward, and for reasons which I had not learned. Now he began to tell me.

It seemed there had been some disagreement on financial policy between him and Dick Hoyt, chairman of the board. Hoyt had wanted to declare a dividend out of earnings from the Army contract for Hispano H engines; Rentschler had insisted on retaining earnings for investment in engineering development. Finally Rentschler had resigned. It had been rumored that he and Hoyt had disagreed over the acquisition by Wright of the Lawrance engine, but Rentschler now made no reference to this. After his resignation from Wright he had intended going back to Hamilton, Ohio, to his father's foundry business, the firm of Hooven, Owens, Rentschler. His father had been certain that the aviation business held no future, but aviation had got into his blood. During a spell in the hospital, he had made up his mind to stay in the game and had given consideration to what he might do to help out.

It was his considered opinion that we needed more competition than we could possibly get under present circumstances. The Curtiss company had no serious interest in air-cooled engines; on the contrary, they were committed to liquid-cooled. Wright, he thought, was unlikely to progress as rapidly as we required, especially under its present management. He knew the inside thinking of both Curtiss and Wright, and was certain that an ultimate merger of the two companies was not an impossibility; as a matter of fact, if the Wright air-cooled engine got threatening, Curtiss might move toward merger and control. The import of his remark was not lost on the Engine Section.

For in taking the decision to support the air-cooled program in competition with the more advanced liquid-cooled development, we had counted heavily on competition in private industry as the vital spark. This merger idea, somewhat new in that era of private initiative, was of course wholly unexpected by such business amateurs as then comprised the Engine Section. The threat to our whole air-cooled program was so immediate, however, that we listened with rapt attention to our visitor.

He now proposed to organize a company to design and construct air-cooled aircraft engines for the Bureau. He had interested the Niles Tool Company in his project, and had their approval to his taking over certain vacant loft areas in the huge plant of the Pratt and Whitney Tool Company, of Hartford, Connecticut. That company, having expanded its facilities to meet excess demands in World War I, now rented the extra space for use as a tobacco warehouse. He had received assurances as to the necessary capital; Pratt and Whitney had idle funds it could advance to a new enterprise willing to rent its excess facilities. The company had extra machine tools and trained supervision and Hartford was a fine labor market for the machinists and craftsmen so necessary for precise aircraft-engine production. He proposed to select a small group of the most experienced engineers and production men in the business and to build around this nucleus the best organization in aviation. Competition from such a group would give the Navy the superior engines it so badly needed.

As Rentschler completed his airtight proposal, I was struck by the sheer logic of his presentation. He'd apparently thought it all through and made himself letter perfect. But there was one big drawback which I now pointed out to him.

We would welcome competition, but current appropriations would hardly support Wright Aeronautical, let alone a new company. We had tried to make such progress through good leadership as might approximate the benefits of strong competition, and had so far succeeded fairly well. Wright Aeronautical had spared no efforts to make dependable air-cooled engines, but Curtiss had not been pushing their R-1454. This had left us with but one source of supply and made us vulnerable to criticism by Congressional investigation, which might charge us with supporting a monopoly. This took us into the field of policy, which was the province of the chief of Bureau, so we decided that perhaps we had best put the proposal before him.

When we were ushered into the admiral's sunny corner office, I noticed a newspaperman, George S. Wheat, sitting in one of the easy chairs. Quite a crony of the admiral's, he had worked for Wright Aeronautical back in the period when Rentschler had been its president. I now associated him, therefore, with Wright, and was somewhat surprised when he made no move to leave the room. It didn't occur to me at the time that he might be a part of Rentschler's approach to the subject of the new company, and I didn't learn the facts until years later. Then George confessed that Rentschler, prior to invading my office, had inquired about the new chief of the Engine Section, and that George had described me as an opinionated somebody who apparently knew where he was going. But in Admiral Moffett's office that morning, suspecting no connection between the two men, I plunged into my statement.

The admiral listened attentively until I had finished and then made a quick decision.

"This Bureau," he began, "is wide open to criticism for supporting an engine monopoly. We know it isn't so, but that won't prevent our being smeared by headlines. I realize we haven't the necessary appropriations, but you leave that to me; I'll wangle them out of Congress. If you can work out anything reasonable with these men, go ahead; I'll approve whatever you recommend."

As I turned to go, the admiral called me back. Some time earlier he had instructed me to prepare a statement for his presentation to a Congressional committee in support of his proposal to junk the war-surplus Liberties and Hispanos and buy new engines. I had given him a rather technical treatise, pointing out the superior aerodynamic performance to be had with the new engines. This he had promptly tossed back in my lap with a remark that Congress had no interest in performance; they wanted to save cash. Now that incident came to his mind and he inquired if I had made any progress.

"Yes, sir," I replied, "I've looked up the records and found that it costs about a thousand dollars to convert an old Liberty into one incorporating all the new changes. After that we can get seventy-five-hours flying time out of it before we have to put in another converted one. For three hundred hours flying time, we spend four thousand dollars on conversions. Meanwhile we can get a new Wright Whirlwind for about the same money and run it for three hundred hours without overhaul." The admiral smiled.

"That's more like it," he said. "Even I can understand that kind of engineering, and so can a Congressman. It's cheaper to scrap junk than try to save it!"

"Exactly," I replied.

"Well," the admiral smiled, as he waved us out the door, "see if you can dream up something like that on this new engine."

When our party returned to the Engine Section, we gathered once more around my desk. Rentschler asked what size engine we thought he should build and I gave him the background of the Wright R-1200 Simoon, especially the basis on which Chance Vought had written the prescription. However, I intimated, Wright had been working on that nearly a year and might have a prohibitive head start.

Rentschler wasn't so sure; Wright had a heavy load with two new engines and the task of developing the third, the Whirlwind. A good engineering outfit, with no production problems and only one project, ought go places; starting off with a clean sheet of paper and no commitments as to old tools or techniques, they might even have the advantage. But they must be sure of their basic design principles. The Wright R-1200, a scaled-down

P-2, would suffer certain handicaps inherent in the process; the new engine might generate the 350 horsepower on less weight.

It looked to me as though they should try the other way around. Keeping the 650-pound weight Chance had specified, they might put their advantage into greater power. Any airplane man would snap at this advantage and thus become an ally. Furthermore, it seemed to me, if by clever design the new company could build more cylinder capacity into the engine and still keep the specified weight, and if by cylinder refinement they could take out more power for each cubic inch of displacement, they might gain an outstanding advantage. This, in turn, might compensate for some of the time advantage Wright had already gained.

This idea seemed to enlist just a tinge of enthusiasm from Rentschler, who was most serious and calculating. Doing a job seemed a fetish with him and he lacked humor where business was concerned. He moved now to the question of an experimental contract. Since we had given one to Wright Aero for the R-1200 Simoon, he presumed, of course, we would do as much for him.

This was a matter on which I had to throw cold water. Wright, I informed Rentschler, was a going concern complete with management, production facilities, engineering, and experience. His new company was still but a figment of his own imagination and I could not recommend to Kraus that he risk public funds in support of anything so ephemeral. Admiral Moffett had earlier obtained an appropriation of $90,000 from Congress for an experimental engine. The best I could do for Rentschler was to earmark the fund and hold it in reserve for his project. If he built an engine that fulfilled our requirements, the fund would be available to help compensate him; after that the engine would stand on the same basis as the Wright—the best job would take the business.

After this statement, Rentschler sat a long while in thought. I could see he was greatly disappointed.

"Well," he said finally, "if that's the way it is, that's the way it is, but I think you're pretty tough with me."

I didn't agree with him. The moment a contractor accepted a contract with the government he was obliged to grant his customer some control over the project. Such a division of authority was bound to slow a development and might even compromise its integrity. But as long as the contractor risked only his own money, then he had full authority over how he spent it, and no one could interfere. Furthermore, in this case, time was of the essence even more than usual, and when a contractor is wasting his own money and time, he is less complacent about it than if it belongs to Uncle Sam. The medicine might look bitter to Rentschler, but in the long run it must prove more effective. And more important than all, the moment he began risking his own funds for our advantage we inherited a moral responsibility to give him every reasonable assistance—and this we did.

From that date forward, Rentschler made it a point to visit the Bureau from week to week to keep us advised of progress. His first surprise was the news that he had collected a small group of men, mostly drawn from Wright Aero, as the nucleus of his organization; and he had shown rare judgment in picking the ablest of them. There was Don Brown from the shop, Andy Willgoos and George Mead from engineering, Jack Borrup and Charles Marks on the tooling side, and so on, to include upwards of a dozen really competent men. The impact on Wright Aero would prove severe and replacements would be hard to find.

George Mead arrived in Washington early in June on a day when my wife and I had planned to run over to Annapolis for the June Week exercises—we had first met there and loved the little town. Going back and forth in the car, George and I first discussed the design principles for the new engine. Of course the enclosed valve gear and rotary induction of the R-1454 were musts, but we rejected that engine's arrangement of accessories on the front end; we would tuck ours on the rear out of the salt spray. We would split the crankshaft in two pieces, as George had done on an earlier engine, and would divide the crankcase similarly. As we talked, George sketched the ideas on the back of an envelope and captioned them in his precise printed letters. Later, we found some of our principles had already been used in the British Bristol Jupiter, but for the moment we glowed with the enthusiasm of creators of a new art.

Later, as the summer wore on and our engine problems eased up, storm clouds appeared in another quarter. The Engine Section had as one of its problems the Packard installation in the rigid airship *Shenandoah*. Lighter-than-air had always been the admiral's pet hobby and we had spent a lot of effort on two jobs: preventing the cooling water from freezing, and recovering water from the engine exhaust to compensate for the expenditure of fuel. This, in turn, avoided the need for valving precious helium gas—a critical factor in lighter-than-air.

The chief engineer of the *Shenandoah*, Edgar W. Sheppard, was an extremely able young lieutenant, who had served as my Number Two at Great Lakes, and who now spent considerable time with us. From him I learned disturbing things about the Naval Air Station at Lakehurst, headquarters for the rigids *Shenandoah* and *Los Angeles*.

In response to the criticism Billy Mitchell had leveled at the Navy, the Chief of Naval Operations had scheduled a number of western flights in the *Shenandoah* for public relations purposes. Prominent people and news writers had already been taken on junkets, but the expedition scheduled for late August and early September seemed correlated with the country fairs all over the West—and just at the peak of thunderstorm activity. If there was one thing a lighter-than-air pilot disliked, it was thunderstorms—and for good reason. But the pilots had not dared make public confession of their fear, lest they betray a weakness of lighter-than-air that might retard its development. And so they gritted their teeth and tried to suppress the jitters that kept them all on edge.

And now, as the *Shenandoah* departed on her fateful cruise, all of us in BUAERO followed her with anxious hearts. Suddenly a telegram sent from a town in Ohio by one of her crew brought shocking news of one of the greatest disasters in history. Turbulent currents of a line squall had sheared the girders of the great silver ship and split her into three sections. Parts had been free-ballooned to safety, but many of the crew had lost their lives, among them Edgar Sheppard. The ship had broken under his feet; in falling he had seized a girder and held on, 6,000 feet in the air. One of his men, hanging on precariously nearby, had called to him. When Shep extended the helping hand, his own girder failed and he fell to his death. There had been no parachutes. The whole Bureau was stunned.

And then lightning struck in another place. From down in San Antonio, Texas, where Brig. Gen. William G. Mitchell, USA, had been exiled to keep him quiet, newspaper headlines trumpeted charges at both the Army and Navy—charges of "treasonable neglect." The front-page news struck the public like a clap of thunder, and the battle for the separate air force was on in earnest. In BUAERO the whole staff rallied around Admiral Moffett, and embers that had so long smoldered now flamed.

CHAPTER SEVEN
CALVIN COOLIDGE'S TOWN MEETING

Billy Mitchell, handsome, dynamic, fast on the draw, and breathing the spirit of the offensive, personified the knight of the air of World War I. An outstanding pilot, a bold horseman, a soldier's soldier, a courageous crusader, he was the newsman's dream of dramatic copy. And now he assumed the lead in public opinion with the same *sang froid* he had displayed flying Number One of the First American Air Force on its first flight over the St. Mihiel Salient. With a fine sense of timing, he did that thing which every American longs to do—he told off his superiors in no uncertain terms, and with such sheer audacity that he almost got away with it. The public supported him from the start; it looked like a sure thing for his independent air force. Save for certain strategic errors, he would have won in a glide.

By seizing upon the crash of the great rigid airship *Shenandoah* as his take-off signal, Mitchell accepted the risk attendant upon hitting the Navy while it was down. And since lighter-than-air craft had become the personal hobby, and public responsibility, of Rear Adm. William A. Moffett, Mitchell made an implacable enemy of a man who, in the public mind, was no less devoted to the cause of aviation than Mitchell himself. And so, when Bill Mitchell sang out, "Tally Ho!" and started his power dive on Billy Moffett's tail, he suddenly found himself in a dogfight with an opponent quite as wiley as the famous German Baron von Richthofen. Even this was a calculated risk and might not have brought Mitchell down. It was Mitchell's attack on the Army that made him vulnerable. For while the Army might view with tolerant amusement Mitchell's assault on the Navy, it could not countenance insubordination in its own ranks; mutiny is inherently an unpardonable sin. Mitchell may have made a fatal error in not resigning his commission before charging his seniors with "treasonable neglect." By such action he could have martyred himself in the public eye and at the same time avoided the court-martial that finally convicted him without having to let the independent-air-force issue influence the trial. As it was, certain of his seniors, notably the then Chief of Staff, Gen. Douglas MacArthur, who would one day use the Air Force to gain victory in the Pacific, seemed at the time fairly to lick their chops as they assembled to convict General Mitchell.

Over on the Navy side were many naval aviators who had suffered the same frustrations that had aroused Mitchell to a frenzy against the Army. Feeling themselves hamstrung by naval conservatism, they too believed their only hope for advancing their beloved aviation lay in a new deal all around. But steeped as they all were in the ancient tradition of the West Point-Annapolis football feud, their first reaction was to defend their Navy, and the second was to rally around their chief, Admiral Moffett. For General Mitchell to expect aid from them under the circumstances would have been something like a Hatfield trying to induce a McCoy to join up on a squirrel shoot, while the feudin' and the fightin' were at a climax. As it was, Admiral Moffett kept his hotheads in line, including a few who openly favored the separate air force.

Meanwhile Mitchell's quick kick took the Navy high command completely by surprise. And as the political football sailed end over end toward the Navy goal, the only receiver ready was Admiral Moffett. A good open-field runner himself, he was about to take the ball over his shoulder on the dead run and might have sped to a touchdown save that his teammates blocked him out. The Navy strategists decided not to dignify Mitchell with any public recognition; they would just refuse to play.

But in BUAERO, every typewriter began tapping out retaliatory releases for the admiral. In spite of urgings by the latter, the Secretary staunchly refused to comment on the Mitchell attack, even as the press clamored for a reply. It was not until several days had passed that the admiral finally succeeded in drawing a reluctant consent to his own response. Then permission was granted only with the express condition that the admiral should reply on his own account and own responsibility.

Approval came at noon on a Saturday. By then the Bureau had closed for the day and, in addition to the admiral, only two of us remained aboard. One was the admiral's faithful colored messenger, Brown, the other, myself. We were waiting for the admiral in the anteroom to his office when he steamed through the door under full power. On the desk lay a copy of a statement I had drawn up for him. Seizing this, the admiral scrawled across the bottom a blunt postscript, calling William Mitchell a liar and ascribing his recent charges either to hallucinations or delusions of grandeur.

I cut the mimeograph stencil for him on his secretary's typewriter. Brown ran off the copies on a machine across the hall. The admiral waited impatiently until they were done, and then, seizing me by the arm, hustled me out of the building and into my car. We drove uptown to the offices of the Associated and United Press, where the admiral himself handed his statement across the counter to astonished reporters.

The statement hit the front pages of the New York papers. Its publication released all the ancient grudges and conflicts in aviation dating as far back as World War I. The old "airplane scandal" was dragged out and dusted off by crank inventors, claiming they had been robbed of their patents. The cry of "air trust" echoed through the halls of Congress and counsels of investigating committees, scenting headlines, began trying to get into the act.

Up to that moment some twenty-odd inquiries had been held on what to do about aviation. With surprising agreement they had all supported certain concrete recommendations; without exception they had been promptly consigned to the ninth pigeonhole—the one next the wastebasket. In 1924, during the excitement over the controversy between the proponents of the airplane and the supporters of the battleship, a Congressional committee, under the chairmanship of Congressman Lampert, had found that aviation, instead of being stifled by a "trust" was dying of neglect. The United States lacked both a policy for aviation and the legislation necessary to implement it.

The new controversy revived the ancient cry of "profiteer" against manufacturers, already reduced to hungry remnants of a once highly productive group. These now got together in their aeronautical chamber of commerce and sent a delegation to call on the Secretaries of War and Navy to urge that the two departments join in requesting the President to appoint a presidential advisory commission to look into the whole question. At the invitation of the President himself, they later went to the White House to support this recommendation. The President, who had always shown a Yankee sense of orderliness and a willingness to accept responsibility for the conduct of his administration, had been disturbed by the unseemly brawl. He now made no attempt to deny Mitchell the privilege of stating his case to the public, but since the charges reflected upon his own administration, he accepted the industry's proposal as a good way to sift them out. He approved the idea of a sort of New England town meeting on aviation.

His first step was to summon his wise and good friend, Dwight Morrow, and his second was to invite him to head up the inquiry. He then selected a group of men whose standing would warrant public support but was careful not to include anyone who had an ax to grind. The Commission included men from civil life who possessed knowledge of aviation, men from Congress who had had experience in the field, and men from the Army and Navy whose judgment would command public respect and confidence as did that of all other members.

Two of the members, Howard Coffin and William F. Durant, were engineers. From the armed forces were drawn Maj. Gen. James G. Harbord and Adm. Frank J. Fletcher, both retired after distinguished public careers. From Congress came three men, Senator Hiram Bingham, of the Senate Military Affairs Committee, himself a military aviator; James S. Parker, of the House Committee on Interstate and Foreign Commerce; and Congressman Carl Vinson, of the House Committee on Naval Affairs, a Democrat and a man destined to play a statesman's role in the nation's security. With Circuit Judge Arthur C. Dennison, Dwight Morrow, the chairman, completed a compact panel well constituted for the task in hand.

The Morrow Board held numerous public sessions and heard over a hundred witnesses present a wide assortment of views and opinions. Against the background of the Mitchell charges, the hearings received public attention and were widely discussed in editorial columns. Comment by the press was strongly favorable to the Mitchell cause and to all outward appearances, the general seemed on the way to victory. Behind the scenes, the Morrow Board studied the many records of previous inquiries, and by sifting them carefully was able to bring its own investigation to a close in about ninety days.

Over in BUAERO, we burned the midnight oil preparing the admiral's testimony. The spadework consisted in assembling the answers to specific questions propounded by the Morrow Board. Such questions were farmed out to different branches of the Bureau and then assembled for final study. Final editing of these comments fell to Lieutenant Commander Du Bose and myself but the larger issues were debated all over the Bureau. The interested parties were pretty well consolidated in opposition to the independent-air-force proposal, but they were divided almost equally on another organization question: should the admiral favor the formation of a corps of aviators, generally similar to the highly regarded United States Marine Corps?

In support of this idea, many of the old-timers worked hard on the admiral right up to the night before the Old Man was scheduled to appear before the Board. Then as we gathered around the long table for his final decisions, with that important subject all that remained to be agreed upon, I put it up to the admiral.

"Sir," I said, "here is a question that can't be straddled."

The admiral twisted nervously in his chair. Strong pressure had been brought to bear on him by the leading old-timers, men whose friendship he regarded highly, and, politician that he was, he would have given almost anything to be able to accommodate them. But underneath this issue lay certain fundamentals on which he had strong convictions.

He had gone to sea in the old days when the Engineer Corps and the line officers had fought so bitterly in the ancient feud between the "black gang" and the "deck force" that the service had been shaken to its foundations. As the only way out of an impossible situation, the Department had finally amalgamated the conflicting forces by absorbing the engineers into the line. The admiral, recognizing the need for specialization, was firmly convinced that it should be had without putting the specialists in a separate corps where corps loyalties might transcend loyalty to the service. Now he had to face that issue alone; there could be no agreement within his Bureau and this time he could not induce them to persuade him to do what he wanted.

"You are all my friends," he said, lifting his hand in a gesture to include all present, "and I'm sorry not to go along with some of you. The young pilots," he added, "will think I've let them down. But the time will come when they will thank me." He paused, and then with greater earnestness than I had ever heard in his voice, he concluded, "I'd rather see those kids dead than inflict on them the misery I suffered along with everyone else in the old days of deck force versus black gang."

Suddenly his face brightened as he said with a smile, "Hell, we won't secede from the Navy. If we are half as good as we think we are, we'll take it over!" Years later, when "Duke" Ramsey, Forrest Sherman, and Arthur Radford, some of his "boys," occupied the seats of the mighty, I recalled this comment.

Next morning, while the admiral testified at the hearings, I sat at my desk in the Engine Section, trying to concentrate on neglected paper work. But up there in that committee room, decisive events were taking place. The admiral was not impressive on the witness stand of a formal hearing; his strength lay in the give and take of the informal conference. He had little patience with the measured logic of a man like Fred Rentschler; though his own conclusions might derive from similar processes, his brain acted like chain lightning. What looked like snap judgment might have been thought through, but he was too impatient to develop the process for others. Now he would be sitting up there before a solemn board, facing a press table of partisan commentators sold on the Mitchell doctrine, and surrounded by all the high dignitaries of the Navy Department, from Secretary Wilbur and Admiral Hughes, the Chief of Naval Operations, down to Bureau chiefs like himself, most of whom feared he might sell out the Navy and go over to the Mitchell side.

For this had been a trying period for the Navy. Following the Armistice, public opinion had favored the idea of peace through disarmament and the Limitation of Arms Conference had all but emasculated the service. Then the spectacular air attacks engineered by General Mitchell had put the Navy further on the defensive. No one in the high command had developed a flair for public relations and now with Billy Mitchell on the offensive, the Navy had its back against the wall. Much of the enmity aroused by Mitchell's attack now turned inward to BUAERO and even Admiral Moffett. Yet up there before the Morrow Board, if the Old Man would just stick to his testimony as we had written it and not start ad-libbing, he would come out all right. If, however, he deviated it, some hawk like Congressman Carl Vinson, of Georgia, one of the best informed men in Congress, would dive on him at terminal speed.

Then, a little before noon, the admiral himself walked into the Engine Section and slumped down in his chair. All jauntiness was gone; he looked tired.

"They tell me I made a mess of it," he said simply.

It seemed that when he had taken his stand against the independent air force, Secretary Wilbur and others smiled their relief. The newspaper men looked let down. Then on the subject of the air corps, when Congressman Vinson cross-questioned him, he had, as an afterthought, stated that his Bureau should have control of aviation personnel and operations as well as matériel. Quick as a flash, Vinson shot back, "So you do believe in the air corps after all!"

In the subsequent confusion, the admiral had not made his position clear, but had left the matter in a snarl. Even as he finished his jerky report, the telephone rang. It was Marvin MacIntyre, a newspaper reporter who frequently dropped into the Bureau for a story and who had become one of the admiral's cronies. Years later, during the Roosevelt Administration, Mac sat in the White House as Secretary to the President, but back in those days he was just a good leg man.

"What happened at the hearing?" he inquired. "It looked to the press as though the Old Man had something on his chest but, with all that rank around him, got hemmed in."

"Maybe," I replied, anxious to keep the admiral's standing.

"But that break with Vinson made him look bad," Mac wailed.

"I can't see why," I replied. "All it meant was that he should have a bigger voice in personnel and operations but with a little topside cooperation, he doesn't need an air corps for that." The admiral nodded vigorously. Mac shouted over the phone.

"Sure, sure, I get you. Good-by!"

With that the admiral departed, his head up, his step springy. But we weren't yet out of the overcast.

Next morning a group of us sat in Jerry Land's tiny office attending a conference called by the head of the Matériel Division. Bureau business had all but ceased during the inquiry and even now we could not get down to brass tacks. Now a civilian walked right into the conference and brought our discussion to an abrupt halt. It was C. M. Keyes, president of the Curtiss Airplane and Motor Company, and a leader of the aircraft industry. The separate-air-force controversy had agitated them too; many companies favored it, especially those doing business with the Army. Navy contractors either disapproved or kept mum. Clem Keyes, who now stood in our midst, had favored the program.

"It looks like the Morrow Board will not recommend the separate air force," he said. "But there is one thing they will approve, and there's nothing you fellows can do about it." He then went on to say that he would appear for the industry at an early session and that he would support the idea of a government agency to be charged with responsibility for and authority over the design, development, and procurement of all aircraft, whether for the Army, Navy, or civil uses.

The news took my breath, for the thing we feared worst after the separate air force was unified procurement supply and design. Admiral Moffett had taken a strong position against it, but if the industry supported the Army on that, then the Board might accept it as a compromise. The only thing left for us to do was to block such a recommendation. While Keyes went on to support the proposal, I slid out the door and down to the Engine Section.

Here I put in a call for Fred Rentschler, in Hartford. I knew that some weeks earlier, Kraus in Procurement had informally agreed to Pratt and Whitney's proceeding with the purchase of a lot of tools and materials against a contract then being negotiated, and that Pratt and Whitney had already committed itself in advance in the interest of saving time and money. When I heard Fred's voice on the phone, I told him about Keyes's visit and suggested that he might reconsider his advance purchase order; I doubted that Admiral Moffett would sign a contract now for the new engines, since the industry proposed a new agency to do all its buying. I did not pretend to read the admiral's mind, and was talking unofficially, but thought he should be aware of this possibility.

It didn't take Rentschler long to get the point. Within an hour he had been in touch with Chance Vought, Grover Loening, Bill Boeing, and others who had taken similar risks. And when, next day, Mr. Keyes appeared before the Morrow Board to speak as the sole representative of the industry, Chairman Morrow advised him that there had been a change of plan. So many industry members had asked to address the committee that he could allow Mr. Keyes but a reduced period and that period had now expired. Meanwhile the admiral knew nothing of my action and the industry members who looked to the Bureau for business were not talking.

And while we sweated out the hearings, Admiral Moffett moved on another front. None appreciated better than he the influence of public opinion on the whole controversy, and he had found much to worry about in the approval given the Mitchell proposal in the public press. He had, therefore, suggested to George Wheat, now Fred Rentschler's public relations counsel, that he would like to meet the editorial writers and especially the aviation writers of the metropolitan dailies in New York at an informal dinner where he could talk with them, and he invited me to go along.

The dinner, held in a private dining room of the old Waldorf Hotel, started out being a bit stuffy with the natural suspicions engendered in newspaper men by industrialists giving away free food, but Admiral Moffett broke the ice with some delightful personal reminiscences, among them the intimate details of how he outsmarted Billy Mitchell at the Washington Limitation of Arms Conference and won the German rigid airship *Los Angeles* for the Navy. Then as things loosened up, one of the newswriters put the very question he wanted, by asking why we opposed the idea of unified procurement, supply, and design. To the layman, this looked like a natural way to avoid duplication of effort, to prevent competitive bidding between the Army and Navy for the same products and generally reduce expenses.

The admiral warmed to the subject. He recalled that he had once had that idea and had investigated a few successful business enterprises in the effort to find out how they handled it. He had found his answer at General Motors. If any group could have effected important economies by central purchasing, it would seem to be that corporation. To his surprise, the several divisions of General Motors had been decentralized and given complete autonomy. Matter of fact, that had turned out to be the basic policy that had made the corporation successful. G.M. divisions had been encouraged to compete among themselves. No single all-powerful executive had been given the job of deciding things. Instead, General Motors' customers made all the decisions. The financial statements of the several divisions were good barometers of the effectiveness of their management. The customer was always right.

Now, the admiral continued, with each G.M. division held responsible for its own performance, common sense dictated that its officers must have full authority over the tools and materials required to discharge that responsibility. Control of purchasing was one of the first requirements. Automotive line production called for split-second scheduling of material receipts, and this could not be surrendered to some independent agency without danger of breakdown. Besides, while central purchasing might appear to reduce cost through volume purchases, competition between the divisions might do at least as well without endangering deliveries. That was all theory, but obviously a company like G.M., in which central purchasing might appear particularly attractive theoretically, must have come to their decision to decentralize after experience.

Next day, on the train back to Washington, I felt depressed by the almost universal acceptance of the Mitchell plan. Even though the Morrow Board were to turn it down, public opinion would ultimately force its acceptance. The admiral, however, was most cheerful. He thought that if he now had just one man in the Bureau, he could turn the whole thing to his advantage. The man he had in mind was Capt. Henry C. Mustin, a pioneer naval aviator who had died in the service. Henry Mustin, he said, was one of the few men in aviation who combined vision and imagination with practical judgment. It was the latter quality that Mitchell lacked; Mustin had had them all. Before he died he had drawn up a detailed plan for the organization of naval aviation. He had sketched the big carriers with their squadrons flying overhead, their spare planes on deck and the personnel listed down to the last ordinary seaman. That sketch now lay in his safe in BUAERO. When we got back there, I was to get hold of Du Bose, his Financial Division head, and help work out estimates of the cost of creating such a force. We should spread this over a five-year period—make a five-year procurement program for naval aviation.

"And," he summed it up, "don't figure too close. Use your imagination."

When, finally, the long-awaited report of the Morrow Board was published, it came as a distinct letdown to many. The advocates of the independent air force let out loud wails of "whitewash," and the press reflected its disappointment. However, in BUAERO there was satisfaction. The Board rejected the idea of the separate air force at that time. It did, however, recommend an Air Corps status for the Army Air Services, something quite compatible with the Army organization's several branches such as Infantry, Field Artillery, Cavalry, Engineers, Coast Artillery, and so on. The report made separate recommendations for reorganization of the Army and Navy, which would later be enacted into law in the Air Corps Act of 1926. It referred to the need for waiving the requirement for competitive bidding in cases where the public interest required it, a provision that was later so garbled in the Air Corps Act that it became quite impossible to procure aircraft at all without violating the law.

The Board especially turned thumbs down on the British plan of an air ministry charged with responsibility for both military and civil aviation. It took a strong position for the principle that historic American tradition called for armed forces for defense only, and it insisted they should be kept subordinate to the civil government. However, it urged the orderly expansion of air transport, preferably under private management and, to promote the orderly development of civil aviation, it recommended the establishment of a bureau of air commerce in the Department of Commerce, then under Secretary Herbert Hoover. It further recommended the appointment of an additional assistant secretary of commerce for air, to supervise the new bureau.

The Board recommended a policy of continuity of orders for the aircraft industry and proposed a standard rate of replacement of operating aircraft in order to retain a healthy industry. This, it pointed out, must become the nucleus of rapid wartime expansion and should be administered as a continuing source of technological leadership.

If the report proved lacking in sensationalism, it was none the less constructive. If now it could be implemented it might become the Magna Charta of American aviation. President Coolidge transmitted the report to Congress with his own approval and thus started it on its way to being translated into the Air Commerce Act and the Air Corps Act of 1926. These acts, in effect, placed the responsibility for promoting aviation directly upon the shoulders of the government. They made it the duty of those in authority to promote the orderly development of the air forces, our air commerce, and our aircraft industry; and thus, for the first time, enunciated a clear statement of United States air policy.

As for General Mitchell, whose charges had led to the formulation of this policy, he was tried by Army general court-martial and convicted of violation of the ninety-sixth Article of War. He was sentenced to be suspended from rank, command, and duty, with forfeiture of all pay and allowances for five years. President Coolidge modified the forfeiture of pay and accepted the general's resignation, to take effect February 1, 1926. Just ten years later, Billy Mitchell died. But one day the United States Congress did create a separate air force, and by then, General Mitchell's name had been firmly established in his countrymen's minds as a man who had been martyred for his vision.

During the last decade of General Mitchell's life, Admiral Moffett served continuously as Chief of the Bureau of Aeronautics, and there founded the technology of naval aviation. It has been said of the contributions of the two men that "Bill Mitchell's fumble set up the play from which Billy Moffett went on to score." Just at the peak of his career, the admiral gave his own life to his country in the crash of the rigid airship *Akron*.

CHAPTER EIGHT
DWIGHT MORROW ADVANCES THE THROTTLE

The Morrow Board policy, for all its wisdom, might have lapsed easily into innocuous desuetude save for the dynamic character of William A. Moffett. Whereas the Army Air Service proclaimed it a whitewash and a denial of their aspirations, the admiral recognized it for what it was, a golden opportunity. And as usual, when it came to capitalizing it, his timing was precise.

I was sitting behind my desk in the Engine Section one morning engaged in shoveling the avalanche of papers from "Incoming" to "Outgoing" and feeling much like a fireman on the floor plates of a coal-burning destroyer under forced draft shoveling coal into the insatiable maws of a pair of boilers, when the phone rang.

"This is Moffett," came the admiral's voice. "I want you to get hold of Du Bose right away. Grab a taxi and come up here to The Hill. You'll find me in Congressman Butler's office, Chairman of the Naval Affairs Committee. Bring that estimate on the cost of the Mustin plan. Got it?"

"Aye, aye, sir!"

"Wait a minute. Change that!" came the staccato bark. "Tell Du Bose to bring the plan. You call up Marvin MacIntyre; tell him to come to the Bureau. Then you write up a news release for him—one like this: 'The greatest forward step in the history of aviation was taken today when Congressman Butler, Chairman of the House Naval Affairs Committee, announced approval of the Moffett five-year Naval Aviation building program.'"

"Did he really approve it, Admiral?" I interposed.

"Of course not," came the reply. "He hasn't even seen it. But when he reads his name in the afternoon *Star* and looks at the editorial Mac will get for us, he'll think he invented it himself. Shake a leg now, and send Du Bose on the run."

"How did you work it, sir?" I insisted.

"At the hearing this morning," the admiral explained, "Butler was fit to be tied—said the public was clamoring for action on aviation and wanted to know what to do. I told him he ought to approve my five-year program. He wanted to know what it was. I told him the program I'd been trying to sell him for five years. When I'd ask Congress for money, they'd say 'where are your men to man these planes?' When I'd ask BUNAV for the men, they'd want to know where the planes were. Butler got all excited and sent me out of the hearing to get the plan."

The Moffett five-year building program went through Congress with a whoop and a holler, and within a week the Army had one of its own. With this final consummation of the recommendations of most of the twenty-two inquiries that had investigated aviation, the throttle was opened at last. This was true in spite of the fact that in writing the Air Corps Act of 1926, Congress had crossed up the aircraft industry. The manufacturers, having been promised relaxation of the competitive-bidding requirement which had served to hamper research and development, had in turn agreed to a provision in the Act under which the Armed Forces could audit their accounts and thus control profits. This was a privilege heretofore never conceded by private industry, but Congress, lacking the nerve to go through with the agreement in committee, had so garbled the language of the Act and so complicated the procedure that no procurement officer could buy anything without violating some law. However, public support of the policy had been so evident that the more courageous procurement people, like our own Sidney Kraus, were willing to accept the risk.

And so it seemed that almost overnight, aviation, released of its tie-downs and wheel blocks, became airborne again. In BUAERO a significant event was the completion of the first Pratt and Whitney Wasp on December 24, 1926, just six months after its inception. George had sent me a photograph of the new engine as a Christmas card and it was a thing of beauty that was to become literally a joy forever. It came out at exactly the 650 pounds Chance Vought had specified but on block test turned up a nice 415 horsepower instead of the 350 he had asked for.

Meanwhile the Wright Simoon also passed its tests at 350 horsepower though it was already outmoded by the Wasp. In order to give the Simoon the full benefits of an airplane designed to utilize the engine's qualities, Wright had put Hugh Chatfield to work on the design and construction of their own single-seat fighter called the "Apache." On flight test the little craft had shown a performance far superior to the current liquid-cooled pursuit, even in the controversial characteristic of high speed at sea level where, according to the critics, the air-cooled would always be at a serious disadvantage because of its "large frontal area."

Since that airplane would show to even greater advantage with the higher power of the Wasp, we now wangled a deal with Wright. We actually persuaded good-natured Charlie Lawrance to turn his pet airplane over to Chance Vought for the installation of a Pratt and Whitney Wasp with which Lt. C. C. Champion, who had now joined the Engine Section, was to take a shot at the world's record for altitude. With the completion of Chance Vought's own Corsair, we now had a brilliant two-seater that compared favorably in performance with the hottest fighters, and thus gave us a stable with which to make an assault on all the world's records in their classes. The admiral, a highly competitive spirit with a keen appreciation of the value of world's records and racing competition, now made participation in these events a major Bureau project.

The names "Wasp" and "Corsair" had been selected by the Engine Section, in response to requests from Pratt and Whitney and Chance Vought. Little did we know at the time what distinction they would one day attain. The Wright Apache focused attention of other manufacturers on the characteristics of the Wasp; and Boeing, after testing an engine in a converted FB-1 fighter, immediately put a new one in the works to be called the "F2B." Curtiss made a conversion of one of its single-seater Hawks, replacing the D-12 with a Wasp. The first Wasp engine to be flight tested was flown in a Curtiss Hawk and thus became a sort of monument to the reluctance Curtiss had shown by their failure to develop their own R-1454 engine. It also nearly became a monument to the failure of the Pratt and Whitney Wasp.

For on the one-hour endurance test over Long Island, Temple Joyce, then test pilot for Curtiss and one of the best-known figures in aviation, grew tired of the monotony of cruising back and forth and decided to vary the routine with some acrobatics. But when he pulled back the stick and booted the rudder to do a nice snap roll, something snapped in the Wasp and Temp had to make a forced landing on the Curtiss field. The competitive Wasp in a competitor's airplane had gone sour on its test flight! Consternation reigned in the Engine Section—matter of fact, it really poured.

Examination disclosed that the crankshaft counterweight had sailed out through the crankcase. Now the cheek had been designed with ample margins for the stresses of centrifugal force, and the failure remained a mystery until I recalled a lesson learned as a student in the Sperry Gyro Compass School several years earlier. No one had anticipated the effect of gyroscopic forces like those set up in a snap roll. Now George Mead took these in hand and strengthened the shaft to withstand them. With this change, the Pratt and Whitney Wasp came to stay.

One day George and I, feeling happy about this, decided to take a walk through the Smithsonian Institution museum. And there we saw something that cut us back to size. It was the Manly engine, one designed by Charles M. Manly, the pilot and engineer of the Langley airplane, the craft Professor Langley had tried to fly off a catapult years earlier. And marvel of marvels, it was a five-cylinder, single-row, air-cooled radial that antedated the original Wright engine and all the other liquid-cooled in-line engines that had followed it. Charles Manly, having no prior art to befuddle him, had reasoned out the rational form for an aircraft engine and created one forthwith. As we stood looking at the museum piece that included the fundamentals we had used to obsolete years of automotive practice, George grinned sheepishly and remarked, "It all goes to show that every time you think you have discovered America, you find that Columbus was here back in 1492."

With the completion of many flight tests, the Wasp was now ready for production. But Rentschler found himself in a quandary as to what price he should ask for the engines in quantity. He had no experienced costs, for no engine had yet been built in production. We had asked for six engines on the first experimental order and Kraus had paid Pratt and Whitney the $90,000 he had set aside for them. It was estimated that this amount covered about half of the experimental costs, and Kraus was willing to add the remainder to the first production order so as to write off this expense. But no one knew nor had any way of guessing what the unit price should be for the order of some two hundred engines now required for Vought Corsairs and Boeing and Curtiss fighters. And so the price was fixed by that which Kraus had previously paid for a similar number of Packard 1500's—a liquid-cooled engine we had earlier prescribed to replace the Curtiss D-12's in the Boeing FB-5's. For while we had promoted the air-cooled vigorously we had likewise developed the 500-hp Packard as a successor to the 400-hp Curtiss D-12.

Rentschler was not too happy about having the price for his air-cooled engines fixed by that of another contractor for liquid-cooled; he insisted there was no relationship between the two. But in government business, price may be fixed by anything else but merit. The ever-present threat of a Congressional investigation made it impossible to write into the Pratt and Whitney contract any figure higher than the Packard price even though the circumstances might be entirely different. This was but one of the things that made it hard to interest private manufacturers in risking either their equities or their engineering talent in a government speculation; none of the business fundamentals with which they were accustomed to measure their risks applied here.

However, as it turned out, an unexpected event exercised such an influence that Pratt and Whitney not only did not lose money on the first contract but even made an embarrassingly high profit. It all started the morning William E. Boeing, of Seattle—not "Addison Sims"—arrived in the Engine Section.

Bill Boeing, founder of the Boeing Airplane Company, and a successful operator in lumber and real estate, had drawn his airplane-company staff from versatile young graduates of the aeronautical-engineering course of the University of Washington and had picked some good ones. Foremost among these were Claire Egtvedt, his chief engineer, and Phil Johnson, his factory manager. Bill, a pilot himself, had opened an air line between Seattle and Victoria, using a couple of Boeing-built flying boats under the management of Eddie Hubbard. Eddie had persuaded Bill, against the advice of Phil Johnson, to enter a bid for the new Chicago-San Francisco contract air-mail route, and Bill had won the competition with a bid considered absurdly low by his competitors.

As Bill took a chair by my desk that morning, he promptly launched into the background of his low bid. It seems that Claire Egtvedt, who had designed the single-seat fighter F2B around the Wasp, had also made a study of that engine in a completely new mail plane, to be called the "40-B." By doing away with the heavy cooling system of the Liberty in the new design, and availing himself of the other features of the Wasp, he had turned out a mail plane capable of carrying double the pay load on the same horsepower. By converting several hundred pounds of dead load into as many pounds of paying load, he had demonstrated the fact that no operator could afford to use war-surplus airplanes—even as a gift—in face of that kind of competition. Furthermore, Boeing could build the new planes dirt cheap with the same overhead needed for the military business. He thought the Wasp would revolutionize air transport. His problem was how to get hold of about twenty-five new Pratt and Whitneys right away with the entire production booked for the Navy.

This was a matter on which the admiral had already set Bureau policy. Having in mind the fact that if government and commercial business could be lumped, the increased volume could bring reduced costs for both, he had issued instructions to cooperate with commercial operators wherever practicable. All Bill needed was a letter of introduction to F. B. Rentschler.

Out of this episode grew the Boeing Air Transport Company's profitable operation, the ultimate consolidation of Boeing and Pratt and Whitney, to form the nucleus for the United Aircraft and Transport Corporation, and such a profit for Pratt and Whitney on the first order that Rentschler finally came to the Engine Section for advice as to what should be done with the profit. Not the least important factor in this achievement was the breathtaking daring which Rentschler showed in tooling up his shop before the engine had passed its tests and before he had received the contract. This intelligent risk paid such dividends that Rentschler later agreed with Kraus to return what might have been called "excess profits," and in so doing thus established a principle of voluntary profit control that finally became the established policy of the company. The original suggestion for this came from the Engine Section.

The development of the new engines and the creation of new aircraft around them came just in time to ease a serious situation in connection with the outfitting of the new carriers *Saratoga* and *Lexington*. The ships were scheduled for completion in about two years and their squadrons were even then being assembled at the Fleet Air Stations at Hampton Roads, Virginia, and San Diego, California. And while the Wasp put us on easier schedules for the fighters, we were still up against it for the big torpedo-bomber scouts. Our SC's, designed originally around the Wright T-3, had proved cumbersome and heavy and, while operable on twin floats, had lacked the performance desired for carrier use. The large engine had introduced a propeller problem, too—one that for a while had given us a lot of concern.

One of the SC's, equipped with a standard propeller made of laminated woods glued together and finished to form, had let go on take-off at Hampton Roads and the engine had nearly jumped out of the plane. In response to an excited call from Norfolk, I had flown down in company with Charles J. McCarthy, then our stress expert, to see what could be done. Fortunately, about this time the Army Engineering Division at McCook Field had brought along an experimental development, under the supervision of Frank Caldwell, in which a new aluminum alloy called "duralumin" had been introduced as a substitute for wood. So far it had not been fully proved in service but we were in such a right spot that I now authorized the procurement of the first production order for 100 of them.

Now to round out the carrier program we must needs do something about those torpedo bombers. The engine situation began to assume a certain stable pattern that could be used to foster development: Wright had a nice bit of business and without serious competition in the 200-hp air-cooled Whirlwind class; Pratt and Whitney had a similar nest egg in their domination of the 400-hp Wasp category; both companies had undertaken new developments in a larger 500-hp type. At Wright it was the Cyclone; at Pratt and Whitney, the Hornet. But neither of these engines looked big enough for the torpedo-bomber class and every engineer in the industry had solemnly assured me in writing that to build a 600-hp air-cooled radial was completely impossible. In light of this dictum we had installed a Packard 2500, 800-hp liquid-cooled engine in one of the SC's which we had called the "SC-6" but which the mechanics had promptly dubbed the "*Sea Cow.*" Now the time had arrived to give the old girl an endurance test.

The personnel of the Engine Section had undergone some change since my taking over. After Ricco Botta had gone to sea I brought in Lt. L. D. Webb, a naval aviator and experienced engineer. Lee had started his naval career as an enlisted man and had served as an electrician in a submarine. In World War I he had qualified as a pilot and been commissioned in the Reserve. Later he had taken the examinations and transferred to the regular service. He was a burly fellow with a broad back, the kind you like to ride behind in an airplane. With Lee in the cockpit, me in the rear seat, and Capt. Lionel M. Woolson, the Packard experimental engineer, lying on a mattress back in the tail, the *Sea Caw* started her take-off at dawn from the bosom of the Potomac River abreast of the spot where the Presidential Yacht *Mayflower* lay. We were so heavily laden with fuel that we missed the first run after roaring past the *Mayflower* wide open with our eight hundred horses straining. On the second run past, I noticed a figure in a nightgown waving encouragement to us, but a second look revealed it as President Coolidge himself and his clenched fist waved no encouragement.

And as hour after hour we droned up and down Chesapeake Bay, trying to burn out the fuel to determine our real endurance, I began thinking of a scheme that might solve our problem. Certainly the big liquid-cooled Packard didn't make sense; but a 600-hp air-cooled might do the job. Our *Sea Cow* grossed some 12,000 pounds of dead weight with her full load of fuel and was correspondingly big and unwieldy. If someone could build a 600-hp radial he would automatically save nearly a ton right off the bat; and if some smart designer could find a way to build a lighter airplane structure, we might get the whole thing down to something of the order of 7,500 pounds. This would give us a smaller, handier airplane that would still carry the bomb, torpedo, and fuel load we wanted, and thus complete the outfit for our new carriers with an all-air-cooled complement. The problem was how to get the job done—and Old Man Competition was the obvious answer.

The chance of a lifetime came one day with a visit from the dean of our aircraft manufacturers, Glenn L. Martin. Glenn's black mood quite overshadowed his natty dress. He was about to finish his contract for torpedoplanes and had no new business in sight. First thing BUAERO knew he'd have to fire his whole organization and, once they got scattered, their know-how and teamwork would be lost forever. It was up to the Bureau to do something to save Glenn Martin.

"Have you tried creating a new model, Glenn?" I asked innocently enough. Glenn protested that his SC was the last word and that nothing much better could be produced.

"I've had an idea checked out by the drafting room," I said, "and they agree that if some smart airplane manufacturer were to design a new torpedo carrier around, say a new six hundred-horsepower air-cooled engine, he could get it down to about seventy-five hundred pounds gross, provided he could develop some new structural features along the lines that Charles Ward Hall has proposed."

Glenn was skeptical; and besides, he and the others had little confidence in those tricky aluminum structures that Charles Ward Hall proposed; they held out for welded steel. And besides, where could you get a 600-hp air-cooled radial?

"Both the Cyclone and Hornet do five hundred twenty-five horsepower now," I said, "and if a smart airplane designer made a deal with one or the other for a 600-hp type, say a year from now, the direct competition in that class might persuade one or both of them to push the development for you in time to give you the power you need, and by that time you can have your revolutionary model."

Glenn's puckered brow suggested thought. "Do you think the Bureau would finance such a development," he asked, "with an experimental contract?"

"Oh, yes," I agreed, "up at the Naval Aircraft Factory at Philadelphia." Glenn was shocked by the suggestion.

"Have you mentioned this to anyone else?" he inquired.

"Everyone who would listen," I replied. "And Frank Russell, of Curtiss, is coming in this afternoon. I thought that since you had taken his SC design away from him by underbidding him on the production order, he might find a certain satisfaction in doing likewise by you."

By the time I had finished the sentence, Glenn had disappeared through the door.

With the carrier program pretty well rounded up, I began to think of going back to sea duty and general service. If I wasted much more time in the side shows, some future Selection Board would gladly skip me over. No use to ask the admiral's permission; he'd say the job was but half done and he couldn't spare me. A personal visit to the Bureau of Navigation and a request to command another destroyer would do the trick.

But when, shortly afterward, Admiral Moffett called me into his office, I found the atmosphere distinctly chilly. On his desk lay the notice from BUNAV advising him of the intention to detach me and requesting that he nominate a suitable relief.

"What will it take to keep you here?" the admiral asked.

"A nonflying officer has no place in this game," I replied, "and I'm supposed to be too old to learn to fly."

"The pilot course," replied the admiral, "takes nine months and I can't spare you that long." I had not intended to ask for flight training but the admiral assumed that I was putting pressure on him.

"I could send you to Pensacola for two months for training as Naval Observer," he went on, "and that might take the curse off shore duty by making you a part of the aeronautic organization."

My next remark surprised me; certainly it came from my mouth rather than my head, though my heart may have been in it. "If I could wangle a way to complete the pilot's course in two months," I inquired, "would that be acceptable to you?"

The admiral grinned as he held out his hand. "When you arrive at Pensacola," he advised, "drop in on Brooks Upham, the Commandant. He's a personal friend of mine and might be able to do something for you."

Thus quite without prior intent on my part I had talked my way even deeper into aviation. But at home that evening I did not reveal the whole scheme to my wife. Having received word of her mother's serious illness she had left the day before for an indefinite visit at her home.

CHAPTER NINE
THE GOSPEL ACCORDING TO AUNT LUCY

Rear Adm. F. Brooks Upham, Commandant of the Naval Air Station, Pensacola, reached across his flat-topped desk for my formal orders. Behind him through the window, the sun glinted on the leaves of ancient live oaks, and filtered through shreds of gently swaying Spanish moss. The rattle of aircraft engines disturbed the still morning, a signal that flying was being resumed after the September hurricane that had seriously damaged this ancient Civil War navy yard. The admiral welcomed me with a friendly smile.

"I've had a note about you from Moffett," he volunteered. "So," he added, "it's the old story of old dogs and new tricks. Having now reached the ripe old age of thirty-nine," he went on, "you're dead but won't lie down. If you ask me, it's a lot of bunk."

"The Regulations," I reminded him, "set twenty-eight as the maximum age limit for flight training." The admiral reached for the top drawer of his antique desk. A warm breeze floated in from across the Gulf of Mexico. Beyond the signal tower, across the blue harbor, the white sands of Santa Rosa Island gleamed in the sunlight. Still farther out glittered the quiet waters of the Gulf.

The commandant handed me a sheet of paper. I recognized it at once as a few lines of doggerel I had written one wintry December night while the old seaplane tender and kite-balloon ship *Wright* had lain in the Brooklyn Navy Yard. We had been working all day on a miserably cold job of ballasting the *Old Hooker* and had turned the duty over to the aviators as a part of their instruction. Then suddenly someone of them had discovered that none of them had qualified as yet for their 50 per cent increase for "flight pay" and that unless they corrected this fault immediately they would lose the allowance. They had all laid down their tools, both the lighter-than-air and the heavier-than-air pilots, and had rushed over to the Naval Air Station at Lakehurst to ride up and down ten times in a kite-balloon attached to a winch in a warm hangar, leaving the ballasting to the mercies of the ship's company, the so-called "thicker-than-mud." Now I read the verses.

The lighter-than-air are jolly boys,
Who float on wings of gas,
Like helium or hydrogen
And some hot air, alas!
They float about in kite-balloons
A blimp or even a zep.
And draw their extra fifty per cent,
With promptitude and pep.

The heavier-than-air boys zoom about,
And make a lot of fuss,
In F-5-L's and NC boats
And other kinds of bus.
It takes a sort of superman
To learn the air's queer feel—
And draw that extra fifty per cent,
With such consuming zeal.

And then there is another crew,
A silly sort of dud,
It does the heavy dirty work,
The poor old thicker-than-mud.
If one of these guys rams a rock,
Or on a reef gets wrecked,
He never gets his pay increased;
Most likely he'll be checked.

And so we sail the briny deep,
Two live ones and a dud,
The lighter-than-air, the heavier-than-air—
And the poor old thicker-than-mud.

I glanced up to find a smile on the commandant's lips.

"I found it in the desk here," he said, "after I had taken over from Christy."

We had visited the *Wright* in the summer of 1922 after ferrying some F-5-L's down from Philadelphia and someone must have lifted the masterpiece from the bulletin board.

"I had hardly expected to find the author of that among the candidates for flight training," Brooks Upham went on, "but since you are here I'll do my best for you. My aide, young Jimmy Lowry, will take you out for a flight check and if he rates you 'promising material,' I'll see that planes are put at your disposal at any time you may want them. No need for you to fool around with the regular schedule for ground school; you know all that. It's simply a question of nervous and physical endurance whether you can complete the entire course in the two months." He reached for a push button.

"By the way," he added, "my lady asked me to invite you to dine with us this evening—seven o'clock—service uniform."

Within a half hour, Jimmy Lowry and I were down at Squadron Six Beach warming up an N-9 seaplane. The Consolidated NY's had gone into service for land-plane training but the N-9's still survived for work on floats. Jimmy, after a few words of instruction, motioned me into the rear seat and took his instructor's position in front. Then signaling to the "boots" to cast us off, he opened the throttle and taxied out into the stream where he cut the gun and let the little plane idle up into the wind.

He gave her the gun and as the engine took hold we skittered smoothly over the surface and into the air to sail out over the landlocked bay. Below us, the old town of Pensacola nestled among live oaks and Spanish moss now devastated by the hurricane. While I had taken the controls now and then, flying as a passenger, I had never presumed to land or take off and had had no other instruction than the few orders Jimmy Lowry had given me back there at the Beach. Now he shook the controls as a signal for me to take over and, as I did so, held both hands aloft to signal that I had charge.

Jimmy Lowry now put me through all the "checks" in accordance with what I learned later was a well-established routine. He sent me flying over the land at an altitude of about fifty feet and, after we had proceeded too far to permit turning back for a water landing in case of engine failure, he cut the gun and watched my reaction. The only thing I could see to do was to land straight ahead into the palmetto swamp, and this, I learned later, was considered to be good "reaction in emergency." Jimmy opened the throttle again before we tangled with the palm fronds, and then waved me back to Squadron Six Beach. He said nothing as we walked up the ramp and, at the entrance to Bachelor Officer Quarters, simply saluted and walked off toward the commandant's office. Still in the dark as to my future, I hunted up my room in "BOQ" and found my baggage already in it. A colored maid was making up the bed.

She had a wrinkled, light-chocolate old face, framed by kinky white hair held in a tight knot at the back of her neck. Though she was said to have been born into slavery, her erect, almost haughty carriage seemed to deny the story. She turned to bow to me in a curtsy that was dignified and respectful.

"Mawnin', sah!" she said. Her soft voice had the resonance of a singer of Negro spirituals. "Ah's Aunt Lucy," she added. "I takes keer o' dis room for de gempmens what has it. Ah unpacks yo satchel, too, if you likes."

"I'm not sure I'll stay, Aunt Lucy," I replied. "We won't unpack until I hear from Lieutenant Lowry." Aunt Lucy bowed her head as she moved off to dust the window sills. She had that air of quiet dignity, that sense of being wholly at peace with the world, that had characterized the old-time darkies I had known as a midshipman back at little Annapolis. A leader among her people, a deaconess in the church, no doubt, Aunt Lucy seemed a woman distinguished by deep religious faith. I had unbelted my sword after leaving the commandant's office and, after my check flight, had carried it to BOQ in my hand. Now as I laid it on the table Aunt Lucy glanced at it and began humming an old spiritual:

"I'se goin' to lay down my sword and shield.
Down by de riverside,
Down by de riverside,
Down by de riverside.
I'se goin' to lay down my sword and shield,
Down by de riverside
I ain't goin' to study war no mo'."

As she drifted out of the door the telephone rang. It was the commandant. As I reached for the receiver, I could feel a flush creeping up the back of my neck and knew for the first time just how much I wanted a favorable report. Well, I'd soon know, now.

"Lowry has passed your check," Brooks Upham was saying. "He considers you 'good pilot material.' See you for dinner!" I hung up and called down the corridor to old Aunt Lucy.

"I guess you can unpack the satchel," I said.

The Uphams were distinctly Old Navy, part of a small coterie of distinguished senior officers and their wives who had served the Navy through the lean years, on duty that had either taken them to distant foreign stations together or forced long separations. They were men and women who had stood for all that was best in loyalty to their country, their service, and to one another, and who supported the fine traditions of the earlier days. Poor in worldly goods, yet they were rich in experience, having traveled widely and lived close to the people of foreign lands. Money had meant little to them; they had found ample compensation in their knowledge of a public service faithfully performed. Evenings at the commandant's quarters were to prove important events in my training as a naval aviator; and old Aunt Lucy was to leave her mark, too.

For flying was still a hazardous business back in the middle twenties, and tragedy cast its shadow all too often over the little station at Pensacola. Perhaps it was this that focused people's thoughts on things far removed from "pounds per horsepower." After dinner that evening, the commandant and his lady sat with me around the fire that provided the only warmth against the evening chill, and discussed books they had just finished reading.

The commandant had been deep in a treatise on nuclear theory as discussed in a book called *The New Knowledge*. It had been written in a popular and entertaining vein by a scientific author whose name I don't now recall and, besides setting forth clearly the new idea as to the structure of the atom and a theory of electronics, it had developed an absorbing spiritual theme. The author, recognizing the resemblance between the laws controlling the actions of electrons within the atom and those that controlled the astronomy of the universe, had emphasized his own conviction that no conflict existed between religion and science. On the contrary, the more a scientific mind studied the revelations concerning the physical world, the stronger became his convictions as to the existence of an infinite God.

The commandant's lady fingered a book she had just finished but seemed to hesitate about opening a discussion of it.

"If you are like the rest of the students," she smiled, "you'll have your nose buried so deeply in that precious *Flight Manual*, that you'll have no time for anything else."

The commandant was rather proud of that *Flight Manual*. It was the book of instruction for the flight-training course that had been evolved out of long experience with many students. It had been compiled by one of his instructors, Lt. Barrett Studley, who was also writing a book on the subject. Every detail was so well covered in it that it had become a veritable "student's bible." No matter how often he read it and reread it or practiced the maneuvers described in it, every new reading revealed something there he had not previously absorbed. Even the instructors boned the manual— and found new inspiration in doing so.

As Mrs. Upham talked, the commandant stirred the fire until it burned brightly, shining on his wife's serene features.

"My book," she said, "bears on the same theme as the one developed by *The New Knowledge* but approaches it from a wholly different point of view."

She went on to point out that its author, whose name I have forgotten along with the title of the book, had been a successful minister—at least one might judge him so by usual standards. He had managed a large New York congregation, kept the church in repair, and collected substantial sums of money for worthy causes. But after his retirement he had reached the conclusion that his ministry had been a complete failure. Lacking faith in religion, because he had not been able to reconcile the Christian Gospel with his reasoned analysis of it, he had failed in his spiritual leadership.

Deep concern over this had caused him to restudy the Gospels and especially the history of their composition; and he had concluded that in the interim between the death of the Apostles and the compilation of the Gospels, numerous additions might have been made and certain beliefs carried over from earlier faiths might have been interlarded into the basic concept of the Christian idea. He had therefore set about to delete from the Gospels, as recorded, all the inconsistencies with the Gospel as he thought it must have been preached, and had emerged with a kernel so dazzling and completely credible to the rational mind that he had become convinced that it must have been divinely inspired.

For no one man nor group of men could possibly have conceived a faith so wholly consistent and so inspiring as had Jesus Christ himself. The very idea of individual dignity had brought men conviction that they were not meant to be slaves but responsible children of God. With that conviction, human liberty was born. And human liberty was not just a pleasant material situation but the world's most vital, dynamic, and constructive spiritual force. To cast off the rule of tyrants men must only be governed by God.

As the commandant's lady finished her review, she handed her book over to me.

"Since we've been on duty down here," she said simply, "we've come to sense the semireligious fervor with which the lads approach their flying. The hazards seem but to lift up their spirits, for while physically the airplane is mechanical, yet the art of flying has the flavor of high destiny." She paused and glanced quickly at her husband as if for support.

"We haven't succeeded in crystallizing the idea," said the admiral, "but even as professional military people we keep groping for the philosophical import of this new device. The thing is potentially so destructive that unless we find some way, through the spirit, to adapt it to constructive uses, it will surely destroy us."

For a while we three sat silent before the fire. Brooks Upham had expressed the unease that lies heavy on the hearts of military men; they dislike the business of destruction.

When, next morning, I arrived at Squadron Six Beach, my instructor was waiting for me with orders to disregard the routine and feed the subject to me just as fast as I could take it. I had, however, been assigned to Class Twenty-six—youngsters, for the most part, two to three years out of Annapolis. Included in the class, however, were a handful of seniors like "Baldy" Pownall, "Woody" Thomas, Harry Bogusch, and Freddie Kauffman. For Admiral Moffett, having felt the need of a little seasoning in the aeronautic organization, had accepted applications from a selected group of more experienced line officers. Among them were former submarine officers who, thinking that duty a little too hazardous to health, had transferred to the comparative safety of flying.

And thus began a most delightful experience. For the first time in many moons, my responsibilities were reduced to the lowest possible terms. All I now had to do was to maneuver a nice little airplane, one that seemed to sense my intentions and even anticipate them, and to execute turns, glides, and landings smoothly and competently and—to my surprise—without dunking me in the drink. The pullings and haulings of BUAERO, the plot and counterplot of politics, now faded into the limbo. And in their places came the thrill of facing hazards—and overcoming them. Raised as I had been in an era when men had not asked extra compensation for extra hazard in the line of duty, I held a secret hunch that a man should be glad to pay something extra for the privilege of enjoying such a happy and uncomplicated routine. Naturally I did not voice this mutiny to my instructors.

With my solo safely behind me, I moved ahead with renewed confidence and from that day forward averaged nearly five hours solo almost every working day, passing one check after the other and moving steadily along on schedule. Meanwhile an unexpected influence had entered into my training, insinuating itself in a delicate sort of way; it was old Aunt Lucy.

It had started one sunny morning when, standing in front of the mirror to tie my black four-in-hand tie, I had, in sheer exuberance, burst out singing "Swing Low, Sweet Chariot." Aunt Lucy, who seemed to be forever dusting the furniture when I was in the room, and who was always fingering my dress sword, as if fascinated by it, now interrupted my music.

"Oh, no sah!" she protested. "Not dataway! Not dataway!"

And then with one foot tapping and her gay turbaned old head bobbing to the rhythm, Aunt Lucy proceeded to swing that old chariot so low it got dizzy. The song ended, she cackled and waddled off down the corridor, but in response to my vociferous applause she was soon back again, dustcloth in hand, flicking specks off the battered furniture of the bare room.

From that moment, Lucy took my Bible instruction in hand and carried it out through a series of Negro spirituals, with a technique that would have impressed Lt. Barrett Studley, the author of the *Flight Manual*. Shadrach, Meshach, and Abednego in the fiery furnace vied with Joshua, as he fit de Battle uv Jericho, to bring me up to date on "de ole time religion." Then one Sunday morning old Aunt Lucy invited me to witness a baptizin' in a nearby bayou where a white-robed, black-faced preacherman, knee deep on a convenient sand bar, ducked his shouting converts. Next morning I noticed her flitting around my sword, where it stood in the corner, and heard her humming the second verse of the first song she had sung to me.

"I'se goin' to try on my long white robe,
Down by the riverside; down by the riverside; down by the riverside.
I'se goin' to try on my long white robe,
Down by de riverside—
I ain't a goin' t' study wah no moh!"

Of an original class of some thirty students, only about twenty survived the rigorous course. The others either lacked the natural coordination essential to instinctive flying or failed on that other important requirement "correct reaction in emergency." The first could be acquired by early athletic instruction, but the second seemed to be innate in some, wholly lacking in others. It was the unpleasant duty of the check instructor to detect the lack of that attribute before it could produce fatal results. But to men who had natural aptitude in the basic requirements, flying had an extraordinary appeal. There was all the intense satisfaction to be experienced through skill in any art, such as the smooth stroking of a tennis ball, the rhythmic swing of a golf club, or the exquisitely precise casting of a feathered salmon fly— all these were experienced by the student pilot, but with the added thrill that a mistake invited disaster.

During the month of November I graduated from the seaplane beach and moved over into landplanes. My classmates, following the more leisurely normal course, remained behind. In landplanes, we used the new Consolidate NY's and, while they had few of the pleasant flying qualities of the little N-9's, they didn't kill students in crack-ups.

Finally came November 30, 1926, and with it my final check. "Dixie" Ketcham, my check instructor, put me through the paces and then waved me back toward Old Corry Field. I was sitting there calmly enjoying the scenery below, but with one eye, as always, roving about in search of a place to land in case of engine failure, when the engine stopped. Below me lay a tiny cow pasture, the spot in which, no doubt, I was supposed to land. But it was so tiny I felt certain that Dixie would open the throttle again after I had demonstrated the required approach technique. And so I settled down to the "normal approach": a left turn to get downwind, a glide over the tops of the jack pine, a slip to lose altitude, a sunfish to kill extra speed, stick-back to break the glide—but the throttle didn't open and we went on in a nice landing.

As we reached the end of the run, just short of the edge of the field—we had no brakes then, nor did we use flaps—Dixie waved a hand as the signal to go home.

"If you can get into a pasture like that," he said, "you can get in anywhere!"

Back at my quarters in BOQ I walked on air. Aunt Lucy with her everlasting dustcloth fiddled around the gilt sword knot of the class of 1871 prize sword. And as she dusted it, she hummed the final verse of the spiritual she had sung so often for me.

> "I'se goin' to lay down my burden—
> Down by the riverside, down by the riverside, down by the riverside.
> I'se goin' to lay down my burden,
> Down by the riverside.
> I ain't a goin' to study wah no moh!"

Tossing my helmet and goggles onto the bed and reaching for my suitcase, I began packing my duffel for the return trip to Washington. Aunt Lucy was folding my best blue blouse with its shiny three stripes and, best of all, my new gold wings pinned on its breast. Under her breath she kept humming.

"I ain't a goin' to study wah no mo!" I stopped to look at her.

"Aunt Lucy," I demanded, "is it by accident or design that you keep singing that song at me?" Aunt Lucy chuckled.

"Well, sah," she replied in her deep contralto, "ah thought maybe now you done learned to fly like de angels, you might like to think a little about peace."

"Why," I retorted, "that's just what a navy is for—to keep peace."

"Yassah, yassah," Aunt Lucy persisted, fingering the gold pin on my best blouse, "but it jes' seem to Aunt Lucy dat, now de Lord done gib yo' wings, maybe yo' might find better use for dem dan jes fightin'."

The telephone jingled. Western Union had a wire for me. My wife was thrilled by the news of my gold wings; she had left for Washington to reopen the apartment.

CHAPTER TEN
THE TAKE-OFF

Back in Washington, the admiral welcomed me with a grin and promptly assigned me a new job as Chief of the Airplane Design Section. This was a naval constructor's stronghold, and even though we line officers had pretty well dominated design down in the Engine Section, I could have been made to feel like a blacksmith in a glassworks, had it not been for my new wings and my postgraduate engineering course under Dr. Lucke. But by now the vision he had foreseen had begun to come to pass: the "professors" and the "practical men" had got together in the person of the engineer, and the world was already on fire with new developments.

Among other things the great engineering societies, like the American Society of Mechanical Engineers, the Institute of Electrical Engineers, the Society of Civil Engineers, and others, had joined hands to build a new Engineering Societies' Building on 39th Street in New York City, where they had their several offices and conducted their technical sessions. One of these societies extended an invitation to Admiral Moffett to address a joint session on naval aviation and the admiral passed the job of writing the screed on to me. But when I handed the finished product over to him, he glanced at the title "Power Plants for Aircraft," and grinned.

"You read it," he directed.

I read it at a session at Pennsylvania State College and afterward, to my surprise, learned that it had won some kind of award. To receive this prize, I attended a session in the New York auditorium of the society's building and in the course of a little talk, told the story of how George Mead and I, after the "invention" of the air-cooled engine, had discovered its prototype in the Smithsonian Institution in the power plant of the early Langley airplane, the Manly engine. There was a disturbance in the back of the auditorium and a member stood up to remark that Mr. Charles M. Manly was right there in the audience. Amid the shouts that followed, Mr. Manly was belatedly revealed as a great pioneer.

In addition to the journals and technical papers of the booming American societies, we received the best articles from foreign countries.

Among these, the Royal Aeronautical Society of London furnished almost world leadership, while the English magazine, *The Airplane*, edited by an outspoken character, C. G. Grey, published stimulating news and comment. Articles in German and French were translated and distributed through BUAERO in such profusion that it required a lot of homework just to keep up with the ever-changing nomenclature of a rapidly growing art. The most scientific writings came to us from the British National Advisory Committee for Aeronautics, but gradually our own committee with the same name began to forge to the front with selected articles and digests of the best laboratory reports from all over the world.

There was some discussion as to the wisdom of releasing the latest in research or development in this country in exchange for similar data from abroad, but the admiral settled it characteristically. If you couldn't keep ahead of the other fellow by resort to your own initiative and enterprise in a free market, he felt, then you certainly couldn't beat him on a closed circuit. An alert mind could often find something in the other fellow's research which the other fellow might have missed; and if the other fellow beat you to the punch in your own field, you deserved to lose out. The admiral's highly competitive spirit kept the whole Bureau on its toes and a word of commendation from him fired his supporters to play better ball than they really knew how.

This general type of leadership seemed to permeate the Washington atmosphere of the middle 'twenties. The team of Harding and Coolidge had been elected to office on the slogan of a "Return to Normalcy." The American people had tasted the European way in World War I and had found it bitter indeed. Then, after President Harding had died, Mr. Coolidge had taken office and given us an administration founded on New England character and integrity. This had been particularly apparent in the monetary field. We in BUAERO had to supply Admiral Moffett with sound bases for our requests for appropriations, but when we did, the Old Man would come through; he had a rare knack for getting money, especially after he had established the principle of the five-year plan. But we were expected to make our appropriations pay dividends; they weren't handouts for "social" purposes.

We didn't pretend to know anything about the obscure theories of economics, but anyone could understand the soundness of Mr. Andrew Mellon's tax policies. The war had left us with the heaviest debt in the history of the country, and with income taxes at high rates. Mr. Mellon seemed determined to reduce the debt, and to this end he resorted to reduced taxation. Meanwhile Mr. Coolidge sat on the lid in so far as expenses were concerned. In BUAERO we got no sudden slashing, but a quiet mandate that when a vacancy occurred, it would not be filled; the work would either be divided among others or, if unnecessary, be allowed to lapse. And between the two processes, prosperity returned. Reduced taxes made funds available for new enterprises; new enterprises paid new taxes which further reduced the debt. Mr. Mellon now began anticipating this result by further tax reductions, which accelerated the creation of new enterprises and new jobs. And so a boom was born and men talked of the "new economic era."

With the Morrow Board policy and the Moffett five-year building program as its foundation, and the favorable climate of the new economic era as its medium, American aviation seemed to turn around almost overnight. The surviving domestic companies, impelled by the incentive of constructive competition, began forging ahead with their integrated programs of research, development, and production. Foreign designers who had languished in the bad atmosphere of war-torn Europe now began peddling their know-how in the promised land. Mr. Anthony Fokker, the rough-and-ready Dutch designer of the famous German Fokkers of World War I, appeared with a new transport designed around the Liberty engine. It had a welded-steel tubular fuselage and a thick monoplane wing made of plywood. With the Liberty it could be nothing but a "kluck" but with three Wright Whirlwind air-cooled radials, it was a hot number. When Dick Byrd planned to fly over the North Pole I wangled one of them for him which he used with conspicuous success. The smaller Fokker Universal made history in the Canadian bush.

Igor Sikorsky, who, as a pioneer Russian pilot and constructor, had built the first four-engined bomber but had left revolution-torn Russia for free America, now designed a remarkably efficient big bomber or transport and began developing his twin-engined amphibian. Giuseppe Ballanca, after setting up shop in Wilmington, Delaware, produced a single-engined cargo carrier, designed around a single Wright Whirlwind engine with which Lt. C. C. Champion of BUAERO's Engine Section, now headed by Henry Mullinix, won all the prizes for speed and efficiency at the Philadelphia national air races.

And a new crop of American designers sprang up almost overnight. Tom Hamilton, of Milwaukee, built a single-motored, high-wing metal monoplane around the Pratt and Whitney Hornet engine and put it into service on many freight routes. Mr. Henry Ford, inspired by zeal to do something concrete for aviation, supported his chief engineer, William Mayo, in the development of the Ford Trimotor—a high-wing, metal monoplane built around three Wright Whirlwinds—and its sale to budding air transport lines at a price which would permit profitable operations. In this Mr. Ford was not prompted by the modern incentive of "tax loss"—that idea had not been born in an era of American initiative and enterprise.

Numerous other enterprisers like Stearman, of Wichita, Kansas, and Stinson, of Detroit, Michigan, began creating private aircraft to exploit the coming boom in personal flying. Many, drawing the analogy with the automobile, were convinced that this boom had already arrived, and began building airports and flying services all over the country. Much of this building was based on shoestring finance, but some of it was sound. And all of it might have made steady progress except for one thing: speculation permeated the sound core of aviation just as it ate at the vitals of all other industry.

Even naval officers, who up until then had seemed to pride themselves on a certain aloofness to the marts of trade, now began dabbling in "the market." Profits here were sure and swift—provided always you were on the inside. One of our friends had an inside tip on a new graveyard to be constructed within the city limits of Los Angeles, with the advice and consent of the City Council, where profits were quick and sure. The harvest for this enterprise was guaranteed to be as sure as—say, death and taxes. This friend looked down his nose at another man whose mouselike wife had been inveigled by a door-to-door salesman into buying a lot in Long Beach, California. The extra burden of paying for this "investment" was about to break the couple down when someone poked a hole in a nearby piece of ground and the oil field on Signal Hill was born. Now the young wife followed the young husband's battleship around in her private yacht. But none of this seemed to discourage creative enterprise, like the rising aircraft manufacturing and air-transport industries.

Among the newcomers in the manufacturing field, Donald Douglas and "Dutch" Kindleberger began to stand out. Prior to their advent, most of the newcomers had been alumni of the great Curtiss Aeroplane Company, of Garden City, Long Island. But Glenn L. Martin, an early bird who had pioneered American twin-engined bombers with his famous Martin bomber, had collected a stable of promising colts; Don Douglas, Dutch Kindleberger, and Larry Bell had worked for him until some temperamental disagreement sent all three on independent projects. After that, each concentrated his efforts to outdoing the others, and especially the old master, Glenn Martin. We in BUAERO, sitting as we did at the crossroads, could always get the dirt and low-down from the visiting firemen and, after sifting it and appraising it, use our own judgment in how to make it pay dividends in new development. Intercompany competition mixed up with interservice competition and whirled about in the old slipstream might look disorderly and inefficient, but it was motivated by highly creative impulses.

Admiral Moffett kept his own Bureau on its toes by involving us in all sorts of racing or other projects. Back in Bruce Leighton's time, BUAERO had given Don Douglas the job of building an experimental single-engined Liberty torpedo-bomber plane—one with extra large tanks for long-range flying. But after Don had produced a masterpiece, the Army Air Service seized upon the type while the Navy dawdled, and the Army had completed the first 'round-the-world flight. This job, a masterpiece of planning and operations, proved such a pronounced success that it gave great impetus to other projects. It also gave the Navy such pain that Admiral Moffett never got over it.

The classic international seaplane race had long been the Schneider Trophy and the admiral had set his heart on winning it. The expenditure of time, money, and effort could be justified then because it always stimulated technical progress. And so BUAERO created a new class of racers and brought the trophy to America; the admiral, master that he was of the art of publicity, played up the results to the fullest. The Navy had also entered the classic land-plane races using special racers in the "free-for-all pursuit." Then, since turn about had always been fair play, the Army entered Jimmy Doolittle in the Schneider Cup seaplane races and won them hands down. This was the same Jimmy Doolittle who would one day take off in an Army bomber from the Navy carrier *Hornet* in our first air raid on Tokyo. Meanwhile, the middle 'twenties were a free-swinging era of intense competition that pushed American aeronautics to the forefront of world progress. The bursting bubble of stock-market speculation in 1929 squeezed out the small fry, but the big boys went on for a while longer.

Meanwhile I found my new flying ability most useful in my billet as Chief of Design. On a training-plane competition between Boeing and Huff-Daland, I was able to check the trial-board report myself and, being fresh out of Pensacola, to do so with a fair knowledge of the latest edition of the *Flight Manual*. The Boeing developed a characteristic which, until then, was new to us. Pete Mitscher, the same Pete who would one day command Task Force 58 in the Pacific and earn from his mates the reputation for being the ablest air commander of them all, got into a flat spin at 6,000 feet over Washington and windmilled to a crash on the end of Haines Point, where he stepped out of the damaged plane quite unharmed. Had he known about flat spins back in the days of the "Affair Fleet," things would have been more difficult.

Then one of these tests of mine came near to washing me out of aviation's slipstream forever and leaving me as a part of the permanent "slip."

There had been some discussion in BUAERO of a suggestion to equip Pensacola with some advanced combat trainers by taking the Pratt and Whitney Wasp out of the Curtiss Hawk and substituting in it the lower-power Wright Whirlwind. I had argued against this and suggested obtaining the same result by flying the standard Hawks with partly open throttles. And in order to prove the efficacy of this, I went over to the Naval Air Station, Anacostia, where we did our flight testing, to put on a demonstration. When I waddled out in my flying suit and parachute, I found the plane turning up on the line, but the mechanic was dissatisfied with the way the engine was running. It was one hundred revs short of the full-throttle crank speed. Since this might be due to a weak spark plug or some other minor fault and since I intended to fly at half throttle anyway, I got in, taxied out onto the field, and took off.

The Anacostia Naval Air Station occupied about half of a flat strip of land and had its hangars and shops along the river front. The Army Bolling Field occupied the other part of the reservation with its old wartime buildings lying under the hill on which stands St. Elizabeth's Hospital. If the presence of an institution for the insane, overlooking the rival Army and Navy fields on the same plot, had any significance, I was not concerned with it that day. What I had to look out for, however, was the extensive regrading going on, which limited the operating area to a narrow tract.

My take-off was diagonally across the field toward the bluff, and the little Hawk, to my delight, fairly leaped into the air at half throttle, and climbed over the trees. Turning to the left, looking down on the hospital, I noticed the circle that marked the landing area, and promptly cut the switch to make a dead-stick precision landing on it. When this turned out well, I started the engine and repeated the maneuver. On the third take-off, noticing a certain roughness in the engine, I opened the throttle wide, thinking to clear a possible fouled plug. But even as I did so, I felt something let go and noticed the ears of the valve rocker box covers drop below the rim of the engine cowl.

There was a sudden "whoosh" and the cockpit filled with flames. Instinctively I cut back the throttle, slapped off the switch, and pulled the fire-extinguisher knob. As I reached behind me alongside the seat for the fuel cutoff valve, I glanced into the cockpit where the flames were licking my stick hand, and curling up around my ankles beneath my slacks. When I looked out again, we were nearing the end of the field. At such a low altitude I could not jump and now, to get the flames out of my face, I kicked into a steep slip to the left which headed us out over the Potomac River. A water landing to a sailor has more appeal than a crack-up in a thicket, and I held the heading until it was certain I could not stretch the river. Then, close to the ground, I booted the rudder to fishtail her the other way and followed this with four hard kicks alternating left and right until she had lost speed. Now as the burning Hawk touched down hard, I had an overwhelming sense of panic; the next thing I knew I was on the ground on my hands and knees and the plane was crackling behind me. Feeling the heat on the back of my neck, I glanced quickly over my shoulder and then, as the flame seared my cheek, I scrambled out of there on hands and knees.

Clear of the wreck, I got to my feet and looked around. A small car was careening toward me from the direction of the Army hangar. My first reaction was one of embarrassment at being caught by the Army in such an undignified situation. When I looked again at the airplane, it stood there without its engine, burning abaft the cockpit, but headed in a direction opposite to that in which I had landed it. Its engine lay a few yards beyond me, one propeller blade broken off near the hub.

Well, that accounted for the crack-up. When the blade had let go, several of the holding-down stud bosses had broken off, but others had held the engine in the airplane. Then the rough landing had sheared the others; the airplane, freed of its heavy noseweight, had bounced into the air, done a split S, broken my safety belt, and dropped me clear of the fire. Had it happened any other way, I must surely have burned up before I could escape the flames.

I glanced at my hands and saw that the skin was burned deep enough to expose the cords. I felt my face and found burns around my lips and eyebrows; at least I would not be disfigured for life. The careening Army car swung alongside with squealing brakes and I climbed on its running board for a fast run back to Anacostia's sick bay. The soldier in the car said the broken propeller blade had sailed right past him, screaming like a wild thing. Arrived at the sick bay, I was hustled into a ward and told to lie down; the doctor said I was suffering from shock. I lay down on the bunk awhile, and when I looked up, Admiral Moffett stood in the door.

"Have you telephoned your wife?" he asked eagerly.

"No, sir," I replied.

"Better do it yourself," he ordered. "News of this will be all over town. Save her the shock."

But when I tried to get up, I couldn't move. The admiral pushed the bed toward the telephone. When I got our apartment, no prior news had preceded me; my wife gasped and said she'd be right over. The door opened and a doctor walked in to examine my hands.

"I'm afraid you'll never use those again," he said. Then he looked up. "Can you stand a lot of pain?" he asked.

I had never had to stand much. The doctor said he'd try a treatment developed in World War I, one using a solution of tannic acid. It worked and today I have nothing to show for the experience save a few minor scars. Meanwhile, the admiral sat there; for the first time that I could recall, he seemed to droop.

"Things like this," he said, "make you wonder if this cockeyed game is worth the candle." He paused.

"Well," he added, standing up to leave, "there's nothing much we can do about it but play it out. The thing's bigger than any of us and we're in it up to our necks."

CHAPTER ELEVE
A LONE EAGLE SETS THE STANDARD

Among the aviation phenomena of the late 1920's was the outbreak of glorified stunt flying. Barnstormers and wing walkers of the earlier half of the decade now began vying with one another on a world-wide scale, competing for rich prizes offered by various personalities, and for assorted motives. Some courageous souls, quite unprepared, took off in the direction of the wide blue yonder and never came back; others, more successful, returned to bask for a while in the pitiless glare of publicity and then faded out.

But one day, while the whole world seemed to hold its breath and to offer up a little prayer for him, a lone eagle soared out over the broad Atlantic and, after thirty-three hours, let down through the murk over Le Bourget, outside Paris. And after taxiing toward a milling throng so dense he had to cut his engine to avoid injuring someone with his propeller, he remarked, "I am Charles A. Lindbergh."

Perhaps one measure of the character of this performance is the fact that, to this day, in spite of all the strides in airplane development, no person has sought to duplicate a solo flight from New York to Paris.

The impact of Lindbergh's flight on the progress of American aviation is well known; it started an upsurge that carried aviation over a dead center and started it spinning on its way. What is not so well known is the underlying character of the man himself and its influence on American air power. For, just as a community or an enterprise mirrors the character of its pioneers, so has aviation taken on some of the personalities of its immortals.

In BUAERO we were at first inclined to look at this last stunt as more or less a lucky break, until Guy Vaughan came down to tell us about the night take-off. Since Lindbergh was flying a Wright Whirlwind engine, Guy had invited him to dinner. And while he and his wife, Helen, sat talking with Lindbergh, word came from Dr. Kimball, the weather wizard, that things were clearing over the Atlantic. The party drove out to the flying field and when the men had pushed their way into the hangar to look for the *Spirit of St. Louis*, the tiny ship was lighted by a single, dim carbon-filament bulb—

"so dim," according to Guy Vaughan, "you had to strike a match to see if it was burning."

Outside the hangar, Dick Byrd, aided by his ample staff, had also been making preparations. But Guy Vaughan and Charles Lindbergh, using their own hands, topped off the fuel tanks of the *Spirit of St. Louis* and started her rolling out onto the ramp. Guy ascribed Lindbergh's achievement to three things: he was the best pilot in the world, he trusted nothing to anyone but himself, and he took no unintelligent chances.

Admiral Moffett hailed Lindbergh's accomplishment, but feared the Army might make capital of it by persuading Lindbergh, an Army Reserve officer, to say that his feat had obsoleted all navies. Jerry Land, now our assistant chief, got a big kick out of the whole thing; Lindbergh was his nephew. And then, as the flight proved to be far more than just a seven days' wonder and Lindbergh's popularity increased rather than diminished with the passage of time, all sorts of people began getting into the act. When the word was passed around that Lindbergh was coming home on the cruiser *Memphis* and that he was writing a book to be called *We*, the Navy began to take him very seriously. The Secretary of the Navy, Mr. Curtis D. Wilbur, radioed Lindbergh on the *Memphis*, offering to assign a naval officer as his technical advisor in the preparation of the book. Lindbergh accepted the offer with alacrity, and I found myself assigned to the detail. My job was to see that his book didn't sink the Navy with a fragmentation bomb.

On the day of Lindbergh's arrival at the Navy Yard in Washington, all the naval aviators in the vicinity were tolled off to act as a guard of honor for him. I walked through the part, but was so little interested that I neglected to attend the ceremonies at the foot of the Washington Monument, and went home as usual for lunch. But after Lindbergh's tour of the provinces, we began to take notice; not only did his popularity increase, but he developed a knack of being exactly on time for all ceremonies. I had noted, during the time the *Spirit of St. Louis* had been in the hangar at Anacostia, that Lindbergh himself had never failed to check every detail of her preparations. Now his incredible on-time performance, under trying conditions, seemed to bear out Guy Vaughan's estimate; he trusted no one but himself and was the best pilot in the country. Then came the day when Charles Lindbergh returned to Washington.

Jerry Land sent for me to tell me that Secretary Wilbur had placed his yacht *Sylph* at Lindbergh's disposal for a cruise down the Potomac as far as Mount Vernon. A number of dignitaries, including Bill McCracken, Assistant Secretary of Commerce for Air; F. Trubee Davison, Assistant Secretary of War for Air; Ed Warner, Assistant Secretary of the Navy for

Air; and a number of Slim Lindbergh's St. Louis backers, were to make the trip. The idea was to give Lindbergh a lot of good advice on his future conduct and afterward we would all adjourn to the house of Secretary of Commerce Herbert Hoover on S Street, where we would meet an agent of George Palmer Putnam, prospective publisher of the book *We*. I was to go along on the *Sylph* and then do my duty at the Hoover house.

On the junket down the river that day, I sat well out toward the rail, watching Glenn Martin's first T4M torpedoplane overhead with its new Pratt and Whitney Hornet going through its one-hour, full-throttle endurance trial. It was oppressively hot and I was nervous about that engine; we thought Glenn had cowled it too close, trying to get speed at the cost of cooling. Lindbergh sat inboard near a cabin skylight, surrounded by important personages and looking very boyish. And while I watched the T4M, listening to every engine throb, I found myself beginning to take notice of the conversation in which I had expected to find no interest.

The older, more experienced men agreed that Lindbergh had done a swell job so far, but they reminded him that fame was fleeting; if he expected to capitalize on his achievement, he must strike while the iron was hot. Of course he shouldn't try anything dizzy; his job was to prove how safe aviation is. It seemed likely that he might do a good motion picture, a sort of educational movie. He could act out the early history of the flight: the meeting with his backers, the days spent building his plane with Claude Ryan in San Diego, his trials and tribulations, and finally the take-off and landing at Le Bourget. It could be conservative and refined.

To this suggestion Lindbergh replied to the effect that he hated to seem ungrateful, but he had no intention of going into the movies. If he were to go into the movies, someone would try to make a sheik out of him and he didn't think he would make much of a sheik. At this comment, I moved a little closer to the cabin skylight.

His advisors now shifted over to the possibilities of Slim's becoming interested in the air lines. After all, he'd had experience as a mail pilot and could easily take over something big. Maybe Bill Boeing of Seattle would be interested in taking him on—think of all the publicity it would bring.

Lindbergh's reply to this was again that he disliked appearing ungrateful. It was true he had had some experience in air transport, but he wasn't too proud of the fact that he had had to parachute from two of his planes and had lost them both. He didn't know anything much about transportation, and if he went into something he didn't know about he would likely make a fool of himself. He hoped that from here on he might not make any bigger fool of himself than he had made already.

It now began to appear that a lot more sense was coming from the advised than from the advisors; I moved over and sat down near Jerry Land, who grinned proudly at me. Overhead the Martin T4M seemed to be droning along with confidence.

The third suggestion offered Lindbergh had to do with aircraft manufacture. It was suggested that after all the publicity on the *Spirit of St. Louis*, a lot of craft of that model might be sold. Perhaps the men from St. Louis who had backed Lindbergh on the flight to Paris might finance an aircraft manufacturing company in St. Louis of which the young pilot might become the president.

Lindbergh shook his head quickly. He had a crazy idea that he would like to have his Paris flight redound to the benefit of aviation as a whole. If he went into manufacture, that would put him in competition with others in the business; he didn't want to compete with them but rather to help the whole aviation game along. If the flight was worth anything at all, he would like to see it advance aviation. He didn't appear to be interested in trying to make money out of it.

By the time Charles Lindbergh had received his friends' advice, the Martin T4M had finished its run successfully and landed at Anacostia. Soon the *Sylph* put back to the Navy Yard and we all got into cars to ride up to Mr. Hoover's house. Mrs. Hoover met us at the door and showed most of the group out onto the porch. Four of us remained behind to sit down around a table and hear a report from the agent of Mr. George Palmer Putnam.

Charles Lindbergh took his seat at the head of a table. On his right sat a keen young Army pilot, Lt. Robert Douglas, who had been a student aviator with Lindbergh at Kelly Field. I sat down at Lindbergh's left while Mr. Putnam's representative stood at the end of the table opposite him. The man from Putnam's held the galley proof in his hand and displayed considerable pride over it. The galley had been struck off in record time.

It seemed that the book really divided into three parts: the first had to do with Lindbergh's early life; the second part reviewed his flight training, his barnstorming, and his experience as an air-mail pilot; the third part, which covered the technical aspects of the New York-Paris flight, had been prepared by someone in the publicity department of the Wright Aeronautical Corporation, makers of the engine of the *Spirit of St. Louis*.

The first part had been written by a journalist who had accompanied Lindbergh on the trip home in the cruiser *Memphis*. This section of the book was considered to be the meat of the cocoanut and had been well advertised. It was the part of Lindbergh's life not already widely publicized. Mr. Putnam's representative hoped Colonel Lindbergh would not find it necessary to make changes in it; its author would be disappointed. Of course, corrections of typographical errors were in order but extensive revisions would delay publication, and time was of the essence. Some parts of this section might sound a little overdone to the colonel, but, after all, that was what sold books and the publisher had already committed himself to the public in forecasting a few sensations.

Lindbergh sat silent during this discourse and when the galley was handed him, divided it into the three parts. The section on his flying experience he handed to Bob Douglas; the technical section he passed to me; his "early life" he kept to himself. There was a long silence while we three scanned copy. I thumbed through a collection of clichés designed to glorify the Wright Whirlwind, until I found what I had been sent to look for. Sure enough, someone had put into Lindbergh's mouth a quote to the effect that his flight had clearly shown that armies and navies might now be done away with, and the moneys previously wasted devoted to an air force. After a while Lindbergh glanced at Bob Douglas.

"How about your part, Bob?" he asked.

Bob Douglas saw nothing out of line in his section. It had been developed largely from Lindbergh's own reports of his parachute drops from the mail planes in soupy weather, and was quite factual. Lindbergh looked my way.

"To be wholly honest with you," I said, "I was planted here to see that you didn't sink the whole Navy with one little bomb, and here it all is, in quotes." Lindbergh grinned. Some years later I was to learn from a naval officer who accompanied Lindbergh home on the *Memphis* that the young pilot had even then been disturbed by the trend his book was taking and had accepted Secretary Wilbur's offer of technical assistance as a possible way out of his dilemma. Now he listened as I read that part.

"If you think that is crazy," he grinned, "just listen to this." So saying, he began to read aloud from his "early life." As I recall what he read, it stressed Lindbergh's qualities as a daredevil, something that certainly did not coincide with my own estimate of him. He was bold, yes, courageous, undoubtedly, but he was the most painstakingly accurate and precise young pilot I had yet encountered, and these qualities, combined with his unique flying skill, had made it possible for him to undertake the impossible, without being a daredevil. Now as he read the passages, Mr. Putnam's representative nervously interrupted him to interpose the publisher's point of view; this treatment was all just a part of the publisher's job; you had to do it, or the book just would not sell. Lindbergh turned his clear eyes on me.

"If you were in my place, Commander," he inquired, "what would you do?" The room was still as I pondered this question. We could hear voices and laughter from the others of the party as they enjoyed their lemonade out on the porch.

"Colonel Lindbergh," I replied, "I don't believe anyone but you yourself can write *We*."

Without a moment's hesitation he turned to the man from Putnam's. "That confirms a decision I had already taken on the *Memphis*," he said simply. "I'm sorry about all the work that has been done, but it just can't be helped."

And Lindbergh did go off to Harry Guggenheim's place on Long Island, and he did write *We*, all except the final portion which was clearly set apart as the work of Fitzhugh Green. And if fewer copies were sold because the book did not set the world on fire, at least its character was consistent with that of its author. I understand that Lindbergh saw that the journalist, who had done his best under trying circumstances, received full compensation for his unused work.

Meanwhile, Charles A. Lindbergh had become for me the personification of the spirit of aviation. Young, courageous, daring, yet painstaking, competent, and proficient in his art, he had integrity and that quality so rare in this era of rampant materialism, Christian unselfishness.

CHAPTER TWELVE
A CHANGE IN STATUS

As the summer of 1927 came to a close, I began to sense that my own work in BUAERO was coming to its end. The fact was crystallized for me one evening when Fred Rentschler, Chance Vought, my wife, and I sat out on the little balcony of our apartment at 2301 Connecticut Avenue, watching the shadows fall. Fred and Chance had had dinner with us and we could hear the clatter of dishes in the pantry as the maid of all work finished her chores. For when the visiting firemen came to town, we either had dinner with them downtown somewhere or they with us in the apartment. We balanced the social obligations that way.

Our apartment looked out over Rock Creek Park and across the Memorial Bridge toward Wardman Park, and the tiny balcony was the one cool spot in it. In an open space among the trees stood a riding school that was reminiscent of that avid horseman, Billy Mitchell. And though he had lost out in his fight, his spirit still haunted aviation and would continue to do so for all time. He had created the opportunity on which Admiral Moffett had capitalized, and people like Fred Rentschler and Chance Vought had founded their businesses. Now Fred Rentschler, whose consuming passion was business, was talking about it.

"This aviation business," he was saying, "is like no other business in the world."

Chance Vought, sitting with his feet on the porch rail, glanced skeptically at him; Chance delighted in debunking Fred's somewhat ponderous deductions.

"Whoever said it was a business?" he demanded. "The best you can say for it is that it's the 'Aviation Game'; but it's still a lousy racket." A pained expression crossed Fred's serious face.

"Aviation is no longer a game or a racket," he insisted. "It's serious business and the sooner some of you airplane wood butchers wake up to that fact, the better." Chance winked at me and then closed his eyes. He would snore during Fred's discourse on a pet subject, but would probably come to life in time to put the clincher on the evening's lesson.

Fred stressed the fundamental difference between the airplane and other mechanisms. Most things produced in factories would wear out in time and replacement furnished the manufacturer with a continuing source of business. The airplane, on the other hand, would never wear out; the high quality required for dependable service meant that the goods would last forever. The only sources of business were expansion and crash losses, and even these were limited. In other words, even while the aircraft manufacturer must strive to increase his quality in the interest of safety, in the process he works himself out of production.

There appeared to be only one solution to this problem, and that was the factor of obsolescence. In things like clothing, or automobiles, or what have you, the trick was to so modify the styling as to keep the customer "just enough dissatisfied with what he has to persuade him to buy something new." Fred ascribed this precept to his friend "Boss" Kettering, of General Motors.

But the factor of styling, so important in some lines, had no bearing in aviation. Here performance was the key to progress: in military aircraft it was speed, climb, and ceiling; in air transport it was dollars per ton-mile. And the degree to which this last factor was important to the commercial airlines depended upon the intensity of economic competition between them.

Bill Boeing, for instance, might have continued to use the war-surplus Liberty-engined DH's indefinitely, had not competition for the air-mail contract forced him to risk a low bid and then build new aircraft to meet his own standards. And so price competition, which many were beginning to think was cutthroat and destructive, was over-all, the key to progress in aeronautics.

The engine manufacturer, for instance, must experiment with new ideas, conduct research into strange fields, and come up with something so economical that the airline operator can't get along without it. That will obsolete his airplanes, retire them to some embryonic service that cannot yet afford new types, and force him to introduce the newest and latest models— or else go out of business. Competition, Fred insisted, was not destructive, but creative; it was tough on the one who lost his shirt, but favorable to the public at large.

Fred went on to develop the vast difference between the volume-producing industries, where low first cost was the incentive, and the aircraft industry, where low operating cost was the real criterion. The airline operator could afford to pay a high price for high quality aircraft, provided he reduced his operating costs enough to absorb the first cost in a reasonable time. The whole character of the two types of industry differed, and neither could expect to do the other's job. Technological development was the key to the economic security of an enterprise like aviation. The way to keep in the forefront was to stress your engineering; once you got behind you could never catch up, unless the other fellow broke a leg and fell down. Yes, he thought, this aviation was a funny business. At this remark, Chance Vought woke up.

"The thing that is funny about it," he said sleepily, "is that it has at last become a business."

I sat looking out over Rock Creek Park as it faded into the shadows. The conversation had pointed up a new situation in my own affairs. If aviation was now a business, then my job here was finished. You could hardly have called it that three and a half years ago, and the time had come for me to go to sea, lest some Selection Board pass me by. I'd go see Admiral Moffett in the morning.

But in the morning the admiral was, as usual, one jump ahead of me. I found a note on my desk instructing me to see him the first thing. In his corner office he waved a letter at me, one scrawled in longhand in the bold writing of Rear Adm. Joseph M. Reeves, Commander, Aircraft Squadrons, Battle Fleet. It was dated at San Diego, California, on the *Langley*, and it took note of the fact that the carriers *Saratoga* and *Lexington* were scheduled to join the fleet in a year or so. His chief of staff, Karl Smith, was ill and he needed a relief for him. He asked if I could be made available.

"Bull" Reeves was a distinguished officer and an able commander. Only a year or two earlier he had dropped in on me in the Engine Section to inquire if I thought he should accept an invitation to join the aeronautic organization and go to Pensacola for instruction with the ultimate idea of succeeding to command of the Aircraft Squadrons, Battle Fleet. He had graduated from Annapolis into the old Engineer Corps but later, upon amalgamation with the line, had qualified for command. A hero of Naval Academy football, he had been on duty at Annapolis as an instructor while I had been a midshipman, and he had been rated "white" by all hands—the highest commendation an officer could earn from the brigade. During the Spanish American War, he had made a name for himself in the engine room of the old *Oregon* in her dash around the Horn. Admiral Moffett was smiling at my obvious satisfaction.

"Yes," he remarked, "you should be a big help to me out there."

I put in a request for a month's leave and bought tickets for my wife and myself on the Panama-Pacific liner, *Mongolia*, sailing direct for San Diego via the Panama Canal. We sailed from New York where Fred Rentschler,

Chance Vought, Guy Vaughan, and many other friends in the aircraft industry saw us off. After a lovely cruise through the Caribbean and the transit of the Canal, we headed north for the West Coast and San Diego, where my wife and I had first set up housekeeping at the Coronado Hotel, while I served my tour of duty in the old Pacific Torpedo Flotilla. It was there we had made our first contact with aviation.

When the *Mongolia* pushed her nose into San Diego harbor that morning late in October of 1927, the bright sun glittered on the white sands of North Island just as it had done some fifteen years earlier when we had last looked upon this pleasant scene. Meanwhile, however, North Island itself had undergone change. Then it had been a flat, brush-covered expanse on which we had hunted jack rabbits; now a latticed airship mooring mast thrust its height above a cleared surface, and white hangars lined the shores of West Beach. The mooring mast, located there as a haven for Admiral Moffett's rigid airships, lay down near the entrance to the ship channel; the hangars, intended for heavier-than-air craft, faced across the bay to San Diego or across Spanish Bight to Coronado Island's bungalows and cottages. The ancient Hotel del Coronado, with its white sides and red-pinnacled roofs reminiscent of the lush days of the land-and-railroad boom, still dominated the bright scene.

As our ship nosed into the pier on the San Diego side, we could look back at North Island and the Naval Air Station where the experimental carrier *Langley*, alongside her dock, filled the immediate foreground, and the tower of the yellow stucco mission-type Administration Building pierced the blue heavens. Here, less then twenty years earlier, had stood the tent hangars of the pioneer Army and Navy aviation schools, the one operated under the supervision of the Wright Brothers, the other by Glenn Curtiss. Here too had been born the early rivalries that still dominated the aircraft establishment, a pattern of Army versus Navy, and of manufacturer versus manufacturer, that had put the spark in the development of a new art.

Back there, student pilots had taken off at the crack of dawn in their powered box kites to get in their flight time before the gentle southwesterlies could interfere with their training. And if, perchance, a student like my classmate "Spig" Herbster, of the Wright camp, were forced down on the harbor by a failure of the tricky engine of his seaplane, another student like Jack Towers, of the Curtiss camp, waiting for just such an opportunity, would literally fly to his rescue—for the benefit of thrilling headlines in that enterprising newspaper, *The San Diego Union*. To us salts of the Destroyer Flotilla, moored alongside the ferry slip or the "Spreckles Dock," accustomed to night torpedo tactics on the high seas off Coronado Island, the whole thing had looked a bit silly. But to the aviators, news headlines had been the breath of life ever since that day at Kittyhawk when the wise money in the public press had refused to print the news of the first flight because it was too smart to fall for such a hoax.

Now that same Jack Towers was serving as captain of the first flattop, the *Langley*, a vessel named for the professor who had failed to fly, and I recalled the *Langley* when she had been commissioned as the collier *Jupiter* at the Mare Island Navy Yard, under command of Comdr. Joseph M. Reeves. The *Langley* had a revolutionary power plant, the electric drive, and had been equipped with a forest of masts and booms designed to fuel battleships at the rate of 500 tons of coal per hour. Today, fuel oil had replaced coal in all naval vessels and the *Langley* masts had been leveled to make room for a flat landing area for aircraft. And I, who had set out to become a gunnery officer but had been converted into a mechanical engineer, was now a naval aviator. Well, the new job seemed to have possibilities, but just how far-reaching they would prove to be, I didn't even dream.

CHAPTER THIRTEEN
A SALT'S SOLUTION

When, next morning, I buckled on my dress sword and reported at the Naval Air Station, I found Admiral Reeves had gone to Denver to make a speech at the Navy Day celebration there. Then, since Captain Towers was senior officer present afloat, I walked down the *Langley* dock to pay my respects to him. The moment I stepped over the rail onto the steel-decked passageway leading aft under the landing platform, I recognized the unmistakable signs of a "smart ship." Freshly scrubbed paint and gleaming brightwork told its own story. And before the winter had passed, I would learn just how smart the *Langley* really was. For Jack Towers, the naval aviator, was one of the best ship handlers in the whole service. He greeted me outside his cabin and promptly asked me to stay for lunch.

Jack Towers, one of the real pioneers of American aviation, was the acknowledged leader of the younger generation. He had served with distinction in World War I as a member of Admiral Sims's staff in London, and though some of his contemporaries resented his tendency to adopt English mannerisms, his juniors swore by him. Now he invited some of his department heads, old friends of mine, like Pete Mitscher, Monty Montgomery, and Bobby Moulton, to join us for a bull fest. And hardly had we sat down around the mess table before I found myself in the middle of the big issue of the moment.

My personal situation was complicated by the fact that I was a newcomer to aviation and now, by seniority and assignment, in a position of authority over such old-timers as were gathered around the table. No doubt they thought my qualification as naval aviator had been donated by Admiral Moffett, and discounted my flying ability accordingly. With this in mind I had sought to tread softly through the lunch, but the issue now raised must be met head on.

It developed that Admiral Reeves held curious notions about carrier tactics. He was insisting that a 500-foot, 10,000-ton vessel like the *Langley* could earn her salt only by operating sufficient aircraft to make her an effective military instrument. He had mentioned thirty-six planes, or two full fighter squadrons, as the minimum complement. But *Langley* officers had crystallized the opinion that not more than a third as many, say twelve airplanes, could be flown off the *Langley* and received on board without hazard to the lives of pilots. That key factor of safety had been argued out in conferences but "Bull" Reeves had stood pat. The *Langley* officers, now concerned, put the clincher on me.

"It's up to you," someone said, while the Filipino mess attendants passed the coffee.

"How come?" I inquired in some surprise.

"As chief of staff," someone replied, "you've got to prevent the admiral making this mistake." In the silence that followed I realized that on my first day in the Aircraft Squadrons we had already pointed up an issue between the *Langley* officers and the admiral's flag. The fat was in the fire.

"As I understand my job," I said, trying to choose the right words, "it is to help the Old Man carry out his program, not hinder him."

After lunch they showed me the slow-motion movies of carrier landings; not the successful ones, but the crack-ups. These ranged from simple landing-gear collapses to rolling off the deck and over the side into the sea. As we broke up, Bobby Moulton came forward with that glint in his eye that characterized the peculiar brand of humor that permeates naval aviation.

"We're qualifying the new class of carrier pilots next week," he grinned. "You can get yours in before the admiral gets back. Meet me Monday morning down at the West Beach and we'll put you over the jumps."

Not too many pilots had qualified for deck landings back there in 1927. The *Langley* could make only twelve knots, and her deck was so narrow a pilot could not see it behind the engine. He could barely see the signalman out on his platform, and even with a good landing, failures of the airplane or the arresting gear could make him trouble. We used Vought UO's with arresting hooks hung under their tails to catch the crosswires, and cross-axle hooks, long since abandoned, to catch the fore and aft wires.

Three of us constituted the next class. After three days of preliminary instruction on a simulated flight deck at Ream Field, primarily to familiarize us with the flag signals, we went aboard. On the way down the bay, a flock of sea gulls followed in our wake, beady eyes alight for possible garbage, and since they constituted a flight hazard, Emile Chourré, a veteran carrier pilot, perched aft on the signal platform to practice his antiaircraft marksmanship by working on the gulls with a BB gun.

Outside Point Loma the first pilot off—a youngster who had been as hot as a firecracker at Ream Field—went haywire, and after washing out his landing gear was ordered back to the air station where he made a safe belly landing in a shower of sand while surrounded by crash trucks, fire engines, and ambulances. My place was second in the line and, as I scrambled into the cockpit and looked down into the nettings where the whole ship's company had assembled in the hope of seeing a brass hat roll over the side, I thanked my stars that the one thing I could do well with an airplane was to set it gently back on the ground. And so closely did I concentrate on the business in hand that I lost track of my landings and came to only when Tiny Sullivan, a 300-pound chief and an old friend, shook hands with himself as I jolted aboard for the tenth and final landing. Climbing from the cockpit I thumbed my nose at Bobby Moulton and waddled triumphantly toward the disappointed sailormen in the nettings.

While waiting for Admiral Reeves to return from Denver and his Navy Day speech, I familiarized myself with the local setup. The Aircraft Squadrons, Battle Fleet, was a part of the battle-fleet organization whose backbone was a dozen battleships that based behind the breakwater ninety miles farther north at San Pedro or Long Beach, and exercised in the open sea nearby. Duty in the organization constituted "sea duty" but the aircraft squadrons were based on shore at the San Diego Air Station. Nominally assigned to the *Langley* for duty, Admiral Reeves and his small staff were given working quarters in a wing of the Administration Building. All save the admiral lived ashore, either in Coronado or San Diego; the admiral, during Mrs. Reeves's absence in Switzerland, lived in a room off the corner office assigned to him. My office was next to his in the opposite corner of the wing. The air station, built to conform to local architecture, was surrounded by pleasant lawns and attractive plantings. It provided operating facilities and repair shops for FLEET AIR, and while under a separate command, had established a reputation for cheerful cooperation, a circumstance not often encountered in the naval establishment.

The admiral had built up his staff from among the personnel of his squadrons. His operations officer, Frank D. Wagner, more commonly known as "Honus," had come up from Fighting One, the swank combat squadron with a reputation for high hat that one day gave it a replica of a top hat for its squadron insignia. Frank had dragged his feet on leaving Fighting One, but had brought to the staff a unique appreciation of the squadron point of view. Under Admiral Reeves's watchful eye, he had conducted the tactical exercises of the summer concentration, and evolved some advanced tactical concepts for air combat. The admiral's flag secretary was Seth Warner; his flag lieutenant, Les Arnold; and his radio officer, Gordon Rowe. I, as his chief of staff, would supervise the administrative functions and have general charge of matériel.

The aircraft squadrons themselves were in the process of organization. The twelve battle wagons at San Pedro operated three Voughts apiece, and since the battleships constituted three divisions, their aircraft formed three squadrons of the observation wing. There were no facilities at San Pedro for aircraft operations, so the observation wing based at San Diego except when needed aboard their ships for gunnery or the monthly fleet tactical exercises. During the summer months, when personnel shifts took place, all aircraft based at San Diego for the summer concentration period, where they broke in new crews and tried out new air tactics under Wagner.

Squadrons were also being assembled for the carriers. *Langley* units based full-time at San Diego and carried out their protracted gunnery schedules over nearby areas. Some *Lexington* squadrons were being gradually assembled at the Naval Air Station at Norfolk, Virginia, while the *Saratoga* units were being brought together at San Diego. These squadrons would be equipped with the new air-cooled fighters and torpedo bombers we had been developing at BUAERO and manned with new pilots then under training at Pensacola. The whole organization, under the leadership of Admiral Reeves, must be rounded out and trained during the next few years.

The admiral had always been "Bull" Reeves to his contemporaries, from the day when he had created the first football headgear so that he might get into the Army-Navy football game after a serious head injury. His juniors in aviation now called him "Billy Goat" because he wore one of the few beards then extant in the Navy. This beard was a lovely gray Vandyke which, with the admiral's shell-pink complexion, gave him an air of grave distinction that quite belied an uproarious sense of humor. He had a deep, vibrant voice and he spoke with great eloquence—a fact he ascribed to his having once studied for the ministry. Standing before an assembly of his brother officers he could expound the weightiest tactical or strategic doctrines in an entertaining and enlightening manner, speaking always with the obvious relish of a man engaged in an undertaking at which he knows he is competent. He differed from Admiral Moffett in almost every characteristic, but especially in his logical, measured approach to a problem. Though trained as an engineer, he had specialized in tactics and strategy and had brought to these subjects an orderly but very active mind. Even as I slid into the routine of my new job, I looked forward with impatience to the Old Man's return.

On the first morning that we faced each other across the desk in his bare office, Admiral Reeves raised the question of the *Langley's* reluctance to expand her operating complement. Entertaining as he did a high regard for Captain Towers both as a seaman and as a leader, and having in mind the initiative with which Jack had pioneered naval aviation, the admiral surmised that the long list of casualties among pilots had tended to overemphasize the hazards of flying off carriers. The fleet problem that was scheduled for the coming spring would offer an opportunity for an air attack on Pearl Harbor. In light of the probable arrival of the big carriers the following year he wanted to try out some of his ideas on the *Langley*, if only on a small scale. However, the scale proposed by that vessel was too small for any use at all. Our job was to find some way around the difficulty.

CHAPTER FOURTEEN
GERM OF A BIG IDEA

When later the Commander in Chief, Adm. Louis R. de Steiguer, once my captain on the *Old Ark*, finally released his statement of the fleet problem, the attention of all hands was focused on the forthcoming Hawaiian cruise. In April the following year, 1928, the fleet would rendezvous at San Francisco to sail from there for the joint Army-Navy exercises. In preparation for the maneuvers, each unit commander was called upon to submit his own "estimate of the military situation" and to formulate his own decisions and his operation orders. The fleet staff, after analyzing the several solutions, would promulgate the commander in chief's orders. In FLEET AIR, as the Aircraft Squadrons, Battle Fleet, were locally known, we planned to close the first phase of the exercises with a dawn attack on Pearl Harbor by planes launched from the *Langley*.

Appreciating that a dozen tiny fighters in competition with the great guns of the ponderous battle wagons would make little impression on Pearl Harbor, the admiral undertook to expand greatly the number of aircraft to be flown off the *Langley*. To provide living accommodations for their crews he instructed Captain Towers to request the Mare Island Navy Yard to undertake alterations to the vessel during her forthcoming annual overhaul. To increase the fire power of our embryonic air force, presently confined to a pair of thirty-caliber machine guns each, we started our squadrons training in a new tactic.

Dive bombing, first tested against Nicaraguan rebels by the United States Marines, had been further developed against naval targets by Fighting Five, a *Lexington* squadron then being assembled at Norfolk, Virginia. Admiral Reeves waxed enthusiastic over this idea, primarily because it concentrated the attack upon objectives located at the surface, instead of wasting energy on the usual dogfights between knights of the air. Frank Wagner, after scurrying around to lease all suitable training areas in the vicinity, soon had airplanes diving all over the San Diego hinterland.

In order to remove some of the hazards of operating carrier land planes over the sea, we began training our two auxiliary vessels, the former mine planter *Aroostook* and the sweeper *Teal* as "plane guards" for the *Langley*. For protection against losses incident to distant water landings, we equipped all planes with rubber flotation bags and gear to inflate them, when necessary, with bottled gas. Finally we borrowed two fast destroyers from the local squadrons under command of Adm. Thomas J. Senn. Here, though we little appreciated it at the time, was the germ of the big idea of the carrier task force.

With a view to further speeding sea rescue, we asked BUAERO to undertake for us the development of a single-float amphibian gear, interchangeable with the seaplane float of the Vought Corsair. To navigate a single-seater without radio out of sight of the carrier, to engage in combat and then return to a pin-point contact with a roving carrier, demanded real skill. In order to provide some sort of homing device, our radio officer, Gordon Rowe, strung a loop of wires between the wings of a Corsair, thus utilizing the loop-antenna feature, then common in home radio sets. Rowe's device, antedating radar, was intended to avoid the possible loss of precious pilots and planes but it also made the Corsair available as a liaison plane for fighter tactics. With a good carrier-based amphibian we could extend our control of combat units and, at the same time, release them for safe long-range operations.

To gain experience from the Hawaiian cruise, Admiral Reeves felt the *Langley* should operate at least two eighteen-plane fighter squadrons as dive bombers together with six Vought Corsair two-seaters for scouting, rescue, and radio liaison. While the *Langley*, with the space available in her vast, empty coal bunkers, could easily provide ample hangar space and crew's quarters, the restricted area of her flight deck and the limited capacity of her plane elevator introduced serious limitations. How to spot forty-two airplanes on an area believed by *Langley* officers to be adequate for but twelve was something of a problem.

While working on this, I proceeded on another project close to my heart, a recommendation from FLEET AIR for a long-term development and procurement program that would conform to the one I knew to be under way in BUAERO. If we could eliminate some of the local partisanship that frequently obscured the fundamentals of such problems, we might facilitate engineering progress.

When I submitted my schedule to the admiral he approved all of it save one critical item, the construction of an experimental two-seat fighter. The idea had originated in World War I on the Western Front, where the classic form of attack had been a dive out of the sun onto the enemy's tail, to shoot him down when he wasn't looking. Perhaps a tail gunner might guard a pilot from such surprise, but Admiral Reeves would have none of the idea. He thought an alert fighter pilot could do the job by twisting his neck. If he had to lug an extra gun and tail gunner, he would impair the combat performance of his airplane. Besides, during maneuvers, no rear gunner could serve a gun. This was no snap judgment on his part; he had had Wagner try it out during tactical exercises, using Voughts to simulate two-seat fighters. In his judgment there could be no such thing as a two-seat "fighter."

Against such logic I could but argue that many officers in the Bureau favored the project, among them Bruce Leighton, who, having finished his tour at sea, was now head of the powerful Plans Division. Failure to include his pet project in our recommendations would stir up such a controversy as to hazard the entire program. The admiral smiled at me.

"You've been with Moffett so long," he chuckled, "that you've begun to think like a politician yourself." It being hopeless to argue further with this forthright old sea dog, I modified the letter, knowing full well that Bruce Leighton, who had fostered the air-cooled engine against bitter opposition, would not readily abandon his pet two-seat fighter. And so it proved. BUAERO and FLEET AIR split wide open on this single controversial item with the result that the rest of the program fell apart. Before long we were engaged in acrimonious correspondence on almost every subject. Even engineering needs politics for lubrication.

When the *Langley* returned from her overhaul, she brought more trouble in her wake. The alterations for additional crew space had not been approved. When the admiral learned this from Frank Wagner his beard bristled and his eyes flashed.

"Instruct Fighting One and Fighting Six to assemble all aircraft on the *Langley* dock," he ordered. "Collect a dozen Vought Corsairs and advise Captain Towers we will call on him after lunch. We'll soon see," he added ominously, "just how many planes the *Langley* can be made to operate."

When, after lunch, the admiral with his staff bore down under all plain sail upon the *Langley* dock, Captain Towers and his officers met us at the gangway. The admiral, taking personal charge, soon had Wagner and me helping the deck crews to spot planes closer and closer together. When he had finished, he wrung from the *Langley* officers their reluctant admission that forty-two airplanes might be operated, but they expressed their firm conviction that it would be dangerous. As the admiral swept off the flight deck in triumph, he pointed up the moral in a strong, resonant voice.

"Most standards," he said, "are limited by opinion or prejudice. They break down under pressure. The function of a leader," he added, "is to generate the pressure." Turning to me he continued, "Please collect all the artificers in FLEET AIR, every carpenter's mate, shipfitter, and helper. Go in person aboard the *Langley* and construct quarters for the plane crews."

"Without authority from Construction and Repair?" I queried.

"Upon the authority of COMAIRONS," he replied, "and," he added, "on my responsibility."

Arriving at San Francisco, we found Chance Vought waiting with a new Corsair single-float amphibian which he had personally chaperoned all the way from Long Island City in a baggage car. The Naval Aircraft Factory at Philadelphia later supplied two more of a somewhat different design. After testing them, I came in for a good deal of ribbing from *Langley* pilots who, like Chance, insisted I had spoiled good airplanes by overloading them with junk. The craft may have been "klucks" but they lifted a heavy load from the staff conscience.

The fleet sailed on schedule with the aircraft squadrons ready in all respects. Some of our wives, including mine, were to all sail later on a passenger steamer from Los Angeles. With our convertible coupe in the ship's hold and my own recollections of an earlier visit to Honolulu in the old Armored Cruiser Squadrons in mind, we looked forward to a pleasant sojourn.

During passage, the fleet passed the steamer at sea, where the wives got a close-up of the *Langley* launching and receiving planes. We had been assigned a fixed station "6,000 yards astern of BAT DIVS," an order that irked the admiral no end. To launch and receive aircraft, the *Langley* had to leave her station and head into the wind, a fact that seemed to cause acute distress to those elements of the fleet accustomed to cruising in precise formation.

On the slow journey westward, daily exercises, morning and afternoon, developed our flight-deck technique to the ultimate. As a plane floated in over the ramp, to drop into the gear and be brought up with a jerk, squads of deck handlers swarmed out of the nettings, cleared hooks from landing wires, caught wing tips, and hustled the craft forward of the barrier, just in time to clear the gear for the next plane, even then floating down the groove. It was Bull Reeves who pressed always for more speed. Always quick to condemn a miscue or commend smart action, he finally inspired the *Langley* officers until they cut the take-off interval between planes down to ten seconds and the landing intervals to thirty.

At the crack of dawn, one lovely Sunday morning, we headed into the wind to launch aircraft for the assault on Pearl Harbor. We had selected this day in the knowledge that the defenders, after the usual Saturday night festivities, would be sleeping late.

First across the bow was Gerry Bogan of Fighting One; the rest of his flock zoomed after him at ten-second intervals. Fighting Six followed, led by "Injun Joe" Tomlinson. Finally scouts and amphibians roared into the air, leaving the deserted flight deck a bleak expanse of silence. After their attack on Pearl Harbor, the squadrons were to land ashore.

Our striking force, undetected by the defenders, caught Army and Navy pilots flat on their backs in bed, just as their successors were destined to be caught some thirteen years later on Sunday, December 7. It now seems likely that the casual Japanese oil tanker that managed always to find herself in the center of our operating areas off San Pedro, or those "fishing" sampans that busied themselves off Honolulu that very morning, later communicated our movements to the Japanese high command. It was natural for their admiralty to assume that we understood the import of the new weapons we were exercising. They could not have believed the intelligence that our own high command had so discounted the striking power of aerial bombs and submarine torpedoes that they had neglected to equip their vessels with adequate gun defenses. Recognizing in FLEET AIR—as they surely did—a revolutionary instrument of sea power, they sped their own development and hastened to exploit it in the rapid expansion of their East Asia Co-prosperity Sphere.

During the remainder of the Hawaiian exercises, we conducted joint operations with local naval forces and with the Army, polishing our flight techniques at sea. One day, a shift of wind, sweeping yellow volcanic dust from an extinct crater, cut our surface visibility to a dangerous low just after Gerry Bogan, with nine fighter bombers from Fighting One, had roared over the bow to attack a distant enemy fleet. Our worried staff found some comfort in the knowledge that one of our radio-liaison Corsairs was supposed to be plane-guarding the unit, ready to lead the flock back aboard after its mission had been completed. But when we radioed the Vought, the pilot reported he had lost the fighters. After homing the Corsair and taking her aboard, we began really sweating it out, peering hopefully into the yellow spaces, looking for Gerry Bogan. Finally at long last came the drone of engines. One by one the planes lurched into the gear and taxied forward. The admiral sent his orderly for Bogan.

"Where the hell have you been anyway?" he demanded with unwonted truculence.

"Fightin'," replied Gerry.

Years later when I read of Gerry Bogan's fantastic exploits in the Pacific, and especially Bill Halsey's estimate of his courage, I recalled this laconic yet complete answer—as well as the way it had parted Bull Reeves's whiskers in an appreciative grin.

At Pearl Harbor, one day, we got news of the arrival in San Francisco of the long-awaited *Lexington*. She planned to proceed at once to Honolulu on a trial run at thirty knots. Day by day we watched her phenomenal performance, and we admired her from afar as she anchored in triumph off Waikiki with Diamond Head as a fitting backdrop. There her captain, Frank D. Berrien, welcomed us warmly as we transferred aboard.

Whereas on the *Langley* COMAIRONS staff had perched under the flight-deck ramp in temporary cubby holes hung as an afterthought out over the stern, on the "*Big Lex*" the chief of staff rated a living room, bedroom, and bath, a sumptuous suite in which I rattled around like a single die in a wardroom dice box. Messing as we did with the admiral in his big cabin, we luxuriated all the way back to San Diego. There, anchored in the Roads, we found big "*Sister Sara*" under the able command of Capt. John Halligan. Bull Reeves's two-starred flag floated over the world's most powerful carrier force, a smart outfit that already gave signs of great *esprit* in the making.

Meanwhile a number of new aircraft and new pilots had been assembling for the "summer concentration." Our job now was to whip the force into shape for the next fleet operation less than a year away. Captain Towers turned over command of the *Langley* to Capt. Arthur B. Cook, another good skipper, and now returned to BUAERO to become Admiral Moffett's Assistant Chief. We hoped that the stresses and strains of the winter might not complicate our affairs, for we already had a tough problem to solve in the relationship between the carriers and their squadrons. The admiral held that the squadrons should base under him at San Diego and should operate under his command in the monthly fleet tactical exercises; some of the carrier officers, and singularly enough it was the naval aviators now acting as ship's officers, and not the line officers at all, insisted that the squadrons should function with respect to the carriers just as a turret crew works on a battleship. Aside from the fact that it was impractical to base squadrons on carriers and train them there without keeping the carriers continuously at sea, the introduction of carrier skippers into the chain of command tended to slow down air operations.

This was a conflict that raged even more bitterly as time went on and especially after Capt. E. J. King took over command of the *Lexington*. It was complicated by the *Langley* incident and worse still by a political situation even then developing back in Washington. Some of the high brass had gone gunning for Admiral Moffett's scalp—his term of office would expire in a year—and their candidate, as yet unbeknownst to Bull Reeves, was Rear Adm. Joseph M. Reeves.

As the net of complications began to tighten about us, I chafed under them. To me it seemed that grown men ought to learn to bury their pet prejudices and to move ahead on the big ideas in an orderly and cooperative fashion. To Bull Reeves, an older, wiser, and always more philosophical man, these conflicts all seemed part of a plan that somehow produced the right answers where the apparently more orderly processes finally created planned disorder.

CHAPTER FIFTEEN
CREATION OF STRATEGIC CONCEPT

The return of FLEET AIR to San Diego coincided with the commencement of the summer concentration period of 1928, and now with the two big carriers *Lexington* and *Saratoga* anchored off Long Beach, ninety miles to the north, their squadrons trained ashore at North Island under the direct command of Admiral Reeves. Scuttlebutt rumor had it that the next fleet problem would take place off Panama early the coming year, and this directed all staff efforts toward sound preparation for the big show. In all this we felt a certain sense of urgency; now was the time to show the battle wagons what we could do, and thus "sell aviation to the fleet." Underneath the daily routine we somehow sensed that we were dealing with high destiny, though our course was never completely clear. What ultimately developed was not the direct result of anyone's far-sighted vision; it just came naturally out of the conflict of forces and events.

At that period, the Navy had settled down into a certain organization and procedure that had evolved out of years of experience. The fundamental concept of the fleet setup had been derived from a somewhat shallow reading of Mahan and somewhat superficial instruction at the Naval War College in Newport, Rhode Island. Mahan, in the evolution of his thesis on sea power, had made a painstaking analysis of history, and especially of naval history. Since he studiously excluded theory and opinion, drawing his conclusions from the record, he was able to present convincing evidence in support of his thesis that victory in war and prosperity in peace have always resided with that nation which controls communication by sea. The foundation of sea power is maritime commerce.

The United States Naval War College at Newport held classes in naval tactics and worked out tactical problems on the maneuvering board. For their precepts they naturally looked to Mahan's classic studies and thus became imbued with the tactics of the battle line as employed by Nelson, the great English admiral. From a continued emphasis on the battle line and a general understanding of the role of sea power in history, it was easy to conclude that sea power and the navy were synonymous. The modern counterpart of this loose doctrine is the prevalent belief that strategic bombardment is air power.

The administrative organization of the Battle Fleet revolved around the battleships—the so-called "backbone of sea power." The big-gun carriers based at Long Beach behind the breakwater where they found nearby plenty of sea room. The destroyer squadrons, then called DESRONS, the submarine divisions, or SUBDIVS, and the aircraft squadrons, or AIRONS, based on San Diego, ninety miles further south. For purposes of administration and elementary training, each of these units operated separately under the supervision of the commander in chief. Once each month, the fleet as a whole conducted combined tactical exercises off the coast. Yet even here the forces operated largely under the command of their administrative staffs. The idea of breaking up the several administrative units and reassembling them as task organizations so constituted as to bring to bear such a concentration of heavy guns, long-range torpedoes, and mobile aircraft as appeared necessary to the accomplishment of a particular mission had not as yet evolved. It was to grow out of the peculiar conditions that prevailed in the aircraft squadrons: the big carriers could find suitable anchorages and deep-water operating areas only at Long Beach; their aircraft could find adequate training and repair facilities only at the Naval Air Station, San Diego.

It was customary to change personnel just before the concentration, sending about half of them to "shore" or other duty, and receiving a new batch of students from Pensacola to be trained "at sea." Half of the squadron officers changed at this time as well, a fact that dictated a fresh start on fundamental tactics each year. In view of this fact I determined upon a revolutionary procedure. Instead of accepting the ordinary run-of-the-mine officers sent to us by the Bureau of Navigation for duty in certain specified units, we would jump the gun and insist upon the right to select our own squadron commanders and assign other officers to such squadrons as seemed appropriate to us. When we suggested this selective process to Admiral Reeves, he smiled tolerantly and invited us to go ahead, intimating that we would be wasting our time. For the Bureau of Navigation usually selected its officers and made its assignments with little or no regard for their aptitude for the jobs in mind. Someone had long ago worked out a system designed to expose every officer to an equal amount of duty in every line, so as to afford him an equal opportunity to advance in rank, whether or not he possessed qualities of leadership.

But if the factor of leadership had fallen into low estate in Washington, it still rated high in the aircraft squadrons. Frank Wagner and I had observed the vast differences in character displayed by ships and organizations, and had noted that each had seemed to take on some of the personality and character of the man or men who had founded it, and to retain that personality and character no matter who had succeeded to command. If the U.S.S. *Taddlyadlie* started out as a "smart ship," she would always be a smart ship; and if the U.S.S. *Tiddlywinks* started as a "madhouse," her career would become a series of variations of that theme. With that idea in mind, we determined to give the aircraft squadrons a propitious start and began some tall wangling to gain our ends. For this we brought two powerful arguments to bear: the lives of pilots depended upon the quality of the leaders; if we were to be held responsible, we must have authority over our leadership selections. In our tough battle against this leveling system we won every skirmish but one—a squadron that suffered our only breakdown in morale.

While focusing attention on the quality of leadership of our subordinates, we did a little soul searching of our own. The rapid development of gadgetry in the Navy had tended to create a special group of staff-officer specialists who had become "plank owners" on various staffs. Thus the intricacies of steam engineering, or gunnery, or radio communications, or what have you, had become so mysterious to the average line officer that the specialists had taken over a lot of authorities without accepting the corresponding responsibilities. An admiral, for instance, might sign out a long-winded technical document without being able to pronounce the words, or he might let his radio officer sign the paper "by direction." The addressee would turn the masterpiece over to his radio officer for reply, and thus accept responsibility for fundamental decisions fogged up by technical jargon. Even Admiral Reeves had tended to shift the administrative authorities to me and the operations to Frank Wagner. But Frank and I determined to have none of that; we directed these matters right back to the admiral.

Contrary to naval custom we sought to build up the admiral and play ourselves down. For instance, after having prepared an order for the Old Man's signature, we would urge him to call a conference of squadron commanders to indoctrinate them in his plan. A fine speaker, one possessed of unusual knowledge of military history, of policy, strategy, and tactics, he often held us spellbound by his entertaining and instructive discourses spiced by keen wit. Wagner and I would grasp every favorable occasion to suggest a commendatory signal to a subordinate who had distinguished himself; similarly we saw to it that the admiral got word of any complimentary comment from his subordinates. In other words, we made it our first order of business to develop loyalty both ways—up and down. The time soon came when a squadron commander remarked, "If Bull Reeves told us to fly into the side of a mountain, we'd fly—and likely come out safe on the other side!"

We also gave critical attention to our own performance of staff functions stressing especially our communications procedures and techniques. On the matériel side we took extreme pains to train our "mechs" and to emphasize the importance of preventive engineering. Under this doctrine, it became the task of the maintenance crews to discover incipient failures and correct them before they could induce forced landings or other accident. Having good, sound, new equipment to start with, we were able to reduce mechanical failures almost to the vanishing point and to abolish them entirely from over-water operations.

On the important morale side, Frank Wagner was the key to success. Intimately acquainted with the younger pilots as he was, and an active participant in their social affairs, Frank could watch their reactions and recommend actions designed to keep them all at a high pitch of enthusiasm. One day, after we had been pressing hard toward perfection, Frank came to me with a long face; he feared the kids were getting stale. He thought we should secure all flying for several days and actually order the pilots off the station and away from their jobs. When we went in to see the admiral, concealing our misgivings as to this revolutionary idea, the Old Man threw back his head and parted his beard in a laugh that must have carried clear down to the *Langley* dock.

"Go to it!" he shouted. "And Wagner," he added, "a little visit across the Mexican border to Tijauna might help you get a smile back on your own face."

As the summer developed, two special projects helped bring our new outfits to a high degree of precision: the city of San Diego planned to dedicate Lindbergh Field, and the city of Los Angeles would be host to the national air races in dedication of Mines Field. This gave the staff an opportunity to keep the squadrons practicing their close formations, a drill that tended to bore them; they preferred the dive-and-zoom of practical combat exercises. But now, returning from the many operating areas Frank had established in the back country, they passed in review before the admiral's critical eye, flying wing-and-tail in tight parade formations. Tommy Tomlinson, with the first section of his squadron, began practicing section acrobatics, putting on a rhythmic show of breathtaking formation loops, rolls, and dives.

At the dedication of Lindbergh Field, the overcast lay so close to the surface that, save for fine air discipline, we should have had to call off our participation. Instead, we flew some four hundred fleet aircraft in a thrilling fly past, at low altitude, with the tails of the formations lost in the clouds. Later at the National Air Races in Los Angeles, Tommy's Three Sea Hawks stopped the show with their precision acrobatics. The Army responded with their Three Musketeers. When one of their team was unfortunately killed in an accident, Charles Lindbergh, stepping into the lead position, gave the crowd a sample, not alone of his own flying, but also of the quality of his teamwork and personal leadership.

It was in the National Air Races, too, that the air-cooled engine finally triumphed completely over liquid-cooled. A year earlier, Claire Egtvedt had come down from Seattle to get our ideas on the specifications for a new plane to replace his current production F3B. Primed by me, the admiral had given him the requirements for what had since become the first experimental single-seat fighter bomber, the XF4B. Flown by Tom Jeter in the free-for-all pursuit race, this airplane won handily, running away from the special souped-up liquid-cooled entries. Later in a special event promoted by Bill Boeing, a race to altitude from a standing start, Mort Seligman, in the XF4B, executed a triumphant loop over the T4M station ship cruising at 10,000 feet above the thronged grandstand, and dived back onto the field before the nearest competitor could climb to the target. Jim Fechet, Chief of the Army Air Service, followed Bill onto the field to get the Army's first order in ahead of the Navy. In subsequent years this basic airplane served both Army and Navy, the one as P-12, the other as F4B, with variations to suit the special requirements of each.

Returning to San Diego, we spent the autumn of 1928 at gunnery training, interspersed by monthly tactical exercises with the fleet. All three carriers and their squadrons operated in conjunction with cruisers, destroyers, and submarines against a simulated enemy battle line and in support of our own "backbone." Yet even as we developed intricate joint attacks under this time-honored doctrine, we in COMAIRONS began to flirt with a revolutionary concept: maybe our task force could defeat the battle line singlehanded! From here to the fantastic proposal to use battle wagons in support of aircraft carriers was a terrific mental leap. When the detailed plans for the winter exercises became available, we drew a long breath and took it.

CHAPTER SIXTEEN
MANEUVER FOR POSITION

When the commander in chief released the preliminary statement of the 1929 fleet problem, we in COMAIRONS staff wore broad smiles of satisfaction. For while the exercises contemplated a conventional assault on the defenses of the Panama Canal, the problem was so stated as to convince us that the high command was beginning at last to recognize the role of the carrier in warfare at sea. A "red" fleet, comprising the modern battleships then based in the Pacific with its accompanying submarines, destroyers, and train, moving into the Gulf of Panama with the object of attacking the Canal, would be opposed by a friendly "blue" fleet which had just transited the Canal and moved out into the Gulf to defend it. The blue fleet comprised the vessels of the scouting fleet, then based in the Atlantic but reinforced by the *Lexington* and *Langley* from the "battle fleet" of the Pacific. This gave the defenders an air force comprising all the Army and Navy shore-based aircraft in the Panama Canal Zone, the aircraft of the scouting fleet then based on my old seaplane tender, the *Wright*, and the planes of the *Langley* and *Lexington*; it left to the attackers the *Saratoga* and her planes, under the command of Admiral Reeves.

In the past, these Panama maneuvers had been stereotyped battle-line tactics with the battle wagons steaming majestically behind a destroyer-laid smoke screen while bombarding the Canal with their turret guns at maximum range. After the fleet had fired a few blank charges or "primers" to simulate long-range attack and its airplanes had been "shot down" by the local defenders, the vessels would proceed to their anchorage in the Bay of Panama and all hands would go ashore for a big bust at the Union Club. Later there would be a "critique" in which the high rankers would stand up before a congregation of Army-Navy officers and alibi their failures, or try to impress their personalities upon the assembly. Following this, the social whirl would begin and fleet grand tactics would be put aside until another year.

This time we proposed to spring something new. Instead of tying *Big Sara* to the apron strings of the battle wagons, we would propose that she be detached from the slow elements and sent on a wide southerly detour past the Galápagos Islands, along the north coast of South America, into the Gulf of Panama, through the screen of defending vessels, and up to a point where we might launch a predawn sneak attack on the Canal locks. The single drawback to our plan was the fact that the only vessel with enough high-speed cruising endurance to accompany *Big Sara* was the light cruiser *Omaha*, flagship of Adm. Thomas J. Senn, Commander, Destroyer Squadrons. However, Admiral Reeves and Admiral Senn were warm personal friends. Capt. Harold R. Stark, Admiral Senn's chief of staff, and I were on terms of warm regard. We decided to chance submitting the fantastic proposal that a senior unit commander be deprived of his flagship to plane-guard *Big Sara*.

Meanwhile, storm clouds had begun to darken our political horizon. With the close of the concentration period, we had come face to face with the moot question as to the relationships of carrier squadrons to their carriers. Based on our experience we prepared a letter recommending such changes in the Navy Regulations as would permit the commanding officers of carriers to exercise administrative control over their squadrons, yet still preserve their freedom for assignment by the admiral to task forces and give to him the tactical command. By this time, Capt. E. J. King had assumed command of the *Lexington*, and Capt. Harry E. Yarnell of the *Saratoga*. Both were extremely able men but with quite different temperaments. Captain King had positive ideas for which he fought with determination; Captain Yarnell, while equally clear in his opinions, approached the problem with judicious moderation. In both the *Lexington* and the *Saratoga*, the positive convictions that the squadrons should be treated like gun divisions as an integral part of the ship rested largely with the old-line aviators running the air departments. And so we had a major difference of opinion in which senior naval aviators battled to keep the squadrons subservient to the carriers while we line officers, basing our convictions on practical experience, battled to keep the aircraft squadrons free. On the staff, we argued that the carriers existed for the squadrons; on the ships, they seemed to think it was the other way around. This conflict came at a time when our Washington fences were none too secure.

The fact that Admiral Moffett would complete his second full term as a bureau chief early in the coming year had intensified the efforts of his enemies to deny him reappointment. Their candidate for his relief was Admiral Reeves, and as a palliative they suggested that Admiral Moffett take over command of the Aircraft Squadrons, Battle Fleet. To us on the staff, the whole thing looked like a tempest in a teapot and we, of course, took no position. Admiral Reeves busied himself with preparations for the fleet problem and expressed amusement over Washington politics. Then came the news that some of the boys in the Bureau now had a foot out for me, and had represented me to Admiral Moffett as a turncoat—a former Moffett man now gone full out for Bull Reeves. Aside from the impact of this conflict upon our personal fortunes, there was the question as to what position BUAERO would take in the matter of the relationships of squadrons to carriers. But more important still, such a warm front of political turbulence afforded a poor climate in which to make our big play for recognition of naval aviation in the forthcoming fleet problem.

Now at the height of our concern for the future, we got a wallop in the solar plexus that all but sent us down for the count. When the commander in chief finally issued his own estimate of the fleet problem and his operation orders for it, there was no reference whatever to our proposal for a sneak attack with the *Saratoga*. The battle wagons would do their time-honored square dance behind a destroyer smoke screen; they would fire a few gun primers and exercise their fire control; then they would proceed to the anchorage and hit the beach for a big party at the Union Club. When Frank Wagner brought the news to me and we both dropped into the admiral's office, he lifted his beard from his paper work to stare at us with amazement.

"Whatever it is," he boomed, "it can't be as bad as you men look." After Frank had briefed him on the disappointing situation, Admiral Reeves reached for a message blank and drafted a dispatch to the commander in chief at San Pedro, asking for a conference for himself and staff on the subject of the fleet problem.

Next morning COMAIRONS and staff took off for San Pedro in a flight of three Loening amphibians, the admiral riding as my passenger. As we mounted the flagship's side ladder to her quarterdeck, we were met at the rail by the ship's captain, none other than Claude C. Bloch, the man who had counseled my wife to get me out of the side shows and back under the main tent.

Admiral Pratt, his blouse unbuttoned to reveal an old-fashioned stiff-bosomed white shirt, received us in his cabin. Seated behind the usual billiard-cloth-covered table, he inquired courteously in his State-of-Maine accent to what he owed this visit from so distinguished a group. To Admiral Reeves's inquiry whether Admiral Pratt had read our estimate of the situation for the fleet problem, the commander in chief replied in the negative; he had left the matter in the hands of his assistant chief of staff. His earlier rejection of our big idea had been doubly disappointing because we respected him as a sailorman of the old school and a man highly regarded as a strategist and tactician. With the news that he had not known of our proposal, our hopes began to revive.

Admiral Reeves swept in his outline with deft strokes: The *Saratoga* would launch her aircraft two hours before dawn from a point some 150 miles away from the Canal. To reach that point where she would rendezvous with Admiral Pratt's battleships, the *Saratoga* would steam all night at 30 knots, accompanied only by the *Omaha*, her plane guard. In the 10 hours of darkness between sunset and the launching time, the *Saratoga* would cover 300 miles. This, added to the 150-mile launching range, would put her 450 miles from Panama the night before the attack. During the previous day she would have run 360 miles more, and these distances were such that the enemy could hardly scout the possible areas of approach with any certainty of discovering the *Saratoga*. There was an excellent chance that we might get in undetected.

Admiral Pratt listened carefully and then put his finger on the one weak spot. He feared that if we launched aircraft that far at sea and lost even a single pilot, the reaction of public opinion at home might be most unfavorable.

Admiral Reeves replied that when he had offered the same objection I had produced the surprising record of the year's operations. Using the new equipment provided by BUAERO we had gone through a full year without mechanical failure over the sea. Since we were drilling constantly to avoid cockpit failures it was reasonable to expect that we would have a similarly clean record off Panama.

Satisfied by the logic of this, Admiral Pratt began to warm to the whole idea. He suggested that, while it was now too late to change the orders all ready issued, this very fact might be converted to our advantage. The problem could be made a better exercise if we kept the new plan a secret among ourselves while he arranged later to spring a sudden change of orders on his fleet. He proposed to stop the formation somewhere along the west coast of Mexico, send out new orders by guard boat, release the *Saratoga* for her wide southerly detour, and, incidentally, profit by the element of surprise inherent in radio silence.

When COMAIRONS and his staff departed the flagship, we walked on air.

The fleet sailed on schedule, maneuvering down along the Mexican coast, with the *Saratoga* rehearsing her part with predawn take-offs and rendezvous. At the time we had no night-flying equipment and had done little night flying; but we had discipline, which was better than any equipment. Then one day the fleet flag made a signal for the fleet to stop and send boats for mail. When we opened our orders we found that Admiral Pratt had assigned the *Omaha* to us as *Saratoga's* plane guard, but instead of transferring the DESRONS flag to a destroyer, had left Admiral Senn, Harold Stark, and all the staff on board.

As the *Omaha*, lifting in the swell, ranged up alongside the *Saratoga*, Admiral Senn, although Admiral Reeves's senior, hailed the *Big Sara* from his bridge by megaphone. "What do you want me to do, Bull?" he inquired.

Now we began working our speed up to twenty knots, proceeding in company with the *Omaha* leading the way on our epoch-making wide southerly detour. And as the *Big Sara's* decks trembled under the thrust of her great screws, we on COMAIRONS' staff began to feel a tremor around our hearts. Looking back into the vessel's boiling wake we could see the churnings of white water as the vast power of her great motors drove her forward; a portion of the energy went into slip, but by far the largest part of it went into effective forward thrust. In that turbulence we could visualize what went on quite unseen in the slipstream of aviation, that remorseless force which was driving us at such breathtaking speed.

From our lofty perch on the flag bridge we could count sixty-six airplanes trembling there in the breeze that swept across the deck straining them against their lashings and wheel chocks. Out in front stood thirty-six Boeing fighters with air-cooled radial engines, airplanes we had not dreamed about five years earlier when I had sat in the anteroom off Admiral Moffett's office in BUAERO. Behind the fighters ranged twelve Vought Corsair scouts, conceived and constructed by Chance Vought, who had written the prescription for the Pratt and Whitney Wasp. Back on the fantail, their biplane wings folded, nested eighteen Martin T4M torpedo-bomber scouts, three-seaters built around the Pratt and Whitney Hornet, an engine that even George Mead, who had created it, had solemnly stated in writing was "quite impossible."

As the crews milled about on deck, checking a cockpit cover here or a lashing there, the squadron commanders supervised their work. There was cagey old "Skinny" Wick, skipper of Fighting One, the squadron that wore the high hat insignia on its fuselages. Commanding the other fighter squadron was brilliant Art Davis. The celebrated Three Sea Hawks, with Art as their new leader, comprised the first section of this command but the entire outfit could now match the leading section in smooth squadron acrobatics. In command of our scout-bomber squadron we had that rough and ready old-timer, "Squash" Griffen. At the head of our heavy bomber outfit rode the Old Man of the Sea himself, Harry Bogusch, of whom Admiral Reeves had said, "That man is so crazy about flying you'll have to shoot him down to get the squadron out of the sky."

As we sped toward the equator, we speculated on our chances of success. Frank Wagner, appreciating the intelligence of some of the smart aviators on the *Lexington*, feared that, having trained under us and learned our mental processes, they might diagnose our play. If they should take their suspicions to Captain King, and he should pass them on to the "blue" C.I.C. along with a suggestion that he deploy the defending aircraft carriers in the Gulf of Panama to scout for *Big Sara*, the *Lex* could intercept us during our daylight run and strafe our planes on deck.

This fear the admiral discounted. While he had great respect for Admiral King's intelligence and counted him an ambitious leader who had carefully schooled himself in all branches with a view to ultimate command of the fleet in case of war, he rated King a hard driver, one unlikely to invite initiative from his subordinates. To be a good driver you had to know more about your job than anyone else and be on it every minute. This tended to develop fear among your juniors and discourage their enthusiasm for making suggestions.

The most important factor in a campaign, according to the admiral, was a knowledge of the military character of one's opponent. One should not discount his abilities, nor should he overestimate them. War is no exact science and not therefore subject to rational analysis like, say, engineering. War itself is irrational and the conduct of a battle is always a tragedy of errors. One must be prepared to take risks but these must be intelligent risks—where the advantage to be gained is commensurate with the hazards involved. Fighting spirit is a major factor. One must know the weapons and have faith in their efficacy. The admiral thought that King, for all his tour of duty in aviation, was still a battleship man. He doubted if King had real sympathy or enthusiasm for aviation.

"I recall that you used to box at the Academy," he said, looking at me, "and you remember the old instructor there, 'Matchew' Strohm—he of the cauliflower ears, the flattened nose, and the Bowery dialect. 'Matchew' used to say, 'If yer feelin' sick to yer stummick, remember maybe de udder guy is feelin' a leetle sicker. It ain't de headwork, but de last leetle poosh, dat wins de fight!'"

We were now committed to action. We had perfected our technique. From here on out, we'd play it by ear!

Sitting there in the admiral's cabin, yarning around the green-baize-covered table, I became suddenly aware of how far we had traveled in the brief span of twenty years. Two decades earlier, back there in Annapolis, I had been one of a couple of hundred midshipmen facing an uncertain future. Britannia's rule of the waves had brought peace and prosperity to a world from which tyranny had all but disappeared. The Navy had lapsed into innocuous desuetude, after a brief flurry in the Spanish American War, and now offered but little hope of early promotion. Admiral Reeves, then but a lieutenant and an oldish one at that, had taught us "skinny" — physics, electricity, and chemistry. Rated "white" by the midshipmen and known for valor on the football field, he had threatened to grow old in the service with no chance to display his talents.

Today he was the commander of a naval force, totally undreamed of two years earlier, a product of his own conception and creation. And he was discoursing to us on matters of tactics, strategy, military policy, and leadership in terms we could not have comprehended much earlier. I had gone to Annapolis, not for any love of the sea, but because I had thought to save my father the expense of a college training which, at the time, he could ill afford. And chance had thrown me in with men like Dr. Lucke, a leader in the creation of the American technology, Admiral Moffett, a leader who had applied it to aviation, and Admiral Reeves, a leader who had conceived a new philosophy for the naval air force.

The morning we sighted the low volcanic cones of the mysterious Galápagos Islands, I recalled the day precisely twenty years earlier when I had helped reconnoiter this little-known archipelago while a midshipman in the armored cruiser *Colorado*. At the time such a thing as a gasoline engine was quite unheard of in the fleet. I had therefore sailed a whale boat into Post Office Bay and had sought out the barrel in which, it was said, whalers were wont to leave their letters for later transmission to their destination by whomever chanced to pass that way. In order to commemorate the day and emphasize the breathtaking progress of engines, I suggested to the admiral that I might take off in a fighter and touch wheels ashore. The admiral smilingly agreed but as we closed the islands, intermittent squalls and areas of low visibility forced us to cancel the project.

This unsettled weather continued until the evening before the night run to Panama. We had run all day at 30 knots, with a section of fighters on the take-off spot, ready to launch the moment the weather cleared. The *Omaha* had reported running short of fuel, giving us a new worry. Unless she could last the route at full speed, we would have to launch without a plane guard. Cruising along from one squall to the next, elated by the luck that had protected us against prowling *Lexington* scouts, we suddenly broke out into the clear in an area of unlimited ceiling and visibility. It was about 5 p.m. when the fighters roared into the air.

CHAPTER SEVENTEEN
FRIGATE BIRDS

Up until this moment, everything done had been in rehearsal. Now, with the possibility of enemy contact at any instant, the flag bridge took on a new atmosphere of high tension. The admiral stood out on the bridge, binoculars glued to his eyes, while the breeze fingered his beard. Frank Wagner hovered beside him, alert for a suggestion or command, a quizzical expression in his eyes, indicative of his humorous reaction to stress. As we followed the tiny fighters racing directly ahead along our course, we were startled by a quick reversal that brought them racing back to the carrier.

At that time, fighters carried no radio. They zoomed across the bow at low altitude to drop short sections of garden hose as message holders. The fighters had sighted a destroyer dead ahead, an enemy scout, the *Breck*, heading for us on a collision course. Even as we read the message, we made out the ship's mast, dead ahead. We'd been caught.

The *Breck* turned to parallel our course, well out of gun range, and seemed to be looking us over. The flag-chief quartermaster, gazing at her through his long glass, turned to the admiral.

"Sir," he remarked, "it looks funny to me. I wonder if he thinks maybe he's sighted the *Lexington*." The admiral lowered his binoculars and turned to me.

"Well," he asked, "what do you want to do with her?" Now, the lack of a plane-guard vessel for the next morning had lain heavily on my mind. We had enough worries without risking a take-off crack-up and a lost pilot. It must have been this that prompted my facetious reply.

"Tell her to plane-guard us, sir!" I laughed.

Quick as a flash the admiral barked the signal to the flag-chief quartermaster. As the bright flags fluttered in the late afternoon light, the *Breck* answered. Then to our amazement, she turned and swung into position directly astern of us, four hundred yards away. There we might have left her save that Ken Whiting, the official umpire, felt obliged to make a ruling. And so we theoretically opened fire on her with the after ten-inch, and theoretically sank her. Ken signaled the *Breck* that she was now disabled without radio to communicate our position.

We were just congratulating ourselves on this break and sweating out the rest of the daylight, when the *Omaha* reported being attacked by the cruiser *Detroit*. Her captain, Dick White, who had once been my skipper on the destroyer tender *Bridgeport* and was an old friend of Admiral Reeves, had doped out our intentions, and disregarding his orders, had left his scouting station to look for us. Even then he was broadcasting our position in plain English, instead of code, begging the *Lexington* to come and get us.

Ken Whiting now ruled both cruisers out of the action. The *Omaha*, already short of fuel, slowed down, but the *Detroit*, calmly taking up the plane-guard station, began a play-by-play account of *Big Sara's* every move. Well, the fat was in the fire now; Captain Dick knew we needed a plane guard too badly to wave him off, and besides, he knew Bull Reeves too well to worry about any future disciplining.

The tropic night fell on the Gulf of Panama, coming down suddenly at five bells of the first dog watch. All night we steamed at thirty knots with the stars closed in around our darkened decks. At midnight the admiral called me to the flag bridge.

"All the squadron commanders have been up in a body to ask me to launch immediately and not wait for dawn. What do you say?" That was a poser. No doubt, sweating it out down in the ready room, fearful that Army or Navy aircraft might catch them flat-footed on deck during the night, they had come up with their big idea.

"Sir," I replied, finally, "we have no reason to believe that any night fighters or bombers can be out this far. At least we haven't seen or heard any signs. To change a plan involves new risks, and we have enough already."

"You're right," the admiral agreed. "I'll tell them to turn in; we'll stick to the original plan."

Standing on the flag bridge with the seas slapping against the side and the night breeze filtering down our necks, I began to appreciate, for the first time, the kind of courage that was being displayed by this man. A half-dozen rivals, candidates for his job, were sitting back, waiting for a break. It was the old Navy Game, keep your neck in and let the other fellow take the risks. Sooner or later it pays off—if you live long enough. Bull Reeves had never played that game.

"Sir," I began, "there's a lot of brass hats watching us tonight." The admiral inclined his head to hear me above the roar of the wind. "And," I went on, "there'd be many a dry eye tomorrow if you should slip." For a while I thought he hadn't heard.

"I know," he replied slowly, "but a commander who stops to appraise the impact of a military decision upon his personal fortunes has no right to be entrusted with a command."

After a while, dark figures began stirring among the parked airplanes, and the blue lights winked on—flashlights screened by paper torn from packages of absorbent cotton, loaned by the sick bay. Still later, the staccato bark of an engine and red flashes from its short exhaust stacks signaled all mechanics to start their engines.

By now the night air was cold and we shivered as we stood around on the bridge, looking down on an expanse of exhaust flames. Ship's officers had taken their stations, their telephone helmets on their heads. Pete Mitscher and Ken Whiting stood in the wings of the bridge. The roar of engines swelled then ceased as suddenly as it had started.

Without hearing the order, we knew what that meant: "Pilots, man your planes." The radio messenger handed me a signal blank. It was a plain-English broadcast from the enemy cruiser *Detroit*. Dick White was on the air, in his play-by-play account.

"*Saratoga* has started all aircraft engines," it began. "What a sight! A thousand tongues of red fire from their exhausts! I have turned on searchlights and am firing pyrotechnics to indicate present position. Can't someone stop this? It would be a pity, but we can't let them get away with this kind of murder."

Over the bow roared Skinny Wick in the first airplane, her running lights on. She turned toward Panama. Now they were getting off at about ten-second intervals. They were rendezvousing on the course to the Canal. Eighteen had joined up. Off went their lights! They were going in darkened.

Now a second group had joined up and turned out its lights. There went the torpedo planes. They were forming in two nine-plane groups. One eighteen-plane fighter squadron would escort each nine-plane bomber division. Now they'd all disappeared. There came the last group, twelve in all—Griffen's dive bombers. Now they were all gone. The signalman handed me an intercept from Dick White. "It's magnificent. I've never seen such precision. It's breathtaking." With that he signed off.

Each of the fighters was a potential 500-pound dive bomber and if unopposed would dive immediately onto the locks. Afterward he would climb back to his station and protect the heavy bombers on their level-bombing run. Even the two-seaters were potential dive bombers, and if unopposed would also go in to bomb. Thus we had three detachments, timing their approaches so as to appear over the defending observation posts simultaneously in order to throw the defenses into confusion. After the bombers had delivered their attacks and started back to the *Big Sara*, the fighter pilots would remain behind to harass the Army pursuit. With their air-cooled fighters they could sit on top of the Army liquid-cooled jobs, watch them climb below in a futile effort to gain altitude, and finally thumb their noses, as the enemy lost flying speed and spun out of control.

On the *Saratoga* we sweated out the hour-long minutes of the approach. Radio silence was broken when Bogusch and Griffen reported success. We sweated out their return; the run would take all the available fuel. When they started coming aboard we were too busy to exult. Every plane got in safely except Les Arnold's F3B. Les, our flag lieutenant, was right over the deck with a few seconds to go before the "cut," when his engine conked, out of gas. He landed smoothly in the sea. We left him to the mercies of a convenient enemy destroyer we had called in to act as plane guard, and started out to sea.

But too late! For now we found ourselves under the guns of the defending battleships. It seems that Admiral Pratt in our battleship divisions had failed to come up in time to support us. The navigator of the flagship had underestimated the strong current off Cape Mala and the *Saratoga's* screen was nowhere in sight. Every phase of the complex air operation had gone off like clockwork. All our squadrons had reached their objectives unopposed just at dawn, and had caught the defenders on the ground. With the exception of Les Arnold's plane, which had now been recovered with only a ducking for Les, we had no casualties of any kind. Only the mighty battle wagons had missed the boat!

The critique that year was brief. Admiral Pratt took the floor.

"Gentlemen," he began, "you have witnessed the most brilliantly conceived and most effectively executed naval operation in our history. I expect to fly my flag in the *Saratoga* on our return cruise north, partly as a badge of distinction but mostly because I want to know what makes the aircraft squadrons tick."

Nearly twenty years after the dawn attack on Panama, I met Gen. J. B. Mitchell, USA, Retired, the officer who had then commanded the Panama defenses. The general told me that, having gone abroad early that morning in company with his adjutant, long before the alarm had been sounded, he had sighted specks against the sky.

"Frigate birds?" his adjutant had inquired.

"Frigate birds, my eye!" the general had retorted. "Those are enemy aircraft and they've caught us flat-footed."

Our own high-rankers, while appreciating the tactical skill Bull Reeves had shown, had entirely missed the implications of his accomplishment. While the Army Air Service had been talking air power, the Navy had created the first American strategic air force, not one riveted to shore bases but one roving the high seas—on the backs of the fleet! Yet if this revolutionary development was lost upon most Americans, it was not lost upon our potential enemies, the Japanese.

CHAPTER EIGHTEEN
ANOTHER TURNING

Admiral Moffett did not miss the opportunity, afforded him by the *Saratoga's* performance, to press for his reappointment as Chief of the Bureau of Aeronautics. He countered front office maneuvers in the Navy Department through adroit handling of the political angle at which he was past master. Someone on the Naval Affairs Committee let the Secretary know that the admiral's reappointment for a third term was favored by that committee; then someone on the Appropriations Committee inquired when his nomination might be expected—and lo, the whole house of cards collapsed.

The performance of the *Saratoga's* planes created a front-page sensation; *The New York Times* handled the story exceptionally. Hanson Baldwin, himself a Naval Academy man steeped in the Mahan tradition, was on the scene, and went out with us on several demonstrations arranged for fleet officers and distinguished visitors. Charles A. Lindbergh, then at Panama in connection with Pan American Airways' first mail hop from Panama to Miami, spent several days on board the *Saratoga*.

Instead of quartering him in the admiral's cabin, we berthed him down in the wardroom with the squadron pilots and passed the word around that he should be treated like any other visiting Army file. However, since his first act had been to request permission to take off and land on the ship, and further, since approval of his request might convey the impression that there was no mystery attached to being a naval aviator—especially a carrier pilot—I was designated to chaperon him during flight operations and diplomatically to fend him off.

We were standing together on the bridge of the *Saratoga*, watching the evolutions on deck. The very precision of the landings and take-offs was a delight, and the smooth teamwork of the deck crews was breathtaking, even to those who had grown up with the development. Lindbergh, enthusiastic as a kid with a toy airplane, kept up a running fire of questions as to the whys and wherefores of everything. He was particularly curious about the air tactics, and kept Wagner and the admiral busy answering searching questions. Lindbergh's eyes gleamed and his boyish grin widened as the admiral held forth as only he could do.

It was after the operations had been concluded and we were heading back to port that Lindbergh popped the question that was uppermost in his mind.

"Why won't you let me land on board?" he asked abruptly.

"Admiral Wiley is reluctant to accept responsibility for your safety," I replied.

"I'm responsible for myself," he retorted brusquely. "Isn't it a fact that they just don't want an Army officer around a carrier?" he added.

"Of course," I replied. And then I moved on to the counterplan. "You remember the Three Sea Hawks at the Los Angeles air races last year?" I inquired.

Naturally Lindbergh remembered.

"Well," I went on, "Tommy Tomlinson has left the service, but Put Storrs and Bill Davis are here, and the boys thought you might like to lead them in a Section take-off, and fly ashore with them when you go."

Lindbergh nodded. "I'd like that," he said simply.

"It would make a good story," I went on. "'Leader of Three Musketeers takes off with Three Sea Hawks.'" Lindbergh shook his head.

"Not interested in the publicity," he said.

And there, thought I, was a key to his conduct. Lindbergh was so honest, intellectually and in every other way, that the antics of publicity seekers revolted him. Newspaper men, having never before encountered a celebrity who was not avid for publicity, could not be expected to understand this. They made—and broke—celebrities at will. They considered that they had made Lindbergh and most now thought him ungrateful.

With Admiral Moffett's reappointment to the Bureau, we became curious as to Admiral Reeves's new assignment. He had made it a practice never to request duty for himself, and now rather hoped he might get command of the Ninth Naval District, at Great Lakes. But when the news leaked out through the grapevine, it was a dive-bomb hit right amidships. Admiral Reeves was to go to the Navy Yard at Mare Island as Inspector, a job that usually rated a commander or, at most, a captain. The admiral took the news cheerfully as usual.

However, this was but a preliminary "strafing attack," the name the admiral had coined for diving tactics. One day Wagner walked into the admiral's cabin, his face as long as the *Saratoga's* flight deck. Waving a letter in his hand he sank down in his seat at the mess table and announced, with a wry grin, "They're shanghaiing me to Guam!" At first we thought he was simply using the slang phrase, but it turned out to be literally true.

"And as for you," he added, nodding to me with a sudden grin that always signaled the triumph of his humor, "you're headed for Coco Solo."

Coco Solo, the big new base on the Atlantic side of the Canal, would have been most acceptable as a command following a full three years' sea cruise, but I had been but a year afloat and was already on the short side of sea duty. The assignment, had it been carried out, would have been a sentence to oblivion. Admiral Reeves later saw that it wasn't. For when the new Commander in Chief, Battle Fleet, who relieved Admiral Pratt, proved to be Adm. Louis M. Nulton, a friend of Admiral Reeves, the latter promptly dispatched a letter to Admiral Nulton suggesting that he ask for me as his Aide for Aviation on the Battle Fleet Staff. This assignment put me one notch above the Aircraft Squadrons, whose new commander was announced as Admiral Butler, with Ken Whiting in my job as Chief of Staff. And since Admiral Nulton was known as a man for detail, the Aircraft Squadrons Staff saw that they would need a friend on high if they were to retain the freedom of action Admiral Pratt had always given Admiral Reeves.

Meanwhile, it was a gloomy outfit that received Admiral Pratt on the *Big Sara* for the cruise home. The admiral had just been selected for the highest naval command, Chief of Naval Operations, in Washington. En route north he brought up the problem of the "home yard" for the *Lexington*. Norfolk was the *Lexington's* home yard. Admiral Pratt, proposed to return her to the Atlantic in order to balance the work load—in other words keep the yard workmen employed.

Wagner and I took issue with him and I must have pressed too hard on the need for keeping the squadrons together for training, for Admiral Pratt turned on me in some annoyance and barked, "You always see the ultimate objective and want to take it on the first assault. You've got to learn to take minor objectives one at a time, and to hold them till the big one falls in your lap. Otherwise," he added, shaking a finger in my face, "you'll never get anywhere in this man's Navy."

Shortly after we arrived in San Diego, and even before the admiral's relief had reported, Bull Reeves was detached from his command. The day he shoved off, all his squadron commanders and staff accompanied him to the Santa Fe railway station. Overhead FLEET AIR paraded for him in a last formation flight. The Old Man put up a cheerful front until Harry Bogusch shook his hand.

"Admiral," said Harry, "we used to hate your guts for making us fly those tight formations, but that night off Panama we blessed you for the air discipline you had forced on us." With that, two big tears welled up in Bull Reeves's eyes and ran down his nose onto his gray whiskers.

After Admiral Nulton had hoisted his flag on the fleet flagship *California*, I found myself once again on a battleship. Time was when I would have thrilled at the thought. Now it left me numb. To have served with two great leaders in succession and to have lived through the creative period of naval aviation ashore and afloat and then go back to battle wagons cheerfully was too much to expect. I couldn't get into the spirit of it.

When later the *California* spent the summer at the navy yard in Bremerton, Washington, I was completely cut off from aircraft operations except by correspondence. Admiral Nulton and his battle fleet staff tried hard to absorb some of the new ideas, but it was too much to expect them to think and act intuitively, along lines that crisscrossed every preconceived idea.

The end of the summer found us back behind the breakwater at San Pedro, when one day a message came that Fred Rentschler and Bill Boeing had flown down from Seattle in their Ford Trimotor and were at the Los Angeles Biltmore where they would like me to have dinner with them. I knew from the newspapers and from letters that great things had been going on in the aircraft industry. Not only had some of the companies made money on operations, but some of the leaders had become rich as a result of the increased values of their stocks. This was the beginning of the end of that mad period of speculation in which all sorts of mergers and consolidations had prompted the public to get into the market and make a killing. In the aircraft industry, Curtiss and Wright had led off with a merger that had brought together two of the greatest names in aviation and had put two of the biggest operations under the same tent.

In reply Boeing, Rentschler, Chance Vought, and others, fearing the giant thus created, had consolidated in a merger of their own. Unlike the Curtiss-Wright consolidation, which, to them, smacked of Wall Street, the new one was to comprise only sound companies, those which had already proved profitable or seemed likely to continue to do so. The big idea was to bring together, under one leadership, the best in airplanes, engines, propellers, and transport systems in order to coordinate engineering experience in a way that would speed progress. For passenger air transport still seemed to hang on a dead center: it was impossible to reduce rates unless volume could be stepped up, and volume refused to step up until costs came down.

The new outfit, which had taken the name of the United Aircraft and Transport Corporation, planned to get its engineering heads together and create improved aircraft designed to break that log jam. Fred Rentschler and Bill Boeing had come to Los Angeles to look over some of the western companies like Northrup, which had already joined up, and Menasco, which would like to. Reading about the Curtiss-Wright consolidation, I had to smile at the idea I had once had of depending upon those two for air-cooled engine competition. Save for Fred Rentschler and Pratt and Whitney, they would now have us by the neck.

It was an interesting circumstance that the particular group should have joined up in the new outfit. For I had put the bee on Chance Vought that had produced the prescription for the Pratt and Whitney Wasp, and had later sent Bill Boeing to Fred Rentschler for the engines for his mail planes, the very engines that had made possible a tidy profit out of a venture that Bill's competition had called impossible. And save for the Martin torpedo bombers, this group had supplied all the equipment for our carriers, including the engines for the Martins. And the marriage seemed natural from another point of view: the parties at interest were all pioneers with a zeal for aviation and they had all played the game according to Hoyle.

On arrival at the Biltmore I found another old-timer in their company. Thomas Hamilton, like Bill Boeing, had grown up in Seattle, but unlike Bill Boeing he had not had money to spend on airplanes. Instead he had taught himself to fly in a crate of his own construction and had then built his own business. On the outbreak of World War I, Tom had rushed to Washington to get a contract to build airplanes but had been diverted to Milwaukee, Wisconsin, the home of furniture manufacture, to make propellers. He had, however, established his own Metalplane Company and built a high-wing metal monoplane that, he claimed, antedated the Ford. And when the new United Aircraft and Transport Corporation had looked around for a propeller company to round out their line, they had taken over Tom Hamilton, his Hamilton Aero Manufacturing Company, and his Hamilton Metalplane Company. Tom, like every other Tom, Dick, and Harry of that time, had been in the stock market but, unlike some of them, had done well.

At dinner that evening, I noted the changes that had come over these men. The time had been when they had scratched gravel for the last trace of "color" that might lie close to bedrock. Now they flew high, wide, and handsome on the crest of the current boom. They had flown in aboard their own Ford Trimotor; they had taken a suite at the Biltmore and now they ordered the exotic foods on the menu. One advantage of the naval service was that much of this had passed us by; we had security, but no wealth.

These men had wealth but little security, and even at the height of the great boom of the late 'twenties, Fred Rentschler, at least, clearly foresaw the ultimate outcome. To him the whole thing was crazy—a house of cards built on a foundation of sand, foredoomed to collapse at the first real tremor. Meanwhile they shop-talked back and forth, discussing their current management problems, one of which seemed to concern Tom Hamilton and his propeller company.

It seemed that after I had taken the decision, away back there in BUAERO, that we would use the new metal propellers in place of the wooden ones, two companies had competed for the business—the Hamilton Aero Manufacturing Company, of Milwaukee, and the Standard Steel Propeller Company, of Pittsburgh. In the middle had sat the Reed Propeller Company, owners of the patents taken out by Dr. Sylvanus Reed. These patents, covering metal propeller blades made of "light alloys, solid throughout the outer half of their length," had been discounted by both Hamilton Aero and Standard Steel, who had declared them invalid. However, the new Curtiss-Wright Corporation had absorbed the Reed Company to put the power of Curtiss-Wright dollars behind the patents.

Meanwhile, Tom Hamilton, of Hamilton Aero, and Harry Kraeling, of Standard Steel, fought their conflict on other grounds. To match Tom Hamilton's propeller-design savvy, Harry Kraeling hired Frank Caldwell, the Army's civilian propeller expert, away from the Army. Frank Caldwell had a few inventions himself and was one of the best informed men in the industry. Both companies sold "two-piece" propellers—that is, duralumin blades mounted in steel hubs that permitted blade-angle adjustment on the ground. The Reed Company held to single-piece, fixed-pitch props made of solid duralumin. It was one of these that had dumped me into the dirt at Anacostia, back in 1926, when a blade had broken off close to the hub. I still kept a section of that blade as a souvenir. Now after United Aircraft and Transport Corporation had acquired Hamilton Aero, of Milwaukee, Standard Steel, of Pittsburgh, had countered by recognizing the Reed patents and taking a license from Curtiss-Wright. Standard paid Curtiss royalties, and in exchange Curtiss agreed to sue all infringers of the patents—including Hamilton.

Fred Rentschler, as president of United, had not relished a patent suit with Curtiss and had therefore bought up Standard Steel of Pittsburgh from its local stockholders. This had given him freedom from the threat of suit because he had acquired the license in the transaction, but it had opened up other problems. The two propeller companies had been so highly competitive, it now seemed unlikely that either Hamilton or Kraeling could consolidate the two outfits into a single company; they needed new and neutral management. Furthermore, since the consolidation had brought the two manufacturers into one group, the action had deprived the Army and Navy of their cherished competitive sources and had substituted instead a potential monopoly.

It was like old times to chin with these friends about their business problems and to become, for an evening at least, a part of the world I had once lived in. In that world, petty personal jealousies had to be subordinated to business principles. Only in a semipolitical organization, such as the Army or Navy, where there was no financial statement to measure the quality of leadership, could men indulge in such extravagances as personal politics. Of course in business, personalities did exercise strong influences, but in the long run, economics seemed to write the answer to the business equation.

After a visit in Los Angeles, Rentschler and Bill Boeing flew to San Diego to call on the Navy. Taking off in my little Vought Corsair, I went ahead to introduce them to the new command down there. Then one evening as we sat together in a bedroom of the old Hotel del Coronado, that relic of the lush boom days of Southern California, Tom Hamilton and Bill Boeing turned in, leaving Fred and me to talk shop. Fred was back on his propeller problem, wondering if I, by any chance, could suggest a possible new president for the consolidated company. He had, of course, kept in touch with the gossip in BUAERO over the controversy with FLEET AIR, and was aware of its influence on my personal situation. The talk drifted naturally to this subject, and before I was aware of its drift, Fred had invited me to take over the propeller job.

"Don't be silly," I laughed. "At forty-two, I'd be crazy to even consider it. In the first place I am devoted to the service and, in the second, there's nothing in a naval officer's training to qualify him for business competition."

"I haven't suggested it," Fred replied soberly, "without first thinking the matter through. I'm sure you have the necessary versatility and resourcefulness."

"I appreciate your interest and thank you for the compliment," I replied, "but frankly I'm sorry you brought it up. If I accepted, which, of course I have no intention of doing, the time would surely come when I would regret it. And in passing it up, I open myself to the certainty that every future setback will make me sorry I lacked the guts to resign."

"Is there no way for you to retire?" he asked.

"No, and if there were, that wouldn't be the way to go about it. Nothing but a complete separation would do, and for me, that is quite out of the question. I've got twenty-five years in on my retirement. Throwing that away would be stupid."

"Well, think it over," he persisted. "And when you're ready, let me know. You could start with the propeller company, and then, if things work out, you could go on from there." I laughed at the idea.

And, at the moment, I was serious about it, but after Fred and Bill and Tom had left, I found I couldn't turn off his voice by a flick of the switch. This was no ordinary proposal to be dismissed forthwith: These men had shown me their stuff on many occasions. They were deep in the technical development of aviation, something close to my own heart. They were getting big things done; I was bogged down in a maze of politics with no clear objective before me, and frustrations wearing me down. I began lying awake nights, analyzing the pros and cons.

Trying to compare advantages and disadvantages like this got me nowhere. The fundamental fact was that if I persisted in working at aviation I must risk my chance for high command. If, however, I gave up aviation and returned to line duty, I would be deserting technical development at the very time it needed the attention of everyone who had acquired experience in it. In private business I could continue the engineering development and, far from impairing my future as an executive, could actually enhance it. For in the new era which had blossomed in the brief fifteen years since Dr. Charles Edward Lucke and Columbia University, an executive with a fundamental engineering training had a better chance to accomplish things in a manufacturing business than one without such training.

The chances of a former naval officer succeeding in business were slim, but the chance was there. The risk of failure was great, but the opportunity to contribute importantly to the advance of aviation was enough to warrant taking the chance. Admiral Reeves would have judged it "an intelligent risk." I submitted my resignation, and received the acceptance in December, 1929.

The stock market had crashed two months before; the world had entered a protracted period of depression. I had bought a complete outfit of brand new uniforms, for duty on the commander in chief's staff. Now I packed them away in a sea chest, along with the prize sword "awarded by the Class of 1871 for proficiency in ordnance and gunnery," and turned my back on the sea. After twenty-five years of naval service, I signed off for life.

Throughout this tortured period of indecision, my wife had taken no other position than the traditional one of the Navy wife, "Whither thou goest!" She had listened with her usual patience to my reasoning, but reserved to herself the intuitive process that proved in the end to be right. For it was only after we had been out of the service some time that I learned a fact that would have made the decision far easier, one that she had sensed all along. In civil life we were free. No longer were we social and professional slaves to every officer and his wife who happened, by accident of date of appointment or scholastic standing at Annapolis, to outrank us on the precedence list. But one basic fact was clear; the slipstream that had sucked me into naval aviation had now blasted me out of the service I had loved, and into civil life.

CHAPTER NINETEEN
NECESSITY, THE MOTHER OF CREATION

When, shortly after the first of January, 1930, Tom Hamilton took me up to Milwaukee to look over the Hamilton Aero plant there, the stock market crash had already enveloped the country in a cold chill. Along the Northwestern Railway's right of way, cold smoke stacks pointed dead fingers toward leaden skies and fear gripped the land. However, we found Tom's modern factory still bright and cheerful for it had been well equipped and was now well run by Arvid Nelson, its manager. While the civilian demand for propellers had collapsed with the boom, military business had continued firm under the five-year Army and Navy building programs.

It was when we went down to Pittsburgh to look over Standard Steel that I got a jolt. The plant, located across the river in Homestead in a former cap-pistol factory, was as drab and cheerless as Pittsburgh itself. With many of the steel mills down as a result of the market collapse, there was less smog than usual along the Monongahela, but the grime of the past still clung to treeless slopes. After a look over the situation there it was clear we must cut the consolidated propeller company back to a size suited to the reduced demand.

While the plant in Milwaukee appeared the better of the two, the State of Wisconsin had a heavy corporation income tax that would have to be included in costs; and besides, Milwaukee lay off the main east-west line of rail communication. At Pittsburgh, Harry Kraeling had just completed a new three-story loft building in which we might concentrate the machinery of both companies, and the plant had a siding to the main line of the Pennsylvania. Here, about halfway between Washington, D.C., and Dayton, Ohio, was a situation that offered such advantages that we decided to consolidate the best equipment and the most skilled workmen there. We would then abandon all excess facilities and endeavor to set up a plant with a break-even point calculated to keep us in the black even with the greatly reduced military production level.

In calculating this setup, I had help from the head office in New York and in the person of Joseph F. McCarthy, controller of United Aircraft. Mac,

I found, was the sort of wizard who could glance at columns of figures and read in them signs and portents such as could be made clear to me only after I had reduced them to engineer's language of graphs and charts. From him I discovered that a financial statement is not just the cold record of past mistakes or triumphs, but also a weather map from which to forecast future trends and to take decisions calculated to reap the abundant harvest.

Using the figures available, we calculated the size of the facility with which we might expect to continue to break even during a period of slow demand but still retain the flexibility essential to reaping a profit when the tide turned. United Aircraft was frankly not in business for its health; it was in business for a fair profit and each of the subsidiaries was expected to stand on its own two feet. By consolidating the financial resources of all its subsidiaries in the parent company, it had in effect broadened the resources of each. Any company in temporary need of funds might look to the parent company without going outside to borrow, but over the long pull it must contribute its share to the over-all income.

Having had no training whatever in accounting or finance, but having been schooled by Dr. Lucke to search for fundamental principles, I now began digging down to bedrock and in J. F. McCarthy, himself, discovered a rich nugget. Profit, it seemed, was not just the excess of receipts over expenditures, a sum to be divided among a few insiders and squandered in riotous living. Profit was, among other things, the great regulator and controller of trade, and trade was the foundation of human existence. Under the free play of natural competitive forces, the compelling need to make a profit or go out of business and starve was what drove men to cut costs of production. If they could reduce costs enough to make the product available to more people they could increase the demand and expand the volume of production. Out of their profits, or the anticipation of profits, they could attract new money with which to buy new machinery designed to cut costs further and expand volume further. All this was a delicate, living process that required good judgment and great skill to nurture.

Profit, it appeared, was like the governor on a steam generator. Increased demand for power would slow down the engine and reduce the voltage were it not for the fact that the governor, sensitive to small changes in speed, now opened the throttle wider to admit the extra steam required to meet the new demand. Contrariwise, when the demand fell off the engine might overspeed and destroy itself, save that the eversensitive governor now reacted quickly to close the throttle, and save the machine.

Profit was therefore no devouring ogre, as some would have us believe, nor was it just the regulator or controller of costs. Men, in seeking to make a profit—and correspondingly to avoid a loss—were ever on the alert to create new devices and new products. If one of these turned out to be useful, or desirable, and if its price proved reasonable, then the device would come into general use and its production and use would become profitable for both its creator and its user, to say nothing of the workmen who manufactured it. If, however, the device or idea failed to measure up to the customer's expectations, or failed to satisfy his tastes, then it would just fade out; nature, it appeared, was highly selective. She believed in enterprise.

When natural law was permitted to function according to principle, corrective forces maintained a degree of equilibrium. To each action there was an opposite and equal reaction and the action contained the germ of the reaction, to the end that the pendulum could not swing too far. It was only when man-made law began hampering natural law that the violent swings took place. No man could understand the workings of the natural law well enough to anticipate the future nor, were he able to do so, could he control the future. Least of all did he have wisdom enough to incorporate the germ of a corrective action in his plans.

As I studied this matter of profit and business cycles, I began to get hold of a truth that seemed to be the answer to a lot of questions about the place of the machine in the economy. Men were beginning to argue that labor-saving machinery would bring about technological unemployment, and as the world-wide depression deepened, the facts seemed to confirm the opinion. However, there was another side to this coin: in a technological age when some engineers were engrossed with the task of cutting costs with machinery, other engineers were busy creating new devices to sell. And when these new devices clicked, they called for the creation of new enterprises, the employment of new money—even the creation of new wealth—and best of all the creation of new jobs for workmen. The automotive industry was one of many brilliant examples of this fact.

Now no man or group of men could possibly have enough wisdom to control the operations of this law. The free play of natural forces was the only intelligent controller. Like the slipstream of an airplane, this process might appear to be turbulent and wasteful, but again, like the slipstream, it was one of the most efficient processes in nature. The best men could do was try to maintain a healthy climate in which the process could flourish, and since the key lay in the incentive for the human spirit, men's chief contribution must come out of faith in the natural process.

All this was a revelation to me in more ways than one. Like most naval officers I had absorbed something of the point of view of the professional man who tends to look down his nose at the tradesman. Overimpressed by the sins of a few profiteers, we considered businessmen mere money grubbers inclined to wink at sharp practices, if not downright dishonesty. To the professional man, especially one in public service, whose compensation does not clearly reflect the results of his own efforts, the real reward lies in his knowledge of a job well done. To some, this provides all the incentive required, but to most it furnishes an excuse to sit on the beach and watch the ebb and flow of the tides. The military man is prone to forget that some hard worker must create the wealth necessary to support him in the honorable estate to which he has become accustomed and that if comparable salaries make his appear modest, Uncle Sam is lavish with the perquisites.

When I sought to probe these matters with J. F. McCarthy, I found a kindred spirit. From the inception of the company, Fred Rentschler had brought Mac into every business discussion and decision; it had been his idea that finance should walk hand in hand with operations rather than bring up the rear with a truck load of old ledgers. He had, therefore, given Mac a high degree of autonomy in financial matters especially in the subsidiaries and Mac had used this so skillfully that everyone in the organization respected his business judgment and admired his integrity.

As time passed, and my responsibilities in United widened, Mac and I expanded our viewpoints together. Shortly after completing the physical consolidation at Pittsburgh, I was made president of the Sikorsky company at Bridgeport. A year later, after Chance Vought had died suddenly, I became head of his company in East Hartford. In less than a year, I, the least experienced businessman in United had fallen heir to its three problem children. As the depression deepened, and vast social changes began to take place, I sensed the far-reaching responsibilities that attach to the head of a manufacturing organization. Aside from the normal headaches incident to managing a competitive enterprise during a period of world-wide depression, there were heavy responsibilities imposed by strange forces unleashed by politicians prying open Pandora's Box. This was an era when American business was placed on trial for its very life.

Our difficulty at Pittsburgh sprang primarily from the fact that the consolidation of the two manufacturers of metal propellers had created a potential monopoly; and there is no business more vulnerable than a monopoly. Our two steady customers, the Army and the Navy, wasted no time in slapping us down; they turned their propeller business over to fly-by-night competitors, and worse still, to government arsenals. My first venture in business was now threatened by unfair competition from sources that contributed nothing to engineering and development and charged their overhead to a government appropriation.

It was somewhat as if Uncle Sam had pirated a manuscript of a best seller and had had it printed in the Government Printing Office or a sweat shop at public expense, and then left the author to starve. The policy is hardly designed to advance the writing art and, in the long run, is sure to prove bad medicine for the government, that is the people, itself.

This fact we endeavored to point out to both Army and Navy, urging that it was to their interest that we continue to live. After all, we were the only organization in the world capable of continuing the development of metal propellers; foreign aircraft still clung to their archaic wooden props, and foreigners were still convinced of their superiority. We tried to point out that the consolidation had been forced by patent considerations and for no other reason, that the new management had been drawn from Army and Navy and had no intention of monopolizing anything but was determined to foster progress in new design. Their reply was to ask to see the color of our new designs.

With survival dependent upon the creation of something new and better, I went upstairs to the engineering department to put the problem before its chief, Frank Caldwell. Frank, a big cinnamon bear of a fellow with a slow Tennessee drawl, had forgotten more about aircraft propellers than most engineers would ever know. While Chief of the Army Propeller Branch at Dayton, he had suggested to Harry Kraeling, then a salesman of the steel alloy Vanadium, that he give up trying to build propeller blades out of welded-steel sheets, and use instead the new aluminum alloy, duralumin. When I put the problem up to Frank, he hoisted his bulk out of his chair and ambled toward a drawing table in the corner of his office. Pushing aside a T square, he peeled the cover back from a large drawing and looked at the black lines with modest pride.

At that time, the Hamilton-Standard duralumin blades were clamped into the sockets of steel hubs in such a way that when an airplane stood on the ground, the blades might be adjusted to whatever setting was desired. However, once set, the blades were not adjustable in the air. This gave the airplane a handicap such as a motor car would have if deprived of its gearshift. The propeller shown in Frank's drawing, however, had a mechanism for adjusting the propeller blade setting in the air. The pilot might use one setting, corresponding to low gear, when taking off, and another corresponding to high, for cruising. Frank visualized his "controllable pitch propeller" as the "gearshift of the air."

The idea of such a propeller was not new. Many people had tried the device and found it sound in conception; the problem was that no one had been able to build one of the things strong enough to stand up under the extremely high centrifugal and vibratory stresses found in propeller blades. The novelty of Frank's design lay in its simple hydraulic control mechanism, in which oil pressure on a piston rotated the blades and locked them in either of two positions, the best setting for cruising or for take-off. Judged by the old engineering adage, "to be good it must look good," Frank's propeller looked to me like the answer to a maiden's prayer.

Now Frank Caldwell was no overenthusiastic salesman. The best he would say for his brain child was to express the quiet hope that it might amount to something some day—provided we could make it hang together. But to me there was no use fooling around; here was just the kind of gadget we needed to pull us out of the hole. I gave orders to shoot the works and rush the development of the "gearshift of the air."

Fifteen years later, after we had become more conscious of the need for corporate social security and after we had got ourselves all bound up in our own red tape, I doubt if United Aircraft would ever have undertaken such a project.

For the problem was not so simple as I have so far stated it. The new propeller must of necessity prove more costly than the old type, and there was no proof that the increase in performance would justify the increased costs. This question did not lend itself to precise calculation, nor could we solve it by trying the propeller on an existing airplane. In order to realize the advantages of the new type we must build a new airplane designed to exploit it, and in those days people just didn't haul off and build airplanes to sell other people's propellers.

The point is that at the moment the controllable-pitch propeller, one day to be recognized as the most revolutionary device in aeronautics, was not then something that men demanded. In fact, current opinion was bearish on the idea just as it had been on the air-cooled engine and still was on reduction gears. In the judgment of the wise men, such devices were bound to be so heavy or so costly that their advantages might at best balance out their disadvantages, so why bother with the complication? Frank Caldwell had thought it through, but, being modest and conservative, he did not try to sell the device to me. My own reaction was intuitive rather than rational.

Though I reported my decision to Fred Rentschler at the New York office, he naturally took little notice of it until our financial statement began showing red ink. Lacking profitable production to support an expensive development, we had begun to show serious losses. Since there was no flight experience available to support my venture, Fred was all for canceling the project to avoid further losses. The sole argument I could bring to bear was the fact that I had installed an experimental prop equipped with magnesium blades in one of the small Sikorsky amphibians, an S-39, which had astonished me with its quick take-off and improved cruising characteristics. Behind my decision, however, had lain the whole background of aviation development. One device after another had been proposed and rejected on the basis of engineering judgment, only to be later perfected by some zealot who refused to recognize handicaps. I expressed confidence in the outcome and offered to gamble my job on it. Fred shook his head in doubt.

"Well," he said sourly, "it had better pan out or it will be just too bad for you."

Now there remained one process by which I might recover some of our investment. The propeller had been developed to the point where we might offer a few of them to the Army and Navy at experimental prices on experimental contracts, a practice long used to foster new and expensive developments. But when I went down to BUAERO I ran into a cold front that iced me up like nothing I had ever before seen. The Plans Division of BUAERO seemed now to have usurped the functions of the Engine Section in developments of this kind, and the head of that division was now Comdr. Richmond Kelly Turner, USN, a Naval Academy classmate of mine and a friend of long standing. "Spuds" Turner was a tough egg, something the Japs were to learn at Tarawa and other South Pacific actions some fifteen years later; I didn't have to wait that long.

Kelly Turner seemed to think that controllable-pitch propellers were no good in general, and to suspect that the one I was trying to sell was probably the least useful of them all. If I had wasted my company's money chasing a will-o'-the-wisp, he had no intention of sending any of Uncle Sam's hard earned cash on a wild-goose chase to try to bail me out of my business mistakes. "Spuds" did not confine his opinions to me in a confidential chat, but took pains to broadcast them all through the corridors of BUAERO in a loud stentorian voice.

Meanwhile, after taking over the Sikorsky job, I had felt the need of a new assistant in Hamilton-Standard and had learned through George Wheat, our public relations counsel, that Raycroft Walsh, a former major in the Air Corps who had resigned to go into business, might be interested. Ray had had an active Army career and, during the Mitchell controversy, had served in the Office of the Chief of Air Corps, Maj. Gen. Mason M. Patrick, as Finance Officer where he had performed some of the functions I had performed for Admiral Moffett. I liked him the moment I met him, and immediately recommended that he be brought into the company.

When Ray took the new propeller to the Army, he encountered a similar lack of interest. Even though he carried his case to the Assistant

Secretary of War for Air, Mr. F. Trubee Davison, and finally to his friend Pat Hurley, Secretary of War, stressing the fact that refusal to help develop the new propeller would prove disastrous to the Army and fatal to Hamilton-Standard, he made no more progress than had I with my friend "Spuds" Turner. It was a kind providence which, taking us by the hand, led us out to Cheyenne, Wyoming, and a new milepost in history.

For prior to the crisis in the affairs of Hamilton-Standard, United Aircraft and Transport Corporation, having in mind the need for building new transport aircraft designed to carry passengers and mail on a profitable basis, had initiated a joint airplane development headed up by Boeing. Based upon the performance of the Boeing "Monomail," a single-engined low-wing monoplane itself partly derived from the earlier work of Jack Northrup, Boeing had taken in hand its new ten-passenger, twin-engined, low-wing monoplane to be called the "Boeing 247." Designed around a new Pratt and Whitney Wasp engine and equipped with Hamilton-Standard propellers, it was intended as a replacement for all other assorted models in use on the line. Boeing, confident of its engineering ability, had released for production a full order of some sixty airplanes without first testing out a prototype. This procedure, if successful, would put the airplane company far ahead of any competitor and would give the transport company a big jump on other airlines such as it had earned by creating the earlier model, 40-B.

At first everything had gone swimmingly, but the day the first ship to fly over the lines essayed to take off with full load from the high-altitude field at Cheyenne, serious trouble developed; the airplane just could not handle full load satisfactorily from such elevations. At first, Boeing had been inclined to blame Pratt and Whitney and the Wasp engine for insufficient horsepower, but when that attempt failed, both parties shifted the blame onto Hamilton-Standard propellers, claiming faulty propeller design. This was the old Indian game of passing the buck around the eternal triangle of engine, propeller, and airplane. When we sent Frank Caldwell to Cheyenne to investigate he went quietly about a demonstration that, we hoped, would prove convincing.

First he adjusted the duralumin blades at best setting for take-off to show how well the ship would perform even at high altitude. This setting, however, was so inefficient at cruising speeds that the nearby mountain peaks echoed and reechoed the whining complaint of whirring blades. To meet this defect, Frank reset the blades to the best angle for cruising, where the airplane, its load having been reduced for take-off, performed perfectly. After this convincing demonstration, he unwrapped his drawings of a controllable-pitch propeller for the 247. While no such prop had yet been air-tested, Boeing brushed the objection aside, confident now that between the two companies, the airplane could be salvaged.

So it was that Frank Caldwell's controllable-pitch propeller not only saved the whole string of Boeing 247's, but in doing so, it opened up the new era of "three-mile-a-minute" air passenger travel and started air transport on its way. After that, even the Army and Navy began to recognize the potentialities of the new propeller; it paved the way for low-wing monoplanes with their high-wing loadings and thus marked the passing of the biplanes.

But prior to the Cheyenne demonstration, Hamilton-Standard propellers dragged bottom. Ray Walsh, who had taken over its management, closed the Pittsburgh plant, reduced the organization to a handful of the ablest men, and moved the shop into a corner of Pratt and Whitney's ample building in East Hartford. Later, when success acclaimed the genius of Frank Caldwell, Ray began expanding his organization to meet new demands and finally built an additional wing on the Pratt and Whitney building to house his new shop. Still later, we moved Chance Vought Aircraft down to Stratford to bunk in with a much deflated Sikorsky, and turned the whole Vought shop over to Hamilton.

Meanwhile, when Ray undertook to sell the rights to manufacture the new propellers in England, he encountered problems both at home and abroad. The British Air Ministry, like our own services, discounted the propeller— this was a time when most Britishers discounted everything American— and our own armed forces threatened to refuse us the right to license them under our patents. Since our government had contributed precisely nothing to the development, and especially since my classmate, Kelly Turner, had broadcast his decision to the whole aeronautic establishment, they were hardly in position to claim much equity or any right to control a device of such obvious interest to commercial air transport.

However, it was in a totally different role that the Hamilton-Standard controllable-pitch propeller attained immortality. The manager of the propeller branch of the de Havilland Aircraft Company, Ltd., our English licensees, was John Parkes, himself a fighter pilot, an Englishmen who retained some of the ancient enterprise and love of innovation. Today he is managing director of Alvis Limited, Coventry, but then he was the moving spirit in the adaptation of the Hamilton-Standard propeller to the British Spitfire fighters, the planes that helped win the Battle of Britain. The Germans had developed their own controllable-pitch propellers and, save for the curious chain of circumstances outlined here, would have hopelessly outclassed the British. When Mr. Churchill paid tribute to the "so few" to whom Britain owed so much, he probably had in mind the courageous fighter pilots but behind them stood, among others, Ray Walsh, Frank Caldwell, and John Parkes.

And so we trace the living process through which our struggle to survive created new devices and exercised profound influences that no human mind could have imagined. The miscalculation of one engineer saved the creation of another engineer just in time to give air transport the necessary fillip, and to provide British fighters with the winning punch. And there is a final point to keep in mind: it was the performance of Hamilton-Standard's controllable-pitch propellers in Boeing transports copied by the Germans that impelled them to develop their own propellers. The moral seems to be that leadership in scientific research and technological development is the key to military security. A laggard faces extinction.

CHAPTER TWENTY
IGOR SIKORSKY SPANS TWO GAPS

On the ninth floor of the New York Central Building, at 230 Park Avenue in the city of New York, Frederick B. Rentschler, president of the United Aircraft and Transport Corporation, sat behind his desk in a corner office that looked out on the Biltmore Hotel, and welcomed me with a grin. It was a May day in 1930.

"We've got a problem in Bridgeport," he began. "It's Sikorsky Aviation Corporation. They need management, and I thought you might like to take it on in addition to Hamilton-Standard."

United Aircraft and Transport, it seemed, had been originally conceived as a consolidation of outstanding manufacturers for military and air transport. However, back in 1928 when it was being set up, Fred had encountered considerable pressure from certain ones "downtown" to include some outstanding private commercial manufacturers as well. Some in Wall Street had become convinced that the day of private flying had already dawned, and they had drawn the analogy with the automobile somewhat closer, it had seemed to Fred, than was warranted by the facts. While he resisted their pressure, he did agree to take over a few outstanding commercial manufacturers like Stearman in Wichita and Sikorsky in Bridgeport.

And when the bottom had dropped out of the stock market, and the fool's paradise that characterized the late 'twenties had faded into the deep depression now steeping the country in gloom and fear, Fred's judgment had been vindicated. At Sikorsky, a flock of "firm orders," with down payments from Curtiss-Wright Flying Service, had been transformed into a big inventory surplus. Somebody must now liquidate that to get enough cash to continue, and somebody must create something to sell to the Army and Navy, the only remaining users of aircraft. That somebody could be me.

"When you get up to Stratford," Fred told me, "you'll find an organization that is unique to say the least."

Practically every one in the company was a Russian—a White Russian refugee who, "come the revolution," had made his precarious way to the

United States. They were all talented, artistic, intellectual, and by our standards at least, wholly impractical.

Igor Sikorsky was their guiding genius, a man around whom all had rallied when the going was tough. Over on College Point, Long Island, at an abandoned chicken farm, they had pooled their resources for the common good and built their first twin-engined bomber. And so successful had this ship been that Arnold Dickinson, an enterprising fellow from Fitchburg, Massachusetts, who had been greatly attracted to the fascinating Russians and much impressed by their cleverness, had advanced them large sums of money. Then came the Sikorsky twin-engined amphibian, one of the first American aircraft to control and maneuver well on either of its two engines, and with its success, United Aircraft became interested in taking the company into the fold. By that time, Sikorsky's backers had built a modern plant for him at Stratford on the Housatonic River, and things had looked promising indeed up until that Black Friday of October, 1929, when the bottom dropped out of the stock market.

It happened that I had flown the Sikorsky amphibian and had met Mr. Sikorsky. He had called on me in BUAERO and left with us a vivid impression of his charm of manner, his intellectual honesty, his resourceful mind, and—unique in our experience—a most becoming modesty. For at a time when fast-talking promoters had beaten paths to our doorway, in the hope of high pressuring us into buying their mousetraps, the Russian designer alone had shown humility with respect to his art and respect for the judgment of others. And with it all, being himself without guile, Mr. Igor Sikorsky had proved himself the most convincing salesman in our rather wide experience. For sitting as we had at the crossroads, we had had the advantage of a good view along all highways.

Now I learned from Fred Rentschler that there was another complication of the kind Mr. Sikorsky later sometimes referred to, in his delightful accent and his literal-English translation of an old American saying—"Somewhere there is a Negro sawing wood." Pan American Airways, during the boom, had advertised a competition calling for large flying boats or amphibians, to be flown on its Caribbean and South American air routes, where practically no airports were available. Sikorsky Aviation, it appeared, had won the award and had agreed to build three of the giant craft at an average price of $125,000 each. After having spent at least that much on engineering alone, they had decided to throw the drawings away and start anew with a clean sheet of paper. Fred Rentschler had been a member of the Pan American Airways board of directors during the competition, and now felt that United was committed to go on with the project. He had reconciled himself to the fact that it would cost United upwards of a million dollars, and had even concluded that the money could be looked upon as an investment. If the planes proved successful, we might get back our money and more too, by selling airplanes, propellers, and engines to the new commercial airline. In a way, one might persuade himself that it was United's duty to make such a contribution to the art.

This idea, while commendable in spirit, seemed to me somewhat fantastic in practice. Some years earlier, "Captain Dick" Richardson, a naval constructor, designer and pilot for the giant NC boats that had crossed the Atlantic, and himself a pioneer pilot, had carefully analyzed the economics of commercial operations and solemnly concluded that airplanes in excess of thirty thousand pounds gross weight could not possibly pay their freight, let alone produce revenue. At that time there had been no controllable-pitch propellers in sight, nor had wing flaps appeared on the horizon; Captain Dick's dictum had become an axiom. In view of this, it seemed to me wise for us to attempt to dissuade Juan Trippe, President of Pan American, from his foolhardy undertaking. When, later on, we tried to do so, Juan could not be sold. He, like Igor Sikorsky, had that intuitive something that motivates the pioneer.

Meanwhile, back there in the New York office, Fred Rentschler continued to explain the complexities of the Sikorsky problem. At this point, J. F. McCarthy, United's controller, who had sat through the whole discussion, began unrolling several of those long yellow ruled sheets of paper on which accountants were accustomed to line up their figures.

Mac had broken the Sikorsky expenses down into the usual three categories, general and sales expense, engineering expense, and manufacturing expense. Now it appeared, the ratios of these expenses to one another and to shipments, sales, and so on, were far out of line with good practice. There were certain items in each that were more or less fixed, but manufacturing expense now looked like the best point of attack; it was a large part of the whole; it had large reducible items and it could be cut without serious harm. In other words my job was to go down to Stratford and fire enough of these attractive Russians to bring the expense into line. Fred summed it up this way:

"There is a limit to the contribution United Aircraft can make to Russian relief."

And so, next day I took a morning train from Grand Central. The new Sikorsky factory lay just below the town of Stratford and just above the point where the Housatonic River empties into Long Island Sound. It was a sheltered spot and had been selected as possessing good seaplane facilities with space for a landing field nearby. From the outside, the high factory buildings looked new and shiny, but as I entered the door I thought that someone had cut corners on the details of construction.

After Arnold Dickinson had arrived, we went to work. Arnold appreciated the problems, but hesitated to move in on them. That remained for me, and now I began the unpleasant task that would burden me for many years. For the good of the organization and the salvation of jobs for the many, I must separate from our companies many delightful people, men who, though warm personal friends, just did not seem to have what it took to keep the wheels turning. The task was heartbreaking but the penalties for shirking it were inexorable. All one could do was try to perform his duty to the company with utmost fairness and kindness, and without impairing the morale of the individual or organization beyond the absolute minimum. This was a job that needed doing all at once; it must not be dragged. And so my first act at Sikorsky was to issue orders that the manufacturing expense be reduced by 20 per cent, and forthwith. The method of accomplishing this would be left to the local management.

That, however, did not work too well at Stratford. The cut in manufacturing expense seemed to create not a single ripple; I soon discovered why: engineering expense had suddenly skyrocketed. And when I ordered it restored to its original level—I did not deem it wise to cut back further for fear it might impair the engineering on the Pan American project—the Sikorsky management "agreed with me 100 per cent" as they were wont to express it in their Russian slang. But I soon found out why; the direct labor skyrocketed. Evidently these Russian intellectuals, refugees from their own land, were so versatile that they could play any position on the team—infield, outfield, or umpire. The organization was like a balloon; you could press your finger on one side and make a dent, but the other side bulged out—and less obviously. And when I took my new organization to task, they always "agreed with me 100 per cent," and then proceeded to do precisely as they jolly well pleased.

Meanwhile, we got on with the Pan American S-40's, as they came to be called, though this project proved to have more angles than the Kohinoor diamond, and threatened to cost about as much. While the specifications for the first Pan American Clippers had been reviewed by Col. Charles A. Lindbergh, Pan American advisor, and incorporated into the contract, they didn't mean a thing. Before Pan American would take delivery on the plane it must be passed by the Department of Commerce and given an Approved Type Certificate as to its airworthiness. Without this ATC, Sikorsky might be left with a million dollars' worth of airplanes and no market. Now Pan American, our sole customer, used this advantage to insist on our incorporating in the ships everything its own engineers or our prolific innovators could dream up, from swivel-handled toilets to back-lighted card tables. Thus our designs were kept in a state of continuous flux—at company expense. Save for the redeeming qualities of Igor Ivanovich Sikorsky himself, it is hard to imagine what might have become of us.

A man of strong convictions, for all his humbleness, he was a brilliant engineer though never a "clever" one. Thoroughly grounded in science and mathematics and accustomed to reason from fundamental principles to valid conclusions, he possessed to an astonishing degree those powers with which to divine a true course even when the signposts were not clearly marked. This capacity he once called "intuitive engineering" without for the moment ascribing that quality of genius to himself.

Thanks to Igor Sikorsky's personal leadership, we finally completed delivery of the first three Pan American Clippers. While United absorbed a heavy loss on them, none of this resulted from changes made necessary by official ATC tests. Unlike other companies that later suffered severe losses from this cause, Sikorsky always managed to pass the tests in a remarkably short time, even though radical design features were involved. As for Pan American, that company used the airplanes to lug tons of mail, cargo, and passengers over the high seas for many years. The ships paved the way for a later model that disproved "Dick" Richardson's formula, hurdled the last long barrier, San Francisco to Hawaii, and pointed the way to overseas air transport by land planes. It is not unlikely that Fred Rentschler's investment paid off in the long run, if not on the books of Sikorsky, on those of Pratt and Whitney and Hamilton-Standard.

With the Clippers behind us, we now had the choice of two courses: first, we could shut down Sikorsky and save further losses; or second, we could reorganize it and try to exploit the genius of Igor Sikorsky without prohibitive losses. There seemed no way to anticipate earning a profit in the near future; whatever we tried must be for the long pull. But one thing we had definitely determined: it was too much to expect our friends, the Russian refugees, to implement the American techniques of production. Not that they could not understand them, for they did understand and admire the extraordinary manifestation of applied science that went under that banner. The problem was rather one of temperament or national character.

It was not until the middle of World War II that I heard this thought advanced by Charles A. Lindbergh, one of Mr. Sikorsky's most devoted friends and an ardent admirer. The conversation took place much later, but before the war had involved this country. By that time I had become president of United Aircraft, and had persuaded Lindbergh to join our organization in the capacity of a personal advisor to me. The conversation took place in our home in Hartford, on one of the many stimulating evenings my wife and I were to enjoy with Lindbergh. He had been outlining those views on the European situation which had involved him in so much misunderstanding. Having been in Russia and Germany and, like his father before him, having ardently hoped for peace for his own country, he had feared that, in joining with Russia to defeat Hitler, we would bring about those very things which have since justified his concern.

He thought that nations, like people, displayed traits of fundamental character that were distinct and unchanging. These had had hereditary origins and had been influenced by environment. They influenced the attitudes of nations toward specific circumstances and conditions and especially tended to determine the attitude of a nation toward war as an instrument of policy and to dictate the methods by which it prosecuted a war. The character of the Russians and that of the American people, he thought, differs as night differs from day. Theirs had been a tradition of compulsion, ours of cooperation. If in competition with them we tried to use their methods, we must prove quite as inept as would they in trying to use ours. But if we had the wit to exploit our own ideology to the limit, we must surely overcome the inferior authoritarian process. He saw the problem in its spiritual rather than material light.

Now if consideration of matters like this appears somewhat academic, the fact remains that they were fundamental to our decision as to what to do with Sikorsky. On the one hand, it was clear that in trying to operate the plant we would assume heavy management burdens with little hope of financial reward; on the other, it was certain that there was a pearl in the Sikorsky oyster which, unless we dived for it, would remain quite undiscovered. Our willingness to accept the risk of further operations there must depend upon our confidence in the collateral benefits. This, in turn, must be based entirely upon the quality of leadership we ourselves could display. And so, after much soul searching, we decided to gamble on our own abilities to direct the genius of Igor Sikorsky so as to benefit the art, if not to swell the treasury.

With this decision taken, we cut the organization back sharply to the double handful of men Mr. Sikorsky himself deemed vital to his success. These included, among others, the brothers Gluhareff, Michael and Serge, Bob Lebensky, of the experimental shop, and Buivid of the laboratory. With the organization set, I stated the problem as that involving the creation of a large flying boat so designed that, when operated on the Pan American system, it could earn its board and keep. In other words, we must move the upper limit of the Richardson formula as high as necessary to gain our objectives. As one contribution to this project, we had the new Hamilton-

Standard controllable-pitch propeller, then under development; as another we had a complementary development of Mr. Sikorsky's, a new wing-flapped airfoil. The propeller could pull more weight into the air and fly it; the flaps could help it into the air and get it back on the water at a reasonable stalling speed. This made the flying-boat hull the controlling factor; its characteristics limited the load we could drag into the air with our new wing and new propellers. To refine the lines of the boat hull, our engineers now devised an inexpensive but effective test rig; they towed a model hull alongside a speed boat and photographed its action in rough or smooth water with slow-motion cameras.

And while we pushed on with our concept of a wholly new design in which we would accept no compromise that impaired the economy of operation, we all sweated out the days and nights of tests and experiments. But there was one critical item on which I did no sweating. Had Mr. Sikorsky revealed to me the fact that the wing loading he had selected would be too high to conform to the current Department of Commerce requirements, and that he would have to sell the Department a new concept of landing in a power stall before he could get his ship accepted, I am sure I should not have had the courage to risk all that money on his persuasive qualities. As it was, he kept me in ignorance of the risk, assumed it wholly to himself, and let me know about it only after he had made his sale. The principle of high wing loadings, involving a new type of approach and landing, is now so thoroughly accepted that few pilots know how it came about. The principle is inherent in current air economics and the limits have gone steadily upward. In 1927 I had solemnly announced for the Design Section of BUAERO that we would not consider wing loadings in excess of 10.5 pounds per square foot. Today, the new Boeing Stratocruiser utilizes loadings eight times that high.

And so Igor Sikorsky built the famous S-42's, forty-passenger flying boats, designed to hop from New York to Bermuda to the Azores and to Portugal on what was called the "stepping-stones" route to Europe. So well did he design the planes that, when the British refused to give Pan American landing rights at Bermuda because they had no similar boat with which to match the service, Pan American turned westward to the Pacific and used the new Clippers to pioneer the run to Australia, the Philippines, and China. On this run the controlling factor was the great distance to Honolulu, 2,400 miles against 1,900 miles from Bermuda to the Azores, but the Sikorsky boat hulls, derived from model-towing tests, could take off nearly 20 per cent more load than that originally contemplated. Thus they removed the last barrier to overseas air commerce.

From the United point of view, while we made no money on the transaction, and, accounting-wise, lost a hundred thousand dollars on the ten ships, cash-wise we bore no out-of-pocket loss. And while the project took a lot of nervous and physical energy out of management, it paid dividends to the aviation art as a whole. Meanwhile we kept our eyes open for a chance to work into some Army or Navy business, though a number of important changes had taken place.

First of all, shortly after President Roosevelt had been inaugurated, Postmaster James Farley had canceled the air-mail contracts and Senators Black and Nye had broken out in a rash of Congressional investigations. These had upset the five-year procurement programs of both Army and Navy and reacted adversely upon many manufacturers. For a while, Admiral Moffett had held the fort, but then a great tragedy had deprived aviation of one of its foremost figures at its time of greatest need.

The admiral, continuing his absorption with the development of lighter-than-air craft, had succeeded in building and operating the *Macon* and the *Akron* and had established a new field near San Jose, California, one that now carries his name. Here the *Macon* carried out operations with the fleet until an unfortunate accident resulted in her complete loss. The Old Man, still faithful to the rigid airship, continued to fly in them himself until the night the *Akron* sailed out over the Atlantic and was destroyed. The admiral was lost at sea along with other gallant airmen, close friends and classmates of mine. The loss was disastrous enough from the personal angle, for Admiral Moffett was loved and admired by all his aeronautic organization to a degree seldom attained by any man. Coming as it did at the time of greatest trial on the political front, it deprived us of the one person who might have guided us through our worst rocks and shoals. The admiral was buried at Arlington along with so many of the young lads he had inspired. With his passing, gloom settled over us all.

When Adm. E. J. King succeeded to command of BUAERO, he brought to it a type of leadership quite different from that which had characterized its thirteen years under Admiral Moffett. Admiral King, who was one day to become Commander in Chief during World War II, was a man of strong convictions who made his own decisions. With his brilliant intellect and decisive manner, he dominated the Bureau completely.

The cancellation of air-mail contracts set off a chain reaction that disrupted the whole United Aircraft and Transport structure. To comply with the law requiring separation of manufacturing companies from transport organizations, United Airlines was split off into a separate company known as United Airlines Transport Corporation. With the transport link between the eastern and western manufacturing groups thus disrupted, we divided them into two separate companies. The four Connecticut companies, Pratt and Whitney, Hamilton-Standard, Chance Vought, and Sikorsky, comprised the new United Aircraft Corporation. The western group took the name of Boeing Airplane Company.

In the reorganization, William E. Boeing severed all his aviation connections. Frederick B. Rentschler resigned the presidency of United. Phillip G. Johnson, deprived by law of his right to manage the airlines, later moved to Canada to create the great Trans-Canada Airlines. Donald L. Brown moved up from Pratt and Whitney to become president of United Aircraft Corporation, and I became its senior vice-president. Thus a Congressional investigation that proved no wrongdoing deprived the country of the services of three outstanding pioneers.

President Roosevelt had, meanwhile, appointed Admiral Reeves Commander in Chief, United States Fleet. Having in mind the progress of events in the Pacific, I had undertaken a study of a big boat designed to scout its vast areas, using available harbors as bases of operations. About the time the job was completed, the admiral invited me to join him on the *California*, at Hampton Roads, to watch the aircraft carriers in operation. Frank Wagner, his Operations officer, met me at Old Point Comfort and the admiral himself greeted me at the gangway. The bulkheads of his cabin had been papered with charts of the Pacific, evidence enough of the Old Man's absorption with that problem. When, after lunch, he developed his estimate of the Pacific situation and asked if I thought it possible to build a flying boat capable of patrolling the area, I was able to produce from my brief case exactly what the doctor had ordered. The hearty laugh with which Bull Reeves greeted this legerdemain brought back memories of the happy days of FLEET AIR.

Under pressure from the fleet, BUAERO, which at this time was absorbed in carrier aircraft and about ready to wash up big boats, invited bids on which Sikorsky won the award. As the designs progressed, BUAERO developed increasing interest in the project and finally authorized a second development by Consolidated Aircraft of San Diego. In the competition for the production order, Sikorsky lost out to Consolidated on price, but the Sikorsky design was selected by the new transoceanic operator, American Export Airlines, for whom we built three passenger ships. The American line, organized and operated under the able leadership of John Slater, provided nonstop flying-boat service from New York to Foynes, Ireland, and during the war provided comfortable berths for many very important people while many others of the same character shivered in bucket seats in hastily improvised land-plane service via Newfoundland, Iceland,

and the Azores. In other words, Sikorsky flying boats showed the way to transoceanic service and, at the moment, actually outperformed the land plane.

However, even under such fair terms as those granted us by American Export Airlines, we did not succeed in avoiding serious losses at Sikorsky. Meanwhile, Pan American had turned to Martin and then Boeing, and each of these able builders had suffered similarly. By that time, too, the aircraft industry had suffered from the political debacle in Washington. We had reached the end of our rope and could no longer afford to contribute either our management or engineering talents, let alone our slender capital, to the subsidization of airline operations. We decided to drop out of the big-boat business.

And when I broke this sad news to Mr. Sikorsky—by then I had become president of United Aircraft—he received it like the great gentleman he is. He understood our problem; he was grateful for all the consideration the company had given him. He wondered if perchance we would grant him one more favor; he would like to go back to his first love—experimenting with helicopters. He thought he might succeed now where he had failed before. A modest sum of money would meet his requirements and he hoped this was not asking too much.

Quite certain that no one could possibly build a successful helicopter but that Mr. Sikorsky at least deserved a try, I magnanimously agreed to back him. Igor Sikorsky did invent the helicopter, just as the Wrights before him had invented the airplane, by diligent study, by painstaking experiment, by teaching himself to fly and then teaching others. In so doing, the man who had given the world the means of vaulting the last barrier to air commerce went to the other extreme to create the only vehicle that can operate in three dimensions without a prepared surface from which to take off or land. Aviation owes much to his creative mind, one that not only finds no difficulty in reconciling science and religious faith, but on the contrary, exercises that intuitive quality that marks real genius.

The moral of this brief review of the history of a representative airplane company is that profit has a counterpart in loss, and both are essential to progress. Again, financial results are not the sole measure of excellence; there is also the intangible factor of stewardship. When the final account is cast up, Igor Ivanovich Sikorsky will rank among the immortals of American aviation.

CHAPTER TWENTY-ONE
THE COURAGE OF CONVICTION

One of the important considerations that had influenced my decision to resign from the Navy had been my desire to work on constructive tasks with men whose competence I had admired. Among these were Fred Rentschler, Bill Boeing, George Mead, Claire Egtvedt, George Wheat, Don Brown, Phil Johnson, and Chance Vought. As fate dealt the cards, however, the decade of 1930 saw the passing of Chance, George, and Don, and of these, Chance was the first. During the summer of 1930, after I had added Sikorsky to my responsibilities, Chance died of septicemia, something which today would respond quickly to the new drugs. With him, much of the sparkle went out of United Aircraft.

By the time I joined United, Chance had already come to realize that his famous Corsair two-seater, which had done so well on battleship catapults and carrier decks, had all but been outmoded by the passage of time alone. And he was at a loss to know what to do about it, and talked far into the night about that problem. His untimely death relieved him of all necessity for further worry, but it also handed the job to me. Worse still, the Vought company, like most other aviation concerns, had always been a one-man show and there were no more Chance Voughts standing around to be hired, even with more jobless men around than the country had ever known. And so we faced the task of creating a new organization—one of a type then new to aviation—of developing some new product and of marketing it in what was becoming a tough market indeed. In this job we pinned our hopes on some of the old-timers in the Vought organization and on a relative newcomer, Charles J. McCarthy.

"C.J.," as we called him, to differentiate the airplane engineer from "J.F.," the financial wizard, had been in BUAERO in charge of the new department called "Stress Analysis" at the time when I had been chief of the Engine Section. It was C.J. who had flown to Norfolk with me the day the Wright T-3 engine jumped out of a torpedo bomber when the wooden propeller flew apart, and it had been out of that experience that we decided to standardize on metal propellers. It was curious how, in the aviation slipstream, we milled around, each trying to add his little push to the effective forward thrust. For Chance had offered C.J. a job in his company, and C.J. had accepted. Now I began to look upon him as my second there, and between us we decided to bring in a new chief engineer.

The newcomer was Rex Beisel, a man who had received good training in the old school of Curtiss Airplane Company but had gone west to create a new private airplane. The stock-market crash had made Rex available and we now promptly scooped him up. We thought Rex a bit opinionated, and expected to have to handle him roughly at times, but we knew there was great capacity there. And in this we were right, for Rex created a strong engineering organization as a substitute for the genius of Chance Vought, and came ultimately to head the Vought Division in his own right. The story of how this was done, like the story of Hamilton-Standard, or Sikorsky, or Pratt and Whitney, or any of the great independent outfits like Grumman, or Martin, or Douglas, or Boeing, is worth a book in itself; but for our purposes here we can sweep in only those high lights that seem to back light the slipstream itself. And though the several stories run concurrently, we are concerned more with events than with precise timing.

There was, however, one vital factor that influenced the performance of every aircraft company, and in the end, imperiled the existence of them all. For while the creative force of the Morrow Board policy carried over beyond the 1929 stock-market crash, it did not survive the ordeal of the New Deal. With the election of President Roosevelt in 1932 and his advent into the White House in 1933, an earthquake hit American aviation. When President Roosevelt ordered the cancellation of the air-mail contracts and directed the Army to take over, the young air-transport business suffered a vital blow. When, after the deaths of several Army pilots who had had no preparation for the complex transport task, the lines were returned to private operations, the blight of Congressional investigation fell upon the whole aircraft industry.

Senator Hugo Black, later a Justice of the Supreme Court of the United States, who had been probing the ocean-mail subsidies, now turned his attention to aviation. The airplane, long a subject of great public interest, crowded the headlines with sensational charges and countercharges, none of which seemed to lead anywhere other than to the glorification of the investigators. Then Senator Gerald P. Nye, not to be outdone in courtesy, dragged out the old myth of the "munitions racketeer" and the "merchants of death" and dusted it off for the more modern treatment of klieg lights and other technological advances in the art of public relations. Whatever else may be said for these hippodromes, they had the effect of knocking down an airplane program just as a killer in the stockyards fells an ox with one neat blow from a maul. Even though the programs remained on the statute books, it would have required a courageous procurement staff, indeed, to make contracts with such apparent renegades as headed the unhappy aircraft companies.

The moment arrived when Chance Vought Aircraft was running out of work. In order to extend the useful life of the old Corsair, we had replaced the Wasp engine with a new Pratt and Whitney Hornet 1690. This gave us a breathing spell while we assembled our engineering team and dreamed up a new model. But BUAERO had now revived the old two-seat fighter project and thrust it on us. Worse still, they had designed the airplane themselves and now looked to us to detail it and build the prototype. Recalling the old fight between FLEET AIR and BUAERO on this subject, back when I had been Admiral Reeves's chief of staff, the whole thing had elements of poetic injustice in it that now aroused me to action. I decided to build their old two-seat fighter, according to all specifications, to exceed their designed performances, and at the same time build the structure strong enough to be used as a dive bomber. This would take a lot of doing, for the performance guarantees were already high, but it would leave us with two strings to our bow, a two-seat fighter that would probably not go into production, and a two-seat dive bomber that probably would. In the latter event, Vought would give the Navy a distinctly new type of airplane, one that could depend upon its guns to penetrate enemy fighter cover and then use its bombs on ground targets.

One of the complications involved was the specification that called for the installation of the new Pratt and Whitney two-row radial, the R-1535. The two-row feature would have introduced excessive drag and cooling difficulties, except that I chanced to read an article by C. G. Grey in *The Airplane*, a British magazine devoted to aviation and to running down everything American. Mr. Grey had recently visited the great Bristol airplane factory and had been impressed with a project for cooling air-cooled engines. Unlike certain foreign engine builders who insisted on blowing large quantities of air in the general direction of their cylinders, Bristol had devised an ingenious contrivance through which they had succeeded in directing a "mere trickle" of air at precisely the required spots, thus saving much drag and improving the cooling no end.

After this tip-off, we set up a joint project using the Sikorsky wind tunnel and staff, under the direction of Chance Vought engineers, to develop a cowl for a Pratt and Whitney engine. Out of this cooperative effort came a new power-plant installation using the "cowl-flaps" which any passenger in any American transport can still see by looking out the window at the engine nacelle and watching the opening and closing of the "gills." This development not only made the two-row radial a success but proved so effective that it has been rated by discerning observers as a development quite as revolutionary in its way as was the controllable-angle propeller.

With the drying up of both military and commercial business in our own country, we must needs look elsewhere or fade out. The export market was the only outlet, and while there were obstacles there, the superiority of our products, built up under the Morrow policy, had put us in a strong competitive position. Even from the point of view of costs and in the face of a preference on the part of some countries for aircraft of their own production, we could still make headway. American automobiles had won leadership in foreign markets because of superior quality and lower price. The idea that we could not compete with "slave labor" had been disproved; the technology of production could support higher wages and still produce low-cost goods of high quality. That was our heritage which we would now exploit.

However, there were other considerations. The control of export permits had been lodged in the State Department, which would not grant such permit without the approval of the military department concerned. In the case of the SBU-1 two-seat dive bomber we had first to obtain permission from BUAERO and then run the gantlet of the State Department and the office of a Mr. Joseph Green. This problem came to the fore when the Argentine Navy sought to acquire some of our planes. Admiral King ruled that since the airplane had the characteristics of a dive bomber it was too secret to permit foreign sale. Of course the only secret about it was that the wings had been made strong enough to take the pull-out loads—something any designer could build in—but that proved enough.

Chance Vought Aircraft now found itself in a tight spot. I camped on the doorstep of the State Department, of BUAERO, and even went to see Adm. William H. Standley, then Chief of Naval Operations, to urge that the matter be viewed from the point of view of the long-term public interest, keeping a vital industry alive and 800 men and women employed. We already had millions on relief without swelling the throng on a technicality, but I was too poor a salesman to make the idea stick. In desperation, I tried another approach.

With my wife as company, I caught a Pan American Airways flight for Buenos Aires, determined to close the contract and then see what Uncle Sam had to say. If he wanted to accept the responsibility for an overt act that would take the food from the mouths of our men, he could do so, but I refused to hold the bag while they gave me the run-around.

We were fortunate in our representation in Argentina. The firm of Jorge Luro y Cia. brought us the experience of Jorge Luro, a distinguished pioneer aviator, and the mature wisdom of Señor Guillermo Leloir, member of an aristocratic Argentine family.

"We Latins," Guillermo counseled me, in anticipation of direct negotiations with Capt. Marco Zar, the director of Argentine naval aviation, "admire your North American enterprise but resent your high-pressure salesmanship."

Marco Zar, a graduate of the Pensacola Naval Air Station, had come to me one day in BUAERO, asking for advice on his procurement problems. His current interest in Vought airplanes was due to his knowledge that I managed the company. An earnest, conscientious officer, he believed that a good deal for his service must needs be a fair deal all around. My tactics during the negotiations were predicated on this fact plus the advice from Guillermo.

Details of our contract were argued out before a large conference of Captain Zar's subordinate officers. The captain won every skirmish pertaining to prices or specification, yet the final conclusions were satisfactory to all concerned. When I returned to Hartford, I passed the word around the shop that the kids could eat for another year, provided Uncle Sam did not refuse us an export permit.

With work for the shop we could direct our attention to a new development. It was already clear that biplanes were being outclassed by monoplanes, but they had persisted longer on carriers because of the space limitations imposed there. As a replacement for our two-seat dive bomber, which could carry a 500-pound bomb, we drew up a proposal to construct a folding-wing 500-pound monoplane dive bomber so designed that a carrier could manage its full complement of the new, faster type. The Bureau considered the proposal for a while, and then, instead of giving us the advantage we deserved for having conceived the idea, got out its own specification and published it to the trade. Then they further complicated the problem by advertising for two types, a 500- and a 1,000-pounder. We submitted proposals for both, and were awarded the 500-pound model. Now in order not to get left at the post in case BUAERO finally decided to buy only 1,000-pounders, we decided to build our ship to meet all the tight specifications for the smaller size but still capable of carrying a 1,000-pound bomb.

The competition from other manufacturers was tough. Every airplane was stressed to the ultimate and no margins were left for error. After winning a design competition, a manufacturer had to submit an article for test by the trial board at Anacostia. If he beat out his competitors there and won a production award, then followed the trials and tribulations of trying to build his brain child without losing his shirt. Then, after the airplane got into service and developed the unforeseen bugs that always show up regardless of previous care, he had the added responsibility for correcting faults on aircraft he might have donated to the government at a substantial loss to himself. After that, all that remained was to dream up a new model to replace the old, and in the meantime, keep service men in the field to show untrained mechanics how to operate a complicated contraption that was fully as high strung as the president of the company that had built it.

After our new SB2U went into service, we shifted our attention back to building a monoplane observation replacement for the battleship and carrier-catapult planes, represented by our original Corsairs. For so well had Chance Vought wrought that his little two-seaters, conceived back there in 1926, remained in service until after Pearl Harbor, some fifteen years later. Our replacement was called the "Kingfisher" and it saw service in World War II. One of them saved Eddy Rickenbacker from a watery grave on the vast Pacific, something that alone compensated us for the painstaking design efforts we had put into a complicated project.

Meanwhile, in the effort to find a product for export sale and, possibly, break into an Army competition, we built a fighter under circumstances so fantastic as almost to belie the telling. Jack Northrup, who had built a sweet little single-seater for the Army, using the Wright 1510 two-row engine, had won high praise from the Army Engineering Division at Wright Field, Dayton, Ohio, in competition with fighters by Curtiss and Seversky. But during an interlude in the contest, after the plane had gone back to California, it had sailed out over the broad Pacific and not returned. There had been gossip at the time that the Japs might have had something to do with it. At any rate, Jack Northrup had decided not to reenter the Army competition, but Jack Horner, sales manager of Pratt and Whitney, suggested that Vought take over the design from Northrup, reconstruct the model around the Pratt and Whitney 1535 engine, and create an export fighter model for United Aircraft.

I conducted the negotiations with Jack Northrup over the telephone and sent our men west by air. Starting with few drawings and no materials, we rushed the airplane to completion in something like forty-five days. During the work at East Hartford, the Connecticut River overflowed its banks and cut off the electric power, but our crews, working night and day, finished the little ship in the light of their automobile headlights.

In the competition at Wright Field, which was based not on the actual performance of the prototype but on what the contractor was willing to guarantee in production, we lost out to Alex Seversky. When we offered the airplane to the Navy, with arresting gear, we were unable to arouse interest. While this put us in the clear for an export permit, we failed to sell any of the craft, at least to countries with cash to buy them. One day our European export representative, Tom Hamilton, brought some Japanese officers to Hartford.

When the Jap pilot put the little fighter through its paces, we looked at one another in wonderment. We had long understood that these boys couldn't learn to fly—they had myopic eyes. But whatever else the Japs had, this pilot had everything; he didn't put on any dive-and-zoom noise show, but checked out the little airplane especially as to its maneuverability at altitude, the characteristic at which it excelled. And so with the full approval of Washington, the plane, which had been rejected by both Army and Navy, was sold to the Japanese.

Later on in the Pacific war, their fighter pilots proved quite proficient in the air. Furthermore, their fleet fighters, the Zeros, could give even our Grumman Wildcats plenty of trouble. Finally one of their Zeros was captured and brought to San Diego where, after passing severe tests by the guards, I was permitted to see it. It was bigger than our Northrup-Vought and powered with a Japanese two-row radial of about the size of our 1830. The engine was of Japanese design but incorporated what the Japs considered to be the best features of the French Gnome-Rhone radials, the British Bristol Jupiter, the Wright Cyclone, and the Pratt and Whitney Wasp. And it displayed beautiful workmanship throughout.

As for the airplane, it looked a good deal like the Northrup-Vought, though it was larger and incorporated some of the best features of other aircraft bought by the Japanese, as well as some neat wrinkles of their own. The power-plant installation was distinctly Chance Vought Aircraft, and the wheel stowage into the wing roots was definitely Northrup. The wing-tip folding was Japanese, and it looked like an idea we should have used. All in all, it was a masterful example of good imitation—they even copied the Navy inspection stamp from the Pratt and Whitney type parts—plus some good Jap innovation which combined to make the product of an "inferior race" all too devastating. As Admiral Reeves had been wont to remark, "One should never discount an enemy."

But while the Japs had been busy with their Zeros, we had not been idle at Vought. I, for one, had not forgotten the lesson of Panama, even though our Navy now seemed to have turned its back on the fighter-bomber idea. Fighter pilots are inherently resentful of any suggestion that they should know how to dive bomb as well as dogfight. But the fact remains that, once they have driven an enemy from the skies, neither they nor their ships are useful unless they can turn a hand at attacking objectives on the ground. With this idea in mind, we set out at Vought to build a new Corsair. She must be able to out-perform enemy fighters and still be readily convertible to a dive bomber; she must have the structural ruggedness and strength to withstand the high stresses of this work. This meant, in turn, that she must be larger than the pure fighter and to this end she must have a more powerful engine. That is just another way of expressing Bruce Leighton's ancient adage about the power plant being the heart of the airplane.

We had such an engine in the new Pratt and Whitney 2800. Originally intended to develop from 1,800 to 2,000 horsepower, this engine was later actually used at from 2,500 to 3,000 in World War II. Around the new power plant we designed a new fighter bomber, and offered it to BUAERO in anticipation of the war that seemed inevitable. But BUAERO was cool to our proposal. Large airplanes could not be carried on the flattops in the same numbers as could the smaller, more compact fighters; number was an important factor in the complement of a carrier. They were willing to let us go ahead on the project, but they could not hold out much hope for ultimate production.

Now I took a long breath and embarked on the gamble of a lifetime. We would commit Chance Vought to a new single-seat fighter, one with such blazing speed and such fire power and such maneuverability that it could blast any enemy from the skies, even though handicapped with all the rigging that goes on a carrier fighter. We would build into it such rugged strength that it could carry heavy bombs in a dive, and still withstand the clumsiness of any horny-handed pilot who might try to pull its tail off.

But in taking this kind of decision we were not alone. Out in Seattle, Boeing had staked its future on the conviction of the Young Turks of the Army that a long-range heavy bomber would one day become the backbone of air power, no matter who said it would not. Farther down the West Coast, Don Douglas risked everything on the future of a new four-engined transport to be called the "DC-4" at a time when the Army remained cold to all transport and the airlines were doing very well, thank you, with the DC-3. Across the city, Bob Gross, at Lockheed, took his chances with a new twin-engined liquid-cooled fighter to be called the "Lightning," at a time when the predominance of opinion was against such craft. Nearby, Dutch Kindleberger of North American, always crazy like a fox, dreamed up a single-seat liquid-cooled fighter around the Rolls Royce Merlin engine, a fighter which was to be called the "Mustang," that would one day become a long-range escort for bombers over Europe. Down at San Diego, Reuben Fleet plugged along with flying boats and amphibians, long after the smart money was all on carrier planes. His Consolidated's Catalinas would one day fight the world over for all our allies. And down Baltimore way the Old Master, Glenn Martin, rode his own hobby of light, fast bombers for ground attack at the very moment when the "Young Turks" seemed about to prevail in their battle for heavy bombardment. Out at Farmingdale, Long Island, the brilliant engineer Kartveli was forging his Thunderbolts, intended as fighters but destined for use in the invasion of Europe as the long-range fighter bombers that broke Hermann Goering's heart because he was sure we couldn't build such planes.

These are but a few of many that come readily to mind. The fact was, no one could guess whom we would fight, to say nothing of how or when. Without a foreign policy, we could shape no military policy, and without a military policy who could guess what airplanes might be called upon to do? But our saving grace lay in the fact that this was a free country where any man might risk his money, or even his neck, in backing his pet idea. When the chips were finally down, Uncle Sam, who hadn't killed his air craftsmen with kindness, found they had supplied him with a wide variety of combat types from which to choose, a variety that made it possible for him to go out and win. In a postwar interview, Hermann Goering was reported to have said that the one thing the Germans had envied us was our flexible system of individual initiative and enterprise.

CHAPTER TWENTY-TWO
REVIEW OF SOME FUNDAMENTALS

During the protracted period when Hamilton-Standard, Sikorsky, and Chance Vought found the going rough as they endeavored to create new products that could be sold to a reluctant government, Pratt and Whitney for a while made much smoother weather of it. The Wasp engine had proved so outstanding that no other power plant had challenged it, and in a field that offered the greatest volume. Subsequent engines, while not outclassing all competition, as had the Wasp, won a fair share of the market. As a matter of fact, it was Pratt and Whitney that had provided most of the resources out of which the other divisions had prosecuted their new developments. But now as the year 1937 arrived, even the bellwether of our flock began to find the pickings scarce.

For certain ones in the Army Air Corps still persisted in advocating liquid cooling, and now, as they began occupying positions of power, they pressed harder than ever, this despite the fact that the brilliant performance of the air-cooled radials had all but driven liquid-cooled in-line engines out of the country. In England, however, where the Bristol air-cooled engines had not attained to the same leadership as had the Pratt and Whitney and Wright radials in America, Rolls Royce had done an outstanding job with a racing-plane engine which they had later developed into a fine pursuit engine. In Germany, where tremendous effort was being made to rehabilitate aviation after the terms of the Treaty of Versailles had been modified, Junkers had taken a license to build Pratt and Whitney engines but, as usual, had not built power plants wholly comparable with the original. Simultaneously B.M.W. had prosecuted the development of their own liquid-cooled engines, a type in which they had background and experience. These facts, plus some new liquid-cooling developments, had encouraged certain men in the Army to promote an American liquid-cooled program.

By using Ethylene Glycol, or Prestone as we know it in our automobile antifreeze mixtures, many of the difficulties inherent in liquid-cooling were ameliorated. The new "pressure-cooling" systems became competitive with the "baffles" of the radials in so far as weight and performance were concerned; they still retained the old handicaps of leaky plumbing. In order to exploit this progress, the Army Engineering Division at Wright Field had designed a liquid-cooled, in-line engine of its own, and turned over the job of building and testing it to the Allison Engineering Company, of Indianapolis, Indiana.

Allison, skilled in automotive experimental work, especially that associated with racing in the speedway, had built up a fine reputation by undertaking highly experimental projects that, for one reason or another, failed to appeal to companies interested in production. Allison's president, "Pop" Gilman, had done a lot of Diesel development, and other clever experimental work for BUAERO when I was chief of the Engine Section, and he had built up a highly competent outfit. After completely redesigning the Wright Field effort, Pop had gone ahead to make a fair engine out of the "Allison."

In addition to their convictions that the United States should develop a good liquid-cooled engine, some men in the Air Forces had always believed that General Motors should become a factor in engine production. Out of this conviction, the time came when General Motors absorbed Allison and put its back into power-plant development. This meant tough competition for the aircraft industry and while we might, by dint of great effort, keep ourselves in the forefront of technological progress, we could not, of course, match the limitless financial resources of "the corporation." With the head start we already held in current engine types, we should more than hold our own, but now with the cold hand of the long depression pressing down on us, we found the new Army-G.M. alliance cold comfort indeed.

Meanwhile, the Army continued its pressure on Pratt and Whitney and Wright Aeronautical, to force both companies to undertake liquid-cooled engines of their own design. The fact that the two types would not mix any better than oil and water, and that for us to divert a portion of our limited energies to something we did not believe in would impair the development of air cooling, seemed to have no weight with a few liquid-cooled fanatics.

And now they dug up a new angle. It seemed that out in Santa Monica, Don Douglas and his engineers were studying a new twin-engined bomber and were leaning toward the idea that, in order to reduce the drag and improve the air flow over the wings, the engines, instead of being mounted outside in the cowls, should be completely housed in the wings. To meet this requirement, the engine must be flat, in the form of a pancake. Our own studies contemplated a twenty-four-cylinder job, and such an arrangement demanded liquid cooling. Under tremendous pressure from Wright Field, where, of course, the purse strings were held, Pratt and Whitney reluctantly agreed to go ahead. Similarly, Wright Aero accepted the inevitable.

This was the situation in the summer of 1937, when, with Chance Vought Aircraft just beginning to round out into an effective team, I was put out of commission by an automobile crack-up that took me out of active service for several months. Coming home after dark in a driving rain from a day of trout fishing at the East Haddam Fish and Game Club, some thirty miles from Hartford, I was smacked so hard by a speeding motorist that my new convertible was reduced to a heap of junk. Only through kind providence was I spared the same fate.

Out of the hospital, I moved from Chance Vought over to the head office at Pratt and Whitney, to undertake a new program. Here I set up a small research department and, with a tight little organization, began collecting all the facts and many fancies, with a view to shaping a new course.

As the brains of this organization I selected John Lee of Vought. The designer of the radical SB2U monoplane dive bomber, John had employed his scientific mind to the company's great practical advantage. He would require at least a year to assemble a body of information that might prove of value in approaching our problem. The time had come for someone, free from administrative responsibilities, to make a considered estimate of the new situation out of which policy decisions might be reached. Of one thing we were sure: there is a definite limit to the number of design projects any one engineering department can handle. The sure way in which to break down even the best organization is to overload it.

In order to get John Lee and his crew started on their study, I set for them the task of making a coldblooded analysis of the liquid-cooled air-cooled controversy. To this end they were to design, from the ground up, a series of single-seat fighters, each of which was to utilize each engine to best advantage. We were not interested in proving a case for either engine, but in ascertaining for ourselves, without prejudice, which engine was best suited to the job. We chose the single-seat fighter because this was the type in which the liquid-cooled appeared to best advantage. John Lee's job was to design a whole family of fighters, orthodox or unconventional, and from this collection make a factual analysis that would resolve our problem for us.

Meanwhile I would make the grand tour of the industry, calling on everyone who might have an idea or an opinion to contribute to our study. Out of such a tour we might gather a few valuable ideas, and hopefully indicate to our customers our own deep interest in their problems. I would approach the matter with an open mind, collect detailed notes of my interviews, and assemble them in such form as would best indicate the thinking of the whole industry on our problem.

And so, while John Lee assembled a handful of selected assistants, I set out on my tour. At Bethpage, Long Island, I interviewed Roy Grumman and Jake Schwoble and visited their shops. Roy, the president of the company, was also its leading engineer—then a rather common situation in aviation—while Jake, a hard-hitting shopman, was more or less the business manager. Here was a competent pair surrounded by an able team, doing a smart job, as we in Vought so well knew through competing with them.

At Seversky's (now Republic's) plant at Farmingdale, Long Island, I was impressed by the sharp contrast between the two Russians, Seversky and Sikorsky. Both were White Russian refugees, both had left their native land, where they were no longer welcome even to live, much less create airplanes, and both had found in free America a climate under which they could employ their talents. Alex P. de Seversky, ably supported by clever engineers led by Kartveli, was a power in the fighter field and, as an ardent advocate of air-cooled engines, had backed Pratt and Whitney exclusively.

On arrival at the Naval Aircraft Factory, Philadelphia, I found many old friends and associates of my days in BUAERO. The factory, in compliance with some legislation that required them to produce a certain percentage of all production, as a so-called "yardstick to private industry," had undertaken to manufacture Wright Whirlwind engines under license. The management had little sympathy with the idea—any such yardstick must be a rubber one—and what with interferences by local politicos and the usual complications inherent in government manufacture, the project had bogged down.

At Glenn L. Martin's plant down near Baltimore, I had a good visit with the old-timer sometimes described as "the dean of the airplane industry." A conservative when it came to design, Glenn had pioneered in volume production processes, and on the financial side had taken numerous risks that proved intelligent. And for all his ups and downs, he had lost none of his zeal for commercial aviation, even though he had lost his shirt as had Sikorsky and Boeing, building Clippers for Pan American Airways.

A visit to BUAERO brought recollections of exciting days under Admiral Moffett and emphasized his inimitable qualities. By now the Engine Section, having lost its sense of direction, had begun to waver in the air-cooled versus liquid-cooled conflict, and no longer wielded its old influence.

From Washington's hazy atmosphere I moved out to the clearer skies of the Pacific Northwest. At Boeing, Claire Egtvedt, though reduced by indifferent health to acting in an advisory capacity, still kept his unimpaired view of the fundamentals of aviation. His orderly, considered estimate of the engine problem was more than worth the trip west; besides, it was stimulating to yarn about the good old days.

Phil Johnson's departure from Boeing had left a big vacuum. Having been banished from the American transport scene, he had undertaken to create his newest masterpiece, Trans-Canada Airlines. Phil had once told me a story about how he had got his first job with Boeing. While still a student in aeronautics at the University of Washington, he had chanced to be alone in the office of the head of the department at the moment when Bill Boeing had called on the telephone to inquire the name of a likely student to fill a job in his new factory. Phil, answering the ring, had promptly replied, "P. G. Johnson!"

Proud of his Scandinavian origin, he delighted in springing a pet question, "What is dumber than a dumb Swede?" His answer, "A smart Irishman."

Down in Los Angeles, where a big segment of the airplane business, attracted by the physical and economic climate, had set up shop, I found Don Douglas at his old stand in Santa Monica, Dutch Kindleberger in a new shop at Inglewood, Jack Northrup in a new establishment at Hawthorne, and Bob Gross at our old flying field at Burbank. These men, though competitive and individualistic, and as different one from the other as night from day, were all animated by the same enthusiasm for aviation and zeal for its advancement.

Don Douglas, conservative as to design, skillful in production, long on timing, and alert as to customer service, had done one of aviation's outstanding jobs. His company, like the others, remained pretty much a one-man show, managed by engineers with good judgment and a limitless capacity for work. Don's was a well-balanced show, founded on sound character, far-sighted vision, and Scotch thrift.

"Dutch" Kindleberger, of North American, a journeyman engineer specializing in military aircraft, delighted in personally contriving ingenious labor-saving devices. A salty citizen, he once summed up the case for the airplane, "There never has been an airplane designed and built that wasn't full of bugs. And you can't delouse an airplane with insecticide. Instead you pick them out the hard way, like hunting fleas on a woolly dog, and when you finally get the one that is making his nose twitch, it is probably biting him under the tail!"

"Dutch," to my shocked surprise, had shifted his allegiance to liquid-cooled engines and was even then mocking up a new power plant installation that threatened serious competition for Pratt and Whitney. However, I remembered that Dutch knew how to give a customer what he wanted, and the Army was his principal customer.

Bob Gross, who had bought Lockheed for a song, had succeeded in giving Don Douglas real competition in air transports. While tending to depreciate his own efforts, he managed an aggressive outfit that placed a high premium on speed. Jack Northrup, having launched a new company, was bubbling with enthusiasm for his newest project, a big bomber designed along the lines of his earlier flying-wing. Always unorthodox, yet extremely practical, he was most helpful to me with my problem.

Following my Los Angeles visit, I flew down to San Diego to look up Reuben Fleet of Consolidated Aircraft, an enterpriser who had lost none of his enthusiasm for, and skill at, making an honest dollar. By this time the Navy had become San Diego's major industry and FLEET AIR filled the skies with formations of carrier aircraft.

Out of this tour around the country, I not only collected every man's point of view as to power plants, but got an interesting cross-section of the industry as a whole. One-man shows for the most part, they were managed by engineer executives, a combination hard to beat when manufacturing was involved. In contrast with the rather studied approach we had in United, they were bold and forthright. Averaging then somewhat under forty-five years of age, they compressed into brief business careers the whole history of aviation.

In a brief span of two decades, they had created a whole new technology, and this had been accomplished in the face of many vicissitudes. Through doing business largely with a few customers like the government or the airlines, they had developed an outlook quite at variance with that of industries dealing with large numbers of individual customers. As an important segment of the national security, it was natural that they should look upon their profession more as a public service, and thus develop an appreciation of public relations. At a time when new enterprises had been almost interdicted by the unfavorable economic climate and they had been singled out for attack, they had still gone on, with youthful self-reliance, with rugged independence, and a competitive spirit, to exploit the freedom of their homeland and create a new art.

And out of my swing around the circuit, I reached clear conclusions with respect to my own problem, aircraft power plants. I had heard nothing to shake my convictions as to the superiority of air-cooled radials. On the contrary, I had heard much to confirm them. If the Air Corps still wanted a source of supply for liquid-cooled engines, they should look elsewhere than Hartford. Furthermore, even if Pratt and Whitney could create the world's best liquid-cooled engine as well as the best air-cooled, it would do little good. The two required different tools, different production processes, in fact separate factories, and we already had our hands full with our own job.

This added up to the fact that in trying to do both jobs we were compromising our ability to discharge our responsibility with respect to air-cooling. We must get back on the beam at the first favorable opportunity and devote our resources to continuing to build the best air-cooled engines in the world.

CHAPTER TWENTY-THREE
A YANKEE PEDDLER

In the spring of 1938, Tom Hamilton, our United Aircraft representative in Europe, came home on one of his periodic visits, to bring himself up to date on new products and to let us in on the low-down in his territory. Ordinarily a buoyant optimist, Tom was much depressed by the developments in Germany. Adolf Hitler had got him down.

Tom had first taken over the European territory at my suggestion back in the early 'thirties. His aviation interests had always been predominantly commercial. While he had built propellers for both Army and Navy at his Hamilton Aero Manufacturing Company, in Milwaukee, he had built only commercial aircraft at his other establishment, the Hamilton Metalplane Company, of the same place. His "Hamilton Metalplane," a high-wing metal monoplane with a single Pratt and Whitney Hornet engine, had been used extensively by Canadian bush flyers and The Isthmian Airways had operated them with signal success across the Isthmus of Panama. This plane, according to Tom, had been the prototype from which the Ford Trimotor had evolved.

At the time Tom had first gone abroad there appeared little likelihood of any real business for United in Europe. European aircraft were considered by Europeans to be vastly superior to the American, and their strong nationalism caused them to prefer to buy at home in support of their own industries. But there was one item in which we had attained leadership— metal aircraft propellers—and even though we might not sell the articles themselves, I thought we might dispose of the right to manufacture under our foreign patents for a good price. The money would come in handy in the development of the controllable-pitch propeller.

Tom had therefore gone abroad as a direct representative of the three companies under my management, Hamilton-Standard, Sikorsky Aviation, and Chance Vought Aircraft. Vought, of course, had nothing to offer at the moment. Upon arrival in Europe, Tom set up headquarters in Paris and laid the groundwork for his business. As a Yankee peddler, Tom displayed all the initiative and enterprise that characterized the American in a foreign land, but combined it with a rare knack of adapting himself to the customs of the country. In character and outward appearance he became quite continental. He set himself up in the George V Hotel in Paris, showed an aptitude for meeting and impressing the right people, and gave to his business entertainment the personal touch of a naturally warm-hearted individual. He exuded the confidence in American products that derived from deep conviction born of intimate knowledge of aircraft production and aeronautical engineering, and undertook the apparently hopeless task of penetrating the European market because he was certain that American production techniques could compete against European cheap hand labor. He had seen the automotive industry succeed in penetrating foreign trade barriers to the benefit of both American industry and American labor, and was confident American aviation could duplicate the feat.

He had not done too well with our propeller license—it took Raycroft Walsh and the controllable-pitch propeller to turn that trick—and when Fred Rentschler visited Europe after a year or so, Tom had to put on his best selling vest to keep Fred from closing out the office. Tom finally won out by suggesting that he give up his salary and continue on a commission basis.

In the interim between the long Armistice and Hitler's renewal of the World War, commercial air transport flourished on the Continent. International competition was reminiscent of the earlier struggle for control of the sea; one nation relied on private initiative, the other sought to capitalize air commerce through government ownership. Earlier in the struggle for sea power, Britain had defeated France through private enterprise. France, under the brilliant Colbert, had staked everything on government support of monopolistic trade associations or guilds. When, finally, Colbert had called in the industrialists to ask what more he might do to help them, they had responded in unison, *"Laissez nous faire!"* (Leave us alone).

But now Britain, having concentrated authority over civil air transport in a separate ministry wholly dominated by an air force steeped in the Douhet doctrine, had abandoned private enterprise, and, following the drift toward state ownership, had put commercial aviation under government control. The effect of this had been clearly set forth in the so-called "Cadman Report," the Report of the British Committee of Inquiry into Civil Aviation, published in March, 1938, which stated unequivocally that, except on Empire routes, that country was backward in civil air transport.

This statement, of course, took cognizance of the rapid progress in America where, following the development of the air-cooled engine, the controllable-pitch propeller, the Boeing and Douglas transports, the Sikorsky boats, and Lindbergh's epic flight, commercial aviation had flourished.

These products now became Tom Hamilton's stock in trade and he peddled them most successfully to independent customers whose decisions were dictated by economic considerations rather than those of national prestige.

When Tom visited Hartford, we often gathered at the close of a business day before the fireplace in our basement recreation room. Its walls were hung with Indian curios and colored prints of Indian warriors, while the corner posts of the fireplace nook boasted accurate replicas of Alaskan totem poles carved under Tom's supervision and decorated by him. Both of us having been raised in the Pacific Northwest, at a time when pioneers still lived to recount tales of their many enterprises, we had absorbed some of their spirit.

The curious turn of events in England, where the most enterprising nation of modern times seemed to have fallen on evil days, came in for much discussion. Tom had accumulated a number of ideas while traveling abroad. For one thing, England, having acquired great wealth, seemed bent on holding onto it, preferably without having to work. Her desire for economic security reflected a human trait that accompanies maturity. Her government, always responsive to business influence, had gradually abandoned free trade in exchange for monopolies and cartels. Meanwhile business had exploited labor as a commodity, a fact disclosed by the character of her industrial cities. The High Street led upwind by way of wide avenues to cultivated gardens; the crooked lane to the workers' cottages wound past bleak habitations blackened by factory smoke. Ultimately, labor in revolt had replaced the business monopoly with one of its own. Labor leaders, having acquired power, became its prisoners. Unless they wielded their power for the material benefit of the workers they represented, someone else would either force them to action or grab their jobs. In time these labor monopolists would feel the force of government in the form of a dictatorship or government monopoly. With the nationalization of industry, initiative and enterprise were sure to be stifled; all incentive would be lost. Tom had witnessed this in France without dreaming it could spread to England. With the vital spark extinguished, the body politic must decay. It always had. Yet while watching the creeping paralysis in England, Tom observed that certain nations continued to exercise their initiative.

In Holland, for instance, where the Dutch, though defeated by the English fleet, had gone on to expand ocean commerce to create an empire in the Indies, the perception of their statesmen and merchants had suffered no obscuration. As far back as October 7, 1918, a month before the Armistice, the Dutch had pioneered with what was to become the world-famous K.L.M. and K.N.I.L.M., outstanding services on the continent of Europe extending to the Dutch East and West Indies. The Scandinavian countries, which behind the sure shield of the Grand Fleet had expanded their sea power, now linked their homeland with the rest of the Continent and with London, and made plans for their forthcoming service to the Americas. In Norway, Bernt Balchen, the well-known explorer, tied the efforts in with American products; in Sweden, Aktiebolaget Aerotransport standardized on American aircraft like the Douglas DC-3.

Similarly, the Belgians, always an enterprising people, covered Europe and reached out for the Congo with their "Sabena." In Italy, the tendency was to use domestic types like the Savoia-Marchettis, but the Italians purchased technical information and took licenses to build American products. In Poland, the Polish Airlines "LOT" operated an extensive service using American equipment. A Jugoslav service covered the capitals of Europe. Finland connected Helsinki with Berlin.

The Germans, after getting the restrictions of the Versailles Treaty lifted, moved rapidly to make up lost ground. Junkers began to manufacture its version of the Boeing 247, and Bavarian Motoren Werke, builders of one of the best in-line liquid-cooled engines extant, took a license to manufacture the Pratt and Whitney Hornet. Junkers took a license to manufacture the Hamilton-Standard propeller, but later abandoned it in favor of their own "V.D.M." The German Lufthansa, equipped with aircraft derived from the American technologies, spread over Europe and reached out to the far comers of the world, like South America.

In France, which we now recognize as a casualty of World War I, the world's strongest air force was dissipated by storing war surplus aircraft and neglecting a living industry. In fact, the French industry, suffering from subversive activities, declined to the point where the government could conveniently nationalize it and, to all intents and purposes, strangle it. French air transport suffered from the internal dissensions which were rife at the time, but Air France attempted to write its name in history with aircraft predominantly of American conception.

In England, even the Empire routes suffered in competition with American aircraft. Thus when Pan American was ready to initiate the Bermuda-Azores-Lisbon transatlantic service, with the new Sikorsky S-42 Clippers, the British delayed granting landing rights in Bermuda to Pan American until they could build a plane of their own, undertaken after Mr. Sikorsky had read a paper before the Royal Aeronautical Society outlining the novel features in his design and setting down its measured performance. During this delay, Pan American shifted its attention to the far Pacific and, using the same Sikorsky Clippers, pioneered the air route to Hawaii and the Orient.

The activity associated with the growth of world air transport provided Tom with just the opportunity he had foreseen. Furthermore, after the American air-mail contracts had been canceled and the American long-term program had broken down, the business Tom had brought to United enabled us to keep our heads above water. Revenue from the sale of technical information provided us with funds with which to keep in the forefront of technological progress. And though we did not realize it, that morning when Tom came home from Europe, his efforts would later provide the sustenance which would save Pratt and Whitney and its organization for a decisive contribution to the coming World War II. It was the war clouds from the cold front in Europe that depressed Tom's buoyant spirit.

"This man Hitler," he said, "is the world's evil genius." We were sitting in my office in East Hartford trying to plan our moves in a game of blind-man's buff.

"You people over here," Tom went on, "tend to discount him because he wears a Charlie Chaplin moustache. But, believe me, he is no tramp. He knows Germans like a book and gives them just the sort of leadership they eat up. It reminds you of the old picture of the donkey with a carrot in front of him and a lash behind him. Hitler knows how to hold out the carrot with one hand and pop the whip with the other."

Tom went on to muse about the curious way thoughts took wing. Here was a former corporal of the Landswehr who had dreamed up a screwy idea and by force of his own conviction had sold it to the German people. Similarly, Lenin had generated an idea and, through sheer fanaticism, had come up from the dregs to impose a new tyranny on a people who had never known much else. Worse still, the cockeyed idea had spread into other lands in the short two decades since the Armistice from a war to make the world safe from such things. In Italy, it was Mussolini; in Japan, Hirohito. Here were four men on horseback, the Four Horsemen of the Apocalypse, and no one was doing anything about a counterattack with a better idea. One was ready at hand in the Christian faith, but subversive influences had persuaded Christians that it was unsophisticated even to talk about it. Protestants were so busy attacking Catholics that they were unwittingly led into an attitude toward communism which, if not sympathy, is at least not outspoken opposition.

Meanwhile at home we buried our heads in the sand. Unable to conceive such an idea as attacking others, we persuaded ourselves that some miracle would protect us. Our only means of counterattack was to pass a law against war and the current nostrum went under the title of "Arms Embargo Act." It had its origin in the ancient myth of the war profiteer, an old wives' tale founded on the idea that greedy munition racketeers in search of profits had fomented World War I. Its approach to keeping the peace was to prohibit the sale of arms to all belligerents. But, as Tom pointed out, it wouldn't work out that way.

To date it had served as a good excuse for French bureaucrats to oppose the purchase of arms in the United States, on the grounds that delivery could be cut off by Hitler; all that was necessary was to declare war on France and convert her into a belligerent. The Act thus became an invitation to Hitler to make war whenever it suited his convenience. The Germans and Italians needed no American help; they had made themselves self-sufficient. From the moment the air-mail cancellations had thrown a rough lock on our own aviation program, they had seized upon the opportunity to expand their own air power as a new weapon with which the have nots could take what they wanted from the haves. Hitler had made no bones about it; such Nazis as Goering, Milch, and Udet bragged about their prowess to every American who visited Germany.

Among these, Charles A. Lindbergh had sought to sound a note of warning when he said to a Nazi assembly in Flyers-House in Berlin in July, 1936,

> Unlike the builder of the dugout canoe, we have lived to see our harmless wings of fabric turned into carriers of destruction even more dangerous than battleships and guns. We have lived to carry on our shoulders the responsibility for the results of our experiments which, in other fields, have passed to future generations.
>
> We in aviation carry a heavy responsibility on our shoulders, for while we have been drawing the world closer together in peace, we have stripped the armor of every nation in war. It is no longer possible to defend the heart of a country with its army. Armies can no more stop an air attack than a suit of mail can stop a rifle bullet. Aviation has, I believe, created the most fundamental changes ever made in war. It has turned defense into attack. We can no longer protect our families with an army. Our libraries, our museums—every institution which we value most, is laid bare to bombardment.
>
> Aviation has brought a revolutionary change to a world already staggering from changes. It is our responsibility to

make sure that doing so, we do not destroy the very things we wish to protect.

Reports as to German preparations by Lindbergh and numerous other competent observers had been discounted at home. A naval air attaché at Berlin had been threatened with orders home and accused of being pro-Nazi because he had made a factual report of German preparations. And at the very moment when Tom could arouse no interest in France or England looking to utilization of American products, the Italians, the Germans, the Japanese, and the Russians had come knocking at his door. At the time it was difficult to be selective. As the Four Horsemen jockeyed for advantage in the race for world dominion, no one knew who would be on our side. As it ultimately turned out, all four were against us at one time, what with the Rome-Berlin-Tokyo axis supported by the Russian nonaggression pact. But United Aircraft did draw the line in one situation; we quoted such high prices for our technical assistance that the Russians refused to buy from us. We knew, of course, that this did not prevent their getting whatever they wanted but at least we kept them out of our plants.

Tom, having long resided in France, had a strong attachment to the country and its people. Now with Hitler arming, he redoubled his efforts to interest the French Air Ministry in an arrangement which would place our facilities at their command in the emergency. After much delay he had finally succeeded in persuading them to test our engines in their laboratories with a view to "homologuing" them and clearing the way for later purchase, if desired. The engines had met all demands and had even got by in spite of some sand and glass which somehow always tended to get into the test engines.

Moving as Tom did in military and diplomatic circles, he had acquired an unusual outlook on the European situation. Yet he had not, as yet, been able to forecast the final line-up. Nazism and communism, though similar under the skin, were natural enemies. If British diplomacy, bent on maintaining the old balance of power on the Continent, could involve Russia and Germany, she might win a respite for western Europe. But if Russian diplomacy could bring Moscow into the Rome-Berlin-Tokyo axis, at least temporarily, Hitler would have a free hand with western Europe—where fifth columns had already penetrated—and might dominate British sea power with an air force based on shore and operating from interior lines. Meanwhile our natural friends abroad scorned our products even as our enemies scrambled to buy our technology.

And so the Yankee Peddler who had set out to advance the new art of air transport, and in so doing expand world trade and promote prosperity, suddenly found himself in the cloak-and-dagger business. The war, he knew, would set air transport back at least ten years to say nothing of incalculable damage in every other aspect of life. We were caught in a net spun out of the idea first suggested by General Jiulio Douhet and later endorsed by other fanatics. And all the while the biggest idea in human existence, the doctrine according to Jesus Christ, lay fallow for lack of ardent advocates.

CHAPTER TWENTY-FOUR
A CHILL SETS IN

Don Brown, our president, who had been in ill health for some time, was now unable to give personal attention to the multitude of matters, and it fell to me to try to get some coordinated action on industry problems. Any sort of joint action by our Aeronautical Chamber of Commerce had long ago been proved impossible, first because joint action called for unanimous consent and no two of our bully boys in the industry could agree on anything. Of course on rare occasions we reached an agreement, and such an occasion developed one day in the office of the Assistant Secretary of War.

Out of the confusion and extravagance incident to the last war, Congress had passed the Army Reorganization Act of 1921, under which responsibility for production planning and mobilization had been lodged in the Assistant Secretary of War. That office had been collecting an array of card indexes which purported to assign some sort of role for mobilization to each manufacturer. After some twenty years of this, the Assistant Secretary, then Mr. Louis Johnson, having decided to take a look at his handiwork, had summoned the aircraft industry. The conference was called to order by General Westover, then Chief of the Air Corps, who was supported by "Hap" Arnold, Assistant Chief, and by Colonel Burns, from the Office of the Assistant Secretary of War.

General Westover stated the situation: the Army would like to have our estimate of the effectiveness of their war plans effort. If, after looking the situation over, we gave general approval, they would ask us to remain over another day to suggest improvements. They wanted our frank opinion of progress. General Westover then introduced General Arnold, who conducted the inquiry.

Hap Arnold was a favorite with the industry. Forthright, courageous, and decisive, he had supported Billy Mitchell at a time when less able men would have taken the easier course. Along with a handful of similarly able men like Hugh Knerr, a classmate of mine and rifle teammate who had transferred to the Army, Louis Brereton, also a Naval Academy graduate, Frank Andrews, Carl Spaatz, Jimmy Doolittle, and others, Hap had preached the air-force doctrine in fair and foul weather. Now he grinned at us across the table.

"Well," he inquired, "who wants to drop the opening bomb?" From the back of the room the salty voice of Dutch Kindleberger resounded.

"If you ask me," he volunteered, "I think you've had twenty years of hogwash." There was a murmur of surprise.

"From time to time," Dutch went on, "you send your bright young men to ask us the same question: 'how many airplanes can you manufacture X days after M Day?' And when I counter that question with another—'what kind of airplanes?'—your young men don't have the answer." As Dutch finished, Glenn Martin put in his oar.

"I agree with Dutch," he began, as a titter greeted the idea that these two might agree on anything.

"You expect us to give you a war plan," Glenn went on, "before you have answered the question; and furthermore, you expect us to give you something worthwhile at no cost. According to my estimate," Glenn continued, "it would cost at least ten thousand dollars for us to get up anything useful, and you apparently expect us to advance it out of profits. It can't be done." As Glenn finished, Hap glanced my way.

My experience with Army was more limited than that of the others. In Hamilton-Standard, Ray Walsh had handled Army business. In Sikorsky and Vought, the dealings had been mostly with Navy. In Pratt and Whitney, "Tilly" Tillinghast, himself a former Army pilot and a favorite with all, had handled Army contacts. However, there were some fundamentals that seemed to apply to both.

"I agree with Dutch and Glenn," I began, adding to the unusual flurry of interindustry agreement, "and I'll go a step farther. For a real test of your war plan, I suggest that you start a staff exercise on mobilization and watch what happens." Hap Arnold flashed me that quizzical Army expression that wonders how any good could come out of the Navy. I went on to explain.

My own experience in naval operations had shown me that in a dress rehearsal it is seldom the high private in the rear rank who falls down. More likely, it's the green second lieutenant in the file closers who gets tangled up in his sword. He's been so busy drilling others, he's forgotten to read his own book. You have to put machinery into operation to find out where it creaks the loudest. In this case, if the Secretaries of War and Navy would order mobilization for drill purposes by designating a certain day as M Day, Headquarters could then announce the types of airplanes it wanted to put into production and the number of each it required, and then procurement officers could go ahead with drill purchase orders, and the contractors could place orders to suppliers, and so on. About here I noticed a flicker in Hap's steely eye.

"I guess Dutch and Glenn are right," he said with a wry grin. "Hell," he went on, "I can't begin to tell you today what airplanes we would want to buy, let alone how many. I don't even know who we expect to fight, nor when, nor where."

From here on the conference moved rapidly to the crystallization of an idea. Since time is of the essence in mobilization, one way to save time was to build the mobilization plan into current purchasing. When the government placed an order for a certain type of equipment, it could include in the original contract an item calling out a detailed war plan to be paid for under the contract. Such a war plan would include options for war quantities and the contractor would place stand-by orders with his own suppliers for the amounts of materials of all kinds required to fill the options. He and his suppliers would go ahead with architects' plans, drawings, and all other paper work incident to creating the expanded facilities required by the options, the idea being to get all contract paper work done, even to the determination of critical materials and priorities. Then, upon a signal of execution designating an option, the machine could start operating, without all the preliminary delays, and still leave the procurement agency free to make its decisions at the last minute.

Hap Arnold listened to the discussion. "Well," he remarked, "I see we won't need that second day for this conference." With that he called in General Westover and Colonel Burns, to whom the general plan was explained. General Westover closed the conference with the statement that he intended to get some such plan in operation, if it was the last thing he did.

But of course, with things as they were, neither he nor anyone else could put such an idea into operation. With the outbreak of the war, responsibility for mobilization was shifted out of the Assistant Secretary's office and into a new and independent agency, which started as the National Defense Advisory Committee and changed its name, at intervals, to the end of the emergency.

Meanwhile, when I got back to Hartford and reported the experience to Don Brown, Don sat a long while looking out the window, across acres that had once been peaceful tobacco fields.

"Well, Skipper," he said finally, "it looks as though you had sold United Aircraft something, whether the Army buys it or not. We'll start building our own war-plans organization and get it ready for trouble." After our estimates of the cost of such a program had come in, we discovered that they totaled just $10,000 per year, the figure Glenn Martin had mentioned down in Washington, but, like Glenn, we had no idea where the money was to come from.

In anticipation of the gradual drying up of government business and with a view to trying to get funds from Congress to help tide us over slack periods, Don Brown had outlined his situation to BUAERO and the Army Air Corps. As a result of efforts by the Armed Forces, Congress had appropriated funds for new engines to be ordered from Pratt and Whitney. It had seemed to us at the time that, with war imminent, the administration might have made better use of relief funds than raking leaves. As a matter of fact, a good deal of relief money was being invested in air fields and armament, but the program was not coordinated; Mr. Ickes and Mr. Hopkins differed as to who was boss. The idea prevailed that peace could be had by just wishing for it. To have spent money for arms, or even to have directed it into the business stream so as to keep the production machine at a high level, would, at that time, have been considered unmoral. On the other hand, spending money wastefully for made work seemed to meet with public approval. The bald fact remained, however, that with war but a few months away, Pratt and Whitney Aircraft, one of the two dependable sources of proved aircraft engines, faced a shutdown, and with it, dispersal of an organization which could never have been reassembled.

To our relief, however, Congress appropriated funds, and the Army notified Pratt and Whitney that it might proceed with the procurement of materials and the production of engines in advance of the formal contract, with the idea of utilizing the allotment to best advantage from the point of view of readiness for emergency. Then, sometime after we had swung into our program, the Air Corps, to our amazement, canceled this informal assurance, and diverted the funds to the procurement of Allison liquid-cooled engines. At that time the General Motors Corporation, owners of Allison, had indicated little need for public relief funds, but to Pratt and Whitney, now almost wholly dependent upon government business, the loss of this critical order was a body blow.

When, later, Don called upon the Assistant Secretary of War, Mr. Louis Johnson, to point out to him the results of his decision, he was advised that the Army had decided to scrap all air-cooled engines in pursuit planes. Next year would probably see the last of air-cooled engines in bombers. He was instructed to start Pratt and Whitney designing liquid-cooled engines at once. To Don, knowing that Allison, equally surprised by the decision, had not yet started tooling, while Pratt and Whitney, already tooled, must remain idle, the decision hardly made sense.

Somewhat bewildered by the change, Don then called on Hap Arnold. Here he learned that the secretary's decision had also taken the Air Force by surprise. Anxious to keep Allison ticking over, Wright Field had built up such a strong case for liquid-cooled, that the secretary had decided to scrap air-cooled. Since recent pursuit planes like the Seversky had been designed for air-cooled, the decision had left them on a spot. Apparently, however, the decision once taken could not be recalled. No one in the Air Force had dreamed for a moment that it would be taken, but here we were, out on a long limb, and war was in the offing.

As the year 1938 came to a close, we began laying off men, dropping first those who could be the more readily spared. But the time came when the organization was being seriously hurt, and the year-end forecast indicated that, by July, 1939, we would reach the end of our production. Since materials must be in hand five to six months ahead of delivery of the finished article, that meant that time had already begun to run out for Pratt and Whitney. We had long since cut back expenses to the bare minimum and there remained nothing but a final decision to suspend manufacturing operations. Yet even then, Don Brown kept the War Plans Division intact.

Now we had but a single remaining hope: Tom Hamilton in Paris. Tom reported by radiotelephone that the French, now reduced to dire straights, still vacillated, but had established financial credits in the United States and would send a purchasing commission to Washington to open negotiations direct with us. Don Brown, sick as he was, went down to Washington with some of our staff to battle through hours of legalistic verbiage, in smoke-filled rooms of Washington hotels.

Here it developed that the United States Treasury would act as a sort of intermediary between the French commission and the American manufacturers, and that Secretary Henry Morgenthau had turned the job over to Capt. Harry Collins, then head of the Purchasing Division of the Treasury. With the Arms Embargo Act still adorning the legislative library, active participation by the Treasury in negotiations between United States arms manufacturers and a possible "belligerent" had certain aspects of incongruity. However, the whole situation was so phony that this detail escaped public attention.

Capt. Harry Collins provided just the *savoir faire* necessary to resolve an impossible situation into a completed contract. Harry had served as supply officer on the ancient destroyer-tender *Iris* back in the dark ages when I had commanded the four-piper *Truxtun*, then based on San Diego. He had resigned his commission to go into business and had there shown the same tact that had endeared him to the temperamental skippers of the Pacific Torpedo Flotilla.

Throughout the negotiations, Don Brown stood fast on the principle that prices to be paid for the equipment should be high enough to permit us to take the necessary financial risks required by the early deliveries specified. The customer should not hamstring us by chiseling prices to the point where our willingness to accept risks was impaired. Fortunately the soundness of this position was apparent to Harry, and his confidence in us enabled him to support it in the discussions with Col. Paul Jacquin of the French commission. The colonel proved to be a man of high character with a sense of fairness and a degree of integrity that finally brought the negotiations to a satisfactory conclusion.

The contract was signed on February 14, 1939, at almost the precise moment when further delay would have done us irreparable harm. As a matter of fact, the time had long passed when a garrison finish might be of any help to France; the chief benefit of this contract lay in the fact that it gave the Pratt and Whitney Aircraft organization a shot in the arm, and put us in such position that when, two years later, the Japs smacked us at Pearl Harbor, we could swing into full-scale production for the American account.

After Don Brown's return to Hartford, his health forced him to turn more and more of his work over to me. In this I functioned, much as I had once done for Admiral Reeves, as a sort of chief of staff, seeking to do things in the way Don himself would have done them, had he been personally on the firing line. Somewhat earlier, when our difficulties had become serious, I urged Don to invite Fred Rentschler to return to our board as chairman where we could call on him for advice and get the benefit of his judgment. Now we three began working closely together—at least as closely as Don's declining health permitted.

Don, a singularly attractive and lovable person, having come upstairs by way of the shop, always displayed a strong sense of responsibility for his men. The specter of shutdown weighed heavily on him and now, as the illness that was to prove fatal began closing in on him, his thoughts were still down on the factory floor.

One day he and I walked along an aisle between the machines. Don made some remark to the effect that he longed to be back there where the problems were of the kind a man could get his teeth into. Behind us we heard the voice of a young kid making some crack about how soft it was for guys that did nothing but sit on cushions in paneled offices and look wise.

Don turned and brushed the kid away from the machine. After running it awhile in obvious enjoyment, he turned to the workman:

"Listen, son," he said, not unkindly, "I'd trade jobs with you any day if I could, but you wouldn't take the responsibility. That's something you fellows never want to accept."

Toward midsummer, we began to hear rumors that the French needed more equipment than our humming plant could deliver. By this time Secretary Johnson's action had reacted to our advantage. The inventory of raw stock, semifinished, and finished parts which they had left on our hands when they canceled our order enabled us to get rolling without the protracted delay which would have been inevitable had our pipe lines been drained before the big freeze. And so, almost overnight, we had the machines humming again and the empty parking spaces around the plant filled up with cars. But this rumor of new plants was a horse of another color.

First of all, we had no capital with which to construct a new addition, nor did it seem likely we could get it had we wanted it—which we didn't. Having faced the cold shadows of a vacant factory, we had no appetite for more of the same. The punitive attitude of our own government had completely dammed up all sources of private capital for expansion of munitions plants. Actually, the long depression had all but dried up investment in any private venture. The fear and uncertainty which had cast such a pall over the land had been intensified by the drift toward government domination of business and the rise of bureaucratic dictation.

Among other things, there was the sensitive factor of profit control. For instance, the Internal Revenue Bureau of Mr. Henry Morgenthau's Treasury Department dictated, through its review of income tax returns and its rules and regulations, the amount a manufacturer might charge against the cost of his product for the use of his tools. The manufacturer, having in mind the many elements of this problem, such as the wear and tear on machines, the life cycle of the product he was selling, and many other complex factors, would charge against each item of manufacture what he judged to be its proper share of the cost of the tools. The more he charged, the less was his profit for a given year. In the long run the whole thing washed out. But the Internal Revenue Bureau, sitting in judgment of each case and anxious to prove high profit in order to assess higher taxes, was interested in reducing this depreciation charge as far as possible. Bearing no responsibility for the survival of a company, and having little knowledge of, or interest in, the technical details of the manufacturer's problem, it tended to set up over-all rules which, even though applicable to one case, might be far out of line for another. And since munitions manufacturers were generally unpopular, they had two strikes on them from the beginning. Real investors, understanding this handicap, were not interested in risking their dollars on this kind of enterprise, nor were the enterprises interested in seeking their money.

Now, if the public policies of the period dried up the flow of capital to private industry, or even reduced it to a trickle, the Arms Embargo Act put the finishing touches upon the process. All Chancellor Hitler had to do to make a "belligerent" out of France was to open war on France, and since the French were now buying aircraft in the United States, the sooner he did the better. On September 1, 1939, Germany invaded Poland; on September 5, France declared war on Germany. President Roosevelt immediately issued his proclamation of neutrality, thus putting the Act into effect and cutting off shipments to belligerents.

Meanwhile, however, the frantic French, desperate by now, had, in a last-minute effort to buy time, insisted upon our creating a new plant and accepting new contracts. Our only course under the circumstances was to insist that they advance the entire amount of the cost of the new facilities, some eight million dollars, and finance the additional contracts for aircraft by advancing working capital under terms agreeable to us. However, under French law, the state was prohibited from investing its funds in a capital outlay on foreign shores. Further, the French, at the time, were pursuing the opposite policy at home; they were expropriating and nationalizing their own industry—a policy that reduced the country from a position of world leadership, following World War I, to one of abject dependence upon American aviation in World War II. How they could agree to go ahead with us under the circumstances we could not see, especially with the Arms Embargo Act hanging over them. But go ahead they did, and under our terms.

Meanwhile, during the protracted negotiations, we went right ahead, in our new War Plans Division, with all the blueprints and schedules, working in close collaboration with our architect, Albert Kahn. We broke ground for the new French plant on October 10, 1939, pushing automobiles out of the parking space on which we had determined to build it. The shop was to have an area of some 300,000 square feet and be tooled to handle about 300 engines per month of our 1830 model. Since this was an engine rated at approximately 1,000 horsepower, we figured that we were going to get 300,000 horsepower per month out of the new plant; in three months we could build enough engines to generate the power of Niagara. Title to the new facility would rest with United Aircraft. On November 5, 1939, Congress repealed the Arms Embargo Act.

Shortly afterward, the British government came into the market for aircraft. This was a surprise, for but a short time earlier, Lord Beaverbrook, then visiting this country, had snorted at the suggestion that Britain might have to look to America for assistance. Yet Sir Henry Self, formerly of the British Air Ministry, arrived in Washington and joined with M. René Plevin of France, in a new coordinated procurement program.

It was shortly after this, on an evening early in 1940 while we were sitting in the library at home, that the telephone rang. It was the watchman over at the plant.

"Secretary Morgenthau has just walked in," he said, "and he would like to see you."

CHAPTER TWENTY-FIVE
AN UNFAVORABLE CLIMATE

As I backed my convertible out of the garage, and eased it from the driveway onto Albany Avenue, I speculated as to what might have brought Secretary Morgenthau to Hartford in the middle of the night. It might, I thought, have something to do with the new British inquiry which had been discussed earlier in Harry Collins's office in the Treasury. There, a number of aircraft manufacturers had met to be introduced to Sir Henry Self and a newcomer to the French negotiations, M. René Plevin. Sir Henry, very British, had tried not to appear condescending to us provincials, but it was apparent early that he had brought his trading vest along, determined to give us a sample of British tradesmanship.

I had noticed at the time that Col. Paul Jacquin, with whom we had had such intelligent dealings, was not present. M. René Plevin, the new Frenchman, looked to me like the story-book Frenchman, suave, polished, and clever. It occurred to me that Colonel Jacquin might need a little help from us, and this was confirmed by the drift of the conversation. Sir Henry Self made it clear that he and M. Plevin would act in unison in all matters of future procurement. They had looked over the earlier contracts and concluded that the terms had not been as advantageous to the customer as must any future terms. At any rate they appeared out of line with what had been customary in Old England. The British were in the market for large quantities of war material, but England was a poor country and we must learn to sharpen our pencils and cut prices. England had shielded us during the first war, but she was not now so strong, etc., etc.

Sir Henry had expressed interest in negotiating for the construction of new facilities from which aircraft engine production could flow; he had wondered if we might not now undertake immediate expansion of our facilities—but of course under more favorable terms to England than we had apparently exacted from France.

To this I pointed out that the French terms had been arrived at after painstaking negotiation under the commission headed by Col. Paul Jacquin. They had not been predicated on chiseling tactics, but designed to give us every incentive to take the heavy risks paramount to quick deliveries. We had found no reason to question that procedure but had, on the other hand, experienced many incidents in which the wisdom of this procedure had been proved. Time had been of the essence and time had proved to be something that could not be bought. With less time now, we could see no basis for further discussion of the terms.

As a matter of fact, I explained, we would not undertake to even negotiate another contract for plant expansion until we saw our way out of our present difficulties. We suffered from chronic indigestion and had no intention of making it acute. And even if the time came when we believed our already overloaded organization might take on greater responsibilities, there was one serious road block that must be resolved. We had accepted the French order without resolving this difficulty because we had been in a serious predicament for business; today we could not accept that handicap.

I referred to the matter of plant depreciation and the rules and regulations of the Treasury Department. Unless these were changed, a sudden cessation of hostilities might leave us with an enormous excess of plant on our hands. The burden of depreciation, however light under maximum output, would prove overwhelming after shutdown. The day-to-day burden of writeoff would force on us serious losses that would, in time, bankrupt the company. I pointed out, of course, that this was a matter for the United States Treasury rather than the British Purchasing Commission, but that we could not undertake to construct new facilities even under terms similar to those in the French contract, until after our Treasury Department had resolved this problem of plant amortization and depreciation.

Now, as I sped down Albany Avenue to North Main Street and turned left there down the Morgan Street hill to the Bulkely Memorial Bridge, I reviewed the atmosphere of that meeting and began to rehearse what I would say to Secretary Morgenthau, should he bring the matter up. I recalled that Sir Henry Self had listened to my statement with an expression of amused tolerance. No doubt he had in mind the power of the Treasury and the influence of the banking fraternity as means of bringing us upstarts into line. But we were under no great obligations to others; we were free— free to do what in our own judgment was in the long-term interest of getting on with our job.

And as I turned into the main gate of the aircraft factory at East Hartford, the lights were ablaze all over the place. I parked my car in the garage under the office building and ran upstairs to my office where the Secretary of the Treasury awaited me. After a greeting, Mr. Morgenthau expressed a wish to see the new French addition, and we walked together down through the main shop and across to the new one. We had scheduled the new building for completion in three months, and three months had seen it finished. The new machinery, earmarked long in advance by War Plans and ordered even before the final contract had been signed, was already coming in. Bare spots revealed the wood-block floor of the vast girdered structure, but millwrights were busy sliding machinery onto prearranged spots and uncrating late arrivals. One complete production line was already set up and working to relieve a bottleneck in the main shop.

After a look-see, the secretary and I made our way back to my corner office upstairs. He sat down in one of the big chairs and I slid into the swivel seat behind my desk. On my walls hung the mementos of bygone days. There in a silver frame was my commission as a commander, and beneath it, all the others from passed midshipman on up; beside it hung my certificate of graduation from the Naval Academy. On other walls were collected the photographs of my friends: Admiral Moffett, pipe in hand, with that alert look; Admiral Reeves, from an oil painting by his own son, bearded like the seamen of the old school and with that gleam in his eye; Chance Vought, dapper with his waxed moustache; George Wheat, wise in the ways of a newspaper man; Comdr. Charles E. Kennedy-Purvis, Royal Navy, a friend of my Grand Fleet days; Hap Arnold, of the Army Air Corps; Jack Towers, of Naval Aviation; and Captain Marco Zar, Argentine Navy. They were a goodly company. The secretary glanced at them and then came to his point.

It was the British matter all right. Time was fleeting and he thought we ought to get down to business and sign the contract. In reply, I pointed out our position. We had accepted the French order without first getting a commitment from the Treasury Department to treat plant depreciation on a more realistic basis. We had, however, set up our own books on the basis of synchronizing the plant writeoff with the shipment of the product called for on the engine contract; on this basis the plant would be completely written down when the product shipments had been completed. That would tend to reduce our taxable income for the period, but it would have the advantage to our own government that all subsequent products of that facility could be invoiced to it at no charge for depreciation of plant. In case we became involved in a war, and that now seemed probable, the government would recover in reduced costs everything it might now lose in taxes.

I had the impression, as I talked, that the secretary did not entirely follow me. I therefore went on to explain the situation more fully. The rules promulgated by the Internal Revenue Bureau might or might not be satisfactory to some ordinary peacetime businesses. I suspected they were not, as the desire to assess taxes currently might easily lead to poor judgment for the long term. This was a serious matter, since it tended to increase product costs by retarding the purchase of improved machinery and thus impaired the whole capital replacement problem. With us it was even more critical because our situation was most unusual and called for broad vision and judgment. I then took a long breath and said the little piece I had rehearsed in the roadster on the way over.

"Mr. Secretary," I said, "for the Treasury to treat this problem in a way other than the one which we have set up would put the Treasury in the position of profiteering—through excess taxation—on munitions contracts let here by foreign governments. We aircraft manufacturers, having been maligned as profiteers, would not like to see our government in the same boat."

The secretary blinked at this, but did not reply.

"Mr. Secretary," I continued, "we feel so strongly about the principles involved here that we have taken a firm decision: we will not go ahead on your British plant, until we have assurance of the treatment we require." The secretary still appeared unimpressed. However, he did reply in his flat voice.

"I will see that it is done."

The problem of plant expansion was but one of our many headaches. In due course we signed the British contract calling for an addition over half again as large as the French addition, and on generally similar terms. For the next several years we waged fierce battle with the Treasury Department over that problem of accelerated depreciation and amortization of emergency facilities, only to learn that the basic law precluded such treatment and could not be amended save by act of Congress. But as luck would have it, when the Treasury finally turned us down, the tax rates had been boosted so high that their adverse decision actually gave us a better break than we would have had with an earlier approval. And though this proved gratifying from the balance-sheet point of view, the principle remained an issue until finally resolved after the outbreak of the European war.

To a harassed manufacturer, intent on production, it seemed incredible that we Americans could be so stupid. At the time, we ascribed it to ignorance. In our shop experience, no deliberate saboteur could throw such backlash into a production line as just comes naturally when a dumb-bunny do-gooder gets to messing around. In the light of subsequent revelations, I am not so sure.

CHAPTER TWENTY-SIX
A SPARK IS STRUCK

Don Brown's death left a big gap in our ranks with no file closers available to fill it. United Aircraft, once the only company in the business with real depth to its management, had got thin on top. In reorganization, the directors elected Fred Rentschler chairman, with responsibility under the by-laws for the general conduct of the business affairs of the company. I was elected president with the authorities and responsibilities of chief executive officer. Raycroft Walsh succeeded me as senior vice-president, and J. F. McCarthy continued as controller with responsibility direct to the board of directors in financial matters. This rounded up a top organization in which the several personalities complemented each other in a way calculated to promote the closest kind of teamwork. In the four divisions, Jack Horner headed Pratt and Whitney, Sidney Stewart succeeded Raycroft Walsh in Hamilton-Standard, and C. J. McCarthy became general manager of the Vought-Sikorsky Division.

Then came May of 1940. The President of the United States in his fireside chat electrified the country with his announcement of a fantastic airplane production program. The total mentioned was 50,000 airplanes. Only two weeks earlier, a House of Representatives' Report on the War Department Appropriation Bill had lopped all but 57 airplanes off the Army Air Corps' own modest request for 496. By that time, some 2,800 airplanes had been contracted for under the previous year's appropriations, of which some 2,200 had been training planes. Practically the entire capacity of the American aircraft industry had been allotted to foreign sales. On the morning following the Presidential foray into the numbers racket, I sat behind my desk working on the mail.

Through the open door to the anteroom, I could see my secretary, Mrs. Dexter, typing out some of the faultless copy with which she kept our business flowing. She had come up to the front office with me from Chance Vought Aircraft, and was one of the leading women of the inner circle of highly trained and competent women who managed the routine of the top executive offices. As the only member of my office staff, she sorted out the mail and handled visitors or outside calls. On the mail, she slid into the wastebasket the bulk of it that was obviously part of the advertising matter which Uncle Sam so kindly subsidizes at great expense to himself and the recipient. A large part of the remainder Mrs. Dexter answered outright—and more effectively than if I had handled it. The part that called for decisions came to me—and even that was enough to keep a man scrambling to try to keep the desk clean. How Mrs. Dexter, singlehanded, could manage the flow of mail and calls was more than I could understand but some wag of a punster had opined that she was dexterous indeed. As I turned to my own pile of papers, the phone bell jingled and she reached for the receiver.

"The Secretary of the Treasury is calling, sir," she said, and then added, "just a moment, Secretary Morgenthau." I lifted my receiver.

"Could you come down to Washington," came the flat voice, "and have supper with me at my home Sunday evening?"

"Certainly, sir," I replied.

"Would you mind," the voice inquired, "if I invited a competitor?"

"Not at all," I answered. "May I ask who you have in mind?"

"Vaughan," came the reply. "Guy Vaughan, of Curtiss-Wright." Something impelled me to try to inject a little humor into the colorless colloquy.

"An honest competitor," I laughed, "but with an inferior line." The phone clicked and I sat back to try to dope out what was going on. A 50,000-plane program and the two big suppliers of aircraft engines dining at the secretary's home on a Sunday night! Shades of Franklin D. Roosevelt, Senator Black, and Postmaster General Brown! Phil Johnson, of United Airlines, had chanced to drop in on an informal conference called in the daytime to take away from him air-mail contracts he had won under competitive bidding and Congress had crucified him for it! It all seemed to depend upon whose political ox was to be gored.

I met Guy Vaughan in the Carlton Hotel on Sunday afternoon. Guy had already scouted the terrain and discovered from "Tommy the Cork," so he said, that the bright boys intended to give us the works at supper and force us to agree to license the government to build aircraft engines under our patents. Why they should resort to the cloak-and-dagger technique remained a mystery; they already had such rights under numberless Army-Navy contracts. But there seemed no mystery about why they wanted the licenses; the big idea was to set up a string of big government-owned-and-operated aircraft factories in the several distressed areas of the country to give relief to the unemployed, and votes to their new employers.

Our quiet little supper party with Secretary Morgenthau did seem to bear out Guy's dope. For afterward, the secretary informed us that since we were already overloaded with the foreign business, our government would have to look elsewhere. He served notice on us that we would be expected to license the government under our patents. Guy Vaughan, on being questioned, advised the secretary that in his opinion Curtiss-Wright could build all the engines the government might require, and stated further that his company would not license the government voluntarily on a program that would put competitors into his business—and at government expense—who would, after the war, put his company out of business. In reply to the same question, I stated that we would license others to build our engines.

The secretary indicated some surprise and inquired what our price would be. When I replied that we would license them without fee, the secretary appeared to disbelieve the statement and remarked that he had never seen anything yet that was worth more than it cost. To this I replied that there was a catch to it, and now the secretary seemed ready to believe me.

From here I went on to point out that the manufacture of an aircraft engine was an art that required skill, experience, and know-how; few organizations anywhere had been successful in this field. If we licensed someone to build our product, we must still accept responsibility for its performance—a responsibility that we had always accepted. And since we accepted the responsibility, then we must insist upon retaining authority over the choice of our licensees. We had thought this through long ago as a part of our war plan; a major war would stop production of many articles and throw men out of employment. It would break up organizations and teams that had the know-how of production and had demonstrated their competence in their own lines. We would train such organizations in the specialized technique of our business and thus get a good job. As examples we suggested such organizations as the Ford Motor Company, of Detroit, the Buick, Chevrolet, or Cadillac Divisions of General Motors, the Nash-Kelvinator Company, the Packard Company, Studebaker—in fact, you could go down the whole list and find a great untapped source of skilled production experts.

I went on to contrast this with the possibility of government undertaking the job. Without mentioning the difficulties peculiar to government business, I stressed the responsibility that goes along with aircraft production. When the engines fail, the airplane cracks up and young men get killed. We had got many gray hairs carrying this responsibility. If the government wanted to take it off our shoulders, that was their privilege, but they should go into it with their eyes open.

It was apparent by now that their eyes were fully open and we said good night with mutual expressions of esteem. Soon George J. Mead, once chief engineer of United Aircraft, then serving as vice-chairman of the National Advisory Committee for Aeronautics, had been appointed to supervise the Treasury Department's functions in the 50,000 program. This was good news indeed. For aside from the fact that George Mead knew his airplanes, there was the further and more important consideration that George knew the Army and Navy each had skilled organizations, schooled in the procurement of aeronautical materials, and was likely, after the details of the still nebulous program had been determined, to give the highly technical procurement job back to the Armed Forces. For had fate left this problem in the hands of one of the political agencies then springing up all over the place, we might today be slaves of Hitler, Mussolini, Hirohito, and Joe Stalin.

The government had either forgotten that the Army Reorganization Act of 1920 placed responsibility for industrial mobilization upon the Assistant Secretary of War, Louis Johnson, or, noting the controversy between him and his chief, Secretary Woodring, had changed its mind. In any event, Bill Knudsen was appointed Chairman of the National Defense Advisory Committee and George Mead took over the aircraft job. At the time, no one was able to enlighten us on the real meaning of the 50,000-plane program; it might be a yearly output, a war total, or anything else the fancy might suggest. Nor could anyone advise us what types of aircraft were contemplated. Scuttlebutt rumor had it that the President had first asked the Army and Navy to submit estimates of the maximum number of aircraft they could use but upon receipt of the figures had been disappointed at their lack of imagination. They couldn't seem to add up to more than a few thousand.

His own first figure, so the gossip went, had been a nice round 25,000, the very number, curiously enough, which had been hit upon back in 1917 as the number required to "darken the skies" over Germany. But later, so ran the story, the President had tried out his fireside chat on Lord Beaverbrook, the same "Beaver" who, not many weeks earlier, had snorted his scorn at the suggestion that England would ever have to look to America for aircraft production. And the Beaver, so we were told, had advised the President not to be a piker—100,000 airplanes would make better headlines—and the President had compromised on 50,000. In any event, BUAERO and Wright Field had now dubbed the announcement "the numbers racket," so the fact that a fellow like George Mead, who not only knew the words and music of aviation but could actually sing the song, was now handling the aircraft program seemed to us an incredibly lucky break.

And so it proved, for George got the two services to agree upon the reasonableness of some kind of program that seemed to add up to 50,000 and then passed the job back to them for execution. This put the ball back in play on a field where we knew the score and where the officials knew the rules and the game. It converted the war from a phony to a shooting war, and gave us the signal for take-off.

Now as the new British addition began to take form, we put our War Plans Division to work on a new American addition. This we decided to create in two steps and to finance with funds to be acquired in the market. Designed to utilize the entire capacity of the East Hartford area, the addition would double the total facilities already in hand. Our carefully prepared war plan contemplated farming out more and more of the work to subcontractors and suppliers as rapidly as they could be trained to manufacture to our high standards of precision and workmanship. The original manufacturing concept of Pratt and Whitney, Hamilton-Standard, and Vought had contemplated utilizing the skills and facilities of other competent shops in peacetime and in the interest of economy; now we embarked on our long-contemplated program of expansion of this technique in the interest of accelerated war production.

The capacity of any working area such as East Hartford is definitely limited by physical characteristics, such as transport, electric power, water supply, labor supply, housing, and so on. These limits, as they existed in peacetime, could be expanded to meet wartime needs by close cooperation with the management of the utilities. The War Plans Division, having foreseen the limitations of the several factors, had provided us with the information on which to approach our numerous suppliers of all kinds. Certain of these, like the power companies, whose normal business contemplated a continuous expansion of facilities to meet normal demands, used the information furnished them to arrive at decisions to advance their schedules wherever necessary to meet peak demands. Now "the aircraft," as we were called in Hartford, moved out of the category of a speculative venture and into the position of the controlling industry of the area. Our whole philosophy of leadership, based as it was on the cooperative process, now paid off, not alone in returns to us but to our neighbors and, in fact, to the whole country.

In this connection, reference can be made to a report on "Industrial Mobilization and Design and Development of Nazi Germany," issued by the Office of Military Government for Germany under date of October 5, 1945. The report is based on an examination of Albert Speer by several officers of the Intelligence Department, and deals with the part Speer played subsequent to the year 1942 when he was directed to take over the administration of German war production. Speer had realized immediately what great fundamental errors had been committed and how small armament output had remained prior to his taking over. The Reichswehr had dealt with armament problems theoretically and industry generally had had no great inclination to participate in preparatory work. The government organizations had become so large that they had managed only to keep each other busy; they committed what might be called mental incest and paved the way for all the mistakes that had later kept armament production at a surprisingly low level.

Speer had gone on to say that the Germans had been at a great disadvantage because their rearmament had been planned too long on a theoretic basis. A strict system of discipline and orders fully in accord with their authoritarian regime had replaced what this apparatus lacked in knowledge and ability. He had written a memorandum to Hitler on July 20, 1944, in which he stated that Russia and the United States were to be envied because external circumstances had forced them to improvise. The United States had had to raise their armed forces quickly and therefore could not do without the active personalities in industry, politics, and public life. In Germany, on the other hand, those who occupied themselves with war production were professional soldiers, a closed corporation without the benefit of fresh outside minds. For this reason, Speer believed that the extended theoretical preparation of German armaments had been mainly responsible for their low level of production until after 1942 when he had restored the principle of individual initiative by putting war production back into the hands of private industry. Within a year he had completed an organization of completely new leading personalities to restore the autonomy of industry and preserve its unity even in the most trying times.

The virus that infected Germany also attacked us, but our rugged constitution enabled us to throw it off.

CHAPTER TWENTY-SEVEN
FOR WHAT IS A MAN PROFITED?

The selection of Bill Knudsen to head up the agency charged with coordinating war production was a happy one. Just as George Mead knew his aircraft, so did Bill Knudsen know his production. Furthermore, he knew the men who knew production and he held their confidence and regard. This was important at the moment when business and industry had reason to fear and suspect government; the drift in this country toward the omnipotent state had aroused intense bitterness and might have bogged down the whole program had not Bill Knudsen attracted to his organization other men who held the respect of their fellow manufacturers. These men began immediately on the complex task of unraveling all the mare's nests that had collected around government procurement.

About the middle of the summer of 1940, Fred Rentschler and I went down to Washington to call on the Grand Old Man and outline to him the key to our whole program. The President's 50,000-plane program, when superimposed on the already staggering foreign purchases, was clearly beyond the total capacity of the New England area. And if we undertook further expansion in other areas, we would impose further burdens on an already hard-pressed staff. The time had now come to bring in the great automotive industry.

Since Knudsen had, until recently, been president of the General Motors Corporation, we saw little hope of interesting him in diverting Buick or Chevrolet to aircraft-engine production just yet. For our automobile manufacturers still remembered the treatment given them back in 1918 when, after the Armistice, their war contracts had been ruthlessly canceled—torn up like so many scraps of paper—and their "war profits" had vanished from view except in the news headlines of the next twenty years. It would take some doing to persuade Bill Knudsen to our cause, and even Bill Knudsen would have his work cut out to get his automotive friends on the beam. As a matter of fact, without Bill Knudsen it could never have been done in time.

For Bill was animated throughout his wartime service by a great motive. He had come to the Land of the Free a penniless immigrant, and had there won not alone riches but the respect and esteem of the great men of the land. And whatever the generation which had inherited liberty might think about it, Bill Knudsen knew what liberty meant; his whole being was imbued with a love for the country of his adoption, with a devotion to the spirit which animated it and an intense zeal to pay back in part some of the privileges it had extended him. And so deeply was this zeal imbedded in his character and so honestly did he seek to pay back his debt that even men grown cynical under the lash of government were impelled to go along. His simple fundamental character combined with his native wit and intelligence gave Bill Knudsen such qualities of leadership at the very moment they were most needed.

The day Fred Rentschler and I walked in on him, we found him leaning over a plain table pawing around among some engine parts with George Mead and Henry Crane. "Uncle Henry" Crane, one of the great engineers of the automotive industry, had been called in for a conference over the failures of the Allison liquid-cooled engine. While Fred and I cooled our heels waiting for experts to decide upon what design changes were necessary to make the Allison run, before they could discuss policy with us, we thought we saw a certain irony in the situation. For the Allison engine was the power plant that had taken the business away from our 1830 engine in the critical months of 1939 when that one contract meant so much to Pratt and Whitney.

When, finally, it came our turn, we broke the news to Bill Knudsen that, with the completion of the new American addition in Hartford, we would reach a saturation point in Hartford and must look elsewhere for new facilities. Bill knew that Wright Aeronautical planned to build a big new shop somewhere in Ohio and presumed, of course, we would go and do likewise, but when we explained the differences in our two situations, he understood. Wright Aero had been formed out of the consolidation of two big engine companies, Curtiss and Wright, and had more topside staff than Pratt and Whitney. Guy Vaughan was still its president, but Don Brown had died. Now when we mentioned licensing the automotive companies, Bill's first question was who did we have in mind. When we told him Ford, he at first shook his head, but when we stressed the point that selling Uncle Henry was his job and that no one except he and George Mead could do it, Bill Knudsen reluctantly agreed to try.

And Bill and George succeeded. Within a few days we received word that Ford Motor would send a group of shopmen to look over the job and see what could be done. Bill Knudsen, familiar with the Ford setup, had suggested that the machinery in the great Ford tool room, along with some six thousand men employed there, would take the Pratt and Whitney job in its stride. To automotive men, the aircraft industry still looked something like the ancient "carriage trade," and they discounted our insistence that our standards of quality and precision were not easily come by in the mass-production industries.

Edsel Ford and Charles Sorenson met with Fred Rentschler and me in the boardroom in East Hartford. Sorenson did most of the talking, though Edsel Ford was president of the company. A rough-and-tumble shopman of the Ford school of give and take, Sorenson wasted few words. His men had looked the shop over and found nothing complicated about it—nothing they didn't savvy. The machine tools seemed standard and the processes excellent. At first his boys had thought the job looked easy, but the more they had seen of our precision, the more they had become impressed with the task before them. At first they had thought we might be overdoing the quality but after a look at the test-shed running and studying the high demands for durability and dependability, they had changed their minds. They realized it was a tough racket but were prepared to go ahead on two conditions.

First, they would have to adopt our technique in every detail and even have to build a complete new aircraft-engine shop; the idea that their tool room would serve was fantastic, the machines wouldn't do at all. Second, they would have to have access to our suppliers and subcontractors for parts; they could not find other sources of supply. He presumed, of course, that we would give them every assistance and even detail our foremen and leading men to duty in the Ford shops as necessary.

Sorenson's requirement as to our suppliers posed a problem; most of them were already overloaded. Some like Wyman Gordon, of Worcester, source of our crankshaft and other forgings, were already suppliers to the automotive industry, and could shift their production from autos to aircraft. This had been a long-time feature of our war plans and it applied to many of our parts. On the others we would share the output with Ford and join him in creating new sources. With that decision we all shook hands and it was a deal.

One thing that had impressed the Ford people was the vast difference between the aircraft and automotive processes. Our production was based on the use of standard machine tools; we had few of the special single-purpose machines designed for low-cost volume production of automobiles. Our practice had been deliberately adopted for several reasons. In expanding for war-emergency production we could expect machine tool builders rapidly to expand delivery of standard machines, where special machines would require much longer. Again, whereas automotive production could be standardized for reasonable periods, in aircraft engines we must be able to incorporate every new design change without seriously retarding production. To accomplish this, we had fitted special jigs and fixtures to our standard machines; for a design change we could scrap the fixtures but keep the machines running. No such flexibility as this could be had with the special machines of the automotive shops, and Sorenson's crew had spotted this right away. In fact, if anyone thought we could learn much about production from the automotive boys, he soon found it was the other way around. They learned from us our secret of aircraft war production, the revolutionary idea of flexibility in volume.

Along with this idea we had developed the aircraft-type assembly of components. Instead of using a conveyer to regulate production rates, we used it to transport materials to the assembly points. Here the workers built up complete units or subassemblies and inspected them on the spot. Aside from the flexibility thus introduced, the idea had an impact on our production workers. We did away with the deadly monotony of repetitive processes, by feeding to the operators such precisely machined parts that even the unskilled could assemble finished devices and test their functioning. And now as we lost our experienced workers to the armed forces and began replacing them with recruits from the white-collar trades, we found this gave a tremendous boost to shop morale. In the development of this process, I found myself thinking frequently of the scene in Charlie Chaplin's picture where he finally uses both hands and both feet to feed nuts and washers into the ever-moving and compelling assembly.

Now after Ford had broken the ice, Bill Knudsen began bringing in other automotive plants to help us. The great Buick and Chevrolet companies of General Motors joined up, followed soon by Nash. After Curtice of Buick and Coyle of Chevrolet and Mason of Nash had worked out general principles with our top management, the jobs were taken over by the keen shopmen who had made all those organizations great. In some cases our new allies took on responsibilities for Hamilton-Standard Propellers and, in the case of Nash, they even went into production on helicopters when, later on, we faced that new demand. Chance Vought teamed up with Goodyear Rubber and others, on the licensing of product and every division of United spread out all over the country to bring in competent suppliers, large and small.

Meanwhile, after Bill Knudsen had set up the aircraft program and George Mead had turned it back to the armed forces for administration, we ran into stormy weather on the matter of deliveries. The schedules set up by the Army and Navy were fantastic. Among other things, the two services had long neglected to buy engines and propellers for training planes and now, of course, immediate delivery of these was called for. Our plants had been tooled for foreign account on the 1,000-hp 1830's, and the trainers called for 400-hp Wasp Jrs. for which we had no jigs or fixtures in quantity. Save for our flexible-production scheme, this problem would have thrown us for a loss, and even then we had to hustle to retool. Before we had learned the rudiments of the expanded program, the politicians had begun scrambling for cover. Even some of our military friends began casting about for excuses to blame the manufacturers for their own shortcomings. Newspaper columnists and radio commentators who had previously castigated us as war mongers now began screaming "too little and too late."

One of the most acid of these, Fulton Lewis, Jr., made a special trip to Hartford to give his public an on-the-spot disclosure of the shortcomings at United Aircraft. His Hartford outlet then was WTHT, *The Hartford Times*, whose publisher, Francis S. Murphy, was familiar with our problems "Over East," as we say up here. Frank suggested that Fulton Lewis call on me, and I, all unsuspecting, gave him a personally conducted tour of the shops and then, back in my office, told him some of our problems. Fulton Lewis, surprised by what he saw, asked me if I would go on the radio with him that night. Afterward, he sold the National Association of Manufacturers on his idea of sending a group of commentators of press and radio on a nation-wide tour of factories to learn the truth about "too little and too late."

As I came to know some of the radio commentators, I was impressed by the skill with which some of them dug the germ of the news out of the ruck and got it over to their listeners. After Cedric Foster left Hartford for Boston to take over his spot on Mutual, he made it a habit to call his old friends for their slants on spot news. My experience with Admiral Reeves having taught me to delve for fundamentals in strategy and tactics, I was able to give Cedric some slants on the progress of the war. I was always impressed by the way in which he put his finger on the key items and summarized the situation succinctly and competently.

Our rate of production was largely dependent upon things outside our control. Both Army and Navy made contracts with us and each administered his own business in his own peculiar way. Each maintained a staff of inspectors at our plants, men who sometimes liked to show their authority over us and to put each other on the spot. Each specified the accessories to our equipment according to his own fancies, and even specified details. On this matter of accessories, the British and French had their own ideas, and in some cases these differed from either Army or Navy. A single model of our engine might have as many variations as there were customers to buy them or airplanes in which to install them, and the permutations and combinations ran into complications of all sorts. In an effort to correct some of this, I used the delivery schedule as a lever.

I agreed to accept their fantastic schedules *in toto*, provided three requirements were met: First, one of the services would handle all contracts for our company and administer them for all the others; second, all the services would standardize their accessories and attachments as well as their specifications so as to simplify models; third, the service administering the contracts would require its inspectors to do all those reasonable things intended to expedite deliveries according to the terms of the contracts and its specifications, rather than operate as an obstacle. To the degree that any or all of these requirements were not met, we now submitted delayed delivery schedules to correspond with each degree. Under this pressure, the services agreed to divide the two engine companies; Pratt and Whitney became the charge of the Navy.

It was when we came to prices for engines that we ran into trouble. After Jack Homer had discussed the problem with BUAERO as to details, J. F. McCarthy and I went to Washington to face the issues with Comdr. L. B. Richardson, then in charge of Procurement. This was not the Captain Dick Richardson of the big-boat formula fame, but a younger Dick with whom I had flown in the service. He knew his business and had positive ideas based on wide experience. On contracts calling for such large volume, the Bureau would expect a far lower price than any we had quoted—and in principle it was right. Our problem was that, pending expansion of the shop, the training of new operators, the testing of tools, and all the other problems of getting into production, we would run into high costs. That had been our experience during the expansion periods with the French and British contracts and now with the likelihood that we would lose even some of our key men to the armed forces, we could expect spoiled work and scrap to skyrocket costs. No one could guess when costs could be brought into line, and it seemed almost impossible to arrive at a price agreeable to both sides.

And this problem of price might have delayed negotiations interminably had we not taken an important decision to break the deadlock. This decision was based on long experience in business for government account and on a background of events that have been herein related. It dated back to that provision in the Air Corps Act of 1926, in which we granted the government the right to keep cost inspectors in our plant. To break the impasse we now proposed that if BUAERO would establish fixed prices on our contracts on the basis of our earlier experience, we would undertake voluntarily to reduce future invoice prices on products yet to be shipped, to the end that we would never accumulate any excessive profit. In other words, since neither we nor the Bureau could stand any future criticism on profits, we would voluntarily renegotiate ourselves to avoid excessive profit. The Bureau's resident cost inspectors, with access to all our books, would furnish the data on which the Bureau could judge the reasonableness of our performance, and we would abide by their judgment.

This fateful decision removed the last obstacle and cleared the right of way to the high ball. The remaining problem was to settle upon a sound principle for determining fair profit. During the busy year 1940, one which could be taken as indicating the return which a plant of our character could earn under other than wartime conditions, we had earned $12,000,000 with a plant provided by our own capital, on sales made of our own initiative, and on shipments that included practically no business with the United States government. If now we were to freeze our annual net earnings at that figure no matter how our sales might soar nor how our plant might be increased at public expense, we would be stabilizing our earnings at an experienced level that seemed capable of justification from the points of view of the stockholder and the public. If in this process we could earn that return and still pay our employees reasonable wages and salaries, then we would be discharging our responsibility to all concerned.

As a measure of the effectiveness of this principle we may have recourse to an incident that occurred some months later, when production had begun to roll and costs had cascaded to unprecedentedly low levels. After assembling the figures, we had advised the Bureau formally that, effective at the beginning of the next quarter, we would reduce invoice prices below the contract fixed prices by a certain figure per engine calculated to avoid any accumulation of excessive profits. The total relinquishment of potential profits was calculated to amount to approximately $10,000,000. Meanwhile, we had adjusted wages and salaries on a merit basis for all except top executives. On the day this news appeared I was making one of my customary tours through the shop when one of the workers detached himself from a big Bullard machine and headed out to cut me off in the aisle.

He was a big brute with beetling black eyebrows and a sullen mouth, yet as he caught up with me the hard look melted away before a big grin and he stuck out a grimy fist.

"Mister," he said, gripping my hand in his big paw, "I'd go to hell for a company that won't profiteer. And, mister," he added, "that goes for a lot of other guys in this shop, too."

Despite the fact that the Air Corps Act of 1926 had made provision for this type of profit control, Congress had passed an amendment to the Vinson-Trammel Act in 1934, imposing a further statutory limit on profits under contracts for shipbuilding and aircraft production. The wartime Excess Profits Tax purported to further regulate profits but of course only created waste. The manufacturer had to add the tax to the price of his product anyway. The act encouraged management to take decisions which, though unsound economically, looked smart taxwise. Expense accounts chargeable to cost of product soared to heights undreamed of in competitive business. Political in character, uneconomic in principle, the Excess Profits Tax swelled the costs of war while giving a false impression of profit limitation.

The Price Adjustment Act, commonly called "renegotiation," was the really effective means of profit control. Under it, competent price adjustment boards set up the ground rules and administered them with justice to those concerned. Yet this legislation, despite the fact that it was fundamentally in the interest of private industry, was passed with such a flavor of punitive action against business that even the wisest industrialists were tricked into fighting it as just another attack on the profit motive. Too many of us, unfortunately, were so busy hating Roosevelt that we forgot how to use our brains.

Under wise leadership the whole thing could have been turned around into a constructive effort. Had the administration called in representatives from the many industries and put the problem squarely before them along with an appeal to their patriotism, there would have been no problem. Voluntary, industry-wide action would have been forthcoming to keep industry on a sound financial basis, and the example thus set must certainly have brought wage rates within bounds. Had a routine been set up under which the government agreed to utilize privately owned facilities on terms that would compensate owners for their use and restore them as nearly as possible to their original status, details could have been handled by price adjustment boards in a cooperative manner. Punitive laws could have been reserved for culprits, and industry would have helped police the economy.

My own convictions as to the efficacy of voluntary processes stem out of experiences in two wars. In World War I, Herbert Hoover, relying upon good leadership to prevent shortages, gave a convincing demonstration of what the American people can do voluntarily in such an emergency. In World War II, at the very moment when my company was being frustrated at every turn by arbitrary controls on men, money, machines, and materials, I acted as chairman of the Connecticut State War Finance Committee and saw the people rally to the brilliant leadership of two able young men in the Treasury Department, Ted Gamble and Bob Coyne, who raised billions of dollars that would never have been forthcoming under any compulsion.

CHAPTER TWENTY-EIGHT
OFF THE BEAM

The German attack on Russia immediately converted a lot of former pacifists into bloodthirsty warmongers. With that everybody began trying to get into the act. We, who had once been crucified for warmongering, now found ourselves charged with "too little and too late." The war cry now became "unconditional surrender," a phrase that had a hollow ring to men who had watched Woodrow Wilson end World War I with his "Fourteen Points" by dividing the German people and the German Kaiser.

In this country everybody became overnight an expert on war production and a critic of the professionals. The professionals, unfortunately, must always bear the responsibility for their actions, while their critics can and do speak with the advantage of irresponsibility. The newspapers now began to ballyhoo the "Reuther plan" as the answer to everything and news commentators belabored the ether with a cacophony of approval. From his office in the War Production Board, Bill Knudsen called us on the telephone.

"You know this fellow Reuther?" he inquired, pronouncing the name as if it spelled Rooter.

Yes, we knew about Reuther from the headlines. With his usual flair for publicity, he had crashed the front pages with the bright idea of putting all the machine tools of the automotive industry, now laying off men to convert to war production, into construction of airplanes under the mass-production principle. To an expert like Reuther, the idea of buying new machinery just to build airplane engines smacked of another grab by the bosses. Its reaction on Bill Knudsen had prompted this call for help.

"Well," he said, with that delightful Danish accent, "what are we going to do about him?"

Fred Rentschler thought a moment. "Send him up here," he replied. "We'll take care of him."

And when Walter Reuther arrived at "The Aircraft" in East Hartford, he was mustered into the board room and received by all the principal officers of the company. After he had stated his case bluntly, sparing no wallops at the "carriage trade," we assured him that if he knew where we could get the kind of tools we needed, he was just the man we were looking for. Maybe he had better quit the union and go to work for us. We had combed the countryside for suitable tools but had not been able to find any. As a mechanic, Reuther would know machine tools, and we would like to have his help.

Reuther descended into the shop with our supervisors, who walked him for miles over the entire layout. On his return he pronounced the verdict. The stored machines he'd had in mind were no good for our job, after all. He'd had no idea we were doing a watchmaker's job. What he didn't know was that watchmakers' tolerances were far too crude for the exacting demands of aircraft engines.

After Reuther had gone back to Washington, one of our old-timers lingered a moment in the board room.

"You've got to hand it to that cocky little redhead," he said slowly. "He sure knows publicity."

But aptitude for show business was not wholly monopolized by either labor leaders or politicians; some industrialists got around, too. Notable among these was Mr. Henry J. Kaiser. After the private shipbuilders had developed their new technique of constructing components for assembly in the finished vessel, it was Mr. Kaiser, the dam builder, who caught the public eye as the boss shipbuilder of them all. And his activities were not limited to shipbuilding; he was into everything. After Igor Sikorsky had finally performed the impossible by creating the helicopter, his fame was almost overshadowed by headlines hailing Mr. Kaiser as the great producer of this new contraption. Again, when the German submarine blockade had attained the peak of its effectiveness, it was Mr. Kaiser who crashed the headlines with that hair-raising proposal of his, calling for the construction of 5,000 huge flying boats weighing 500,000 pounds each, with which to leapfrog the German submersibles.

A recognized aircraft constructor with the temerity to point out that no such craft had even been projected, let alone designed or tested experimentally, or that the industrial capacity of the nation had already been stretched to the elastic limit, would put himself in the position of lacking imagination. And when, finally, the tide of public opinion forced the President to place an order for such a craft, the contract was awarded to Howard Hughes, and Mr. Kaiser, having promoted the idea, stepped gracefully aside. The President afterward testified to the power of such propaganda when he told Don Douglas he had felt compelled to award the contract to get Henry Kaiser off his neck.

The appointment of Sidney Hillman as co-chairman with Bill Knudsen on the War Production Board was consistent with the philosophies of a period that held management responsible for production over which labor exercised authority. The idea that labor should earn the right through production rather than the blackjack was too, too old-fashioned. When, therefore, the big unions moved in on the West Coast aircraft companies in an attempt to dictate industry-wide wage rates, Sidney Hillman, after beating the drums to arouse the tribes to the necessary frenzy, summoned leaders of the aircraft industry to Washington for a little "collective" bargaining. The idea, it was said, was "to put the 'C' in 'D.C.'"

At the moment, this looked like but one of the fantasies of that mad era. In retrospect it takes on definite form. We who had created a vital industry were put on the defensive as profiteers by leaders of a publicly supported labor monopoly, itself bent on profiteering. Whatever profit we might be allowed was a matter of law. As suppliers to the government, we were responsible to the people for keeping costs down. The workers, largely unskilled, were being urged by their leaders to slow down, while the same leaders blackjacked the public for higher wages for less work. All this, in the task of making the tools for the public's defense.

The situation, largely chargeable to the Nye investigation and similar episodes, could have been avoided under leadership of a different character. A clear statement of the fundamentals, accompanied by an appeal to industry, labor, and the public, could have resolved the internal conflict into an all-out cooperative effort, but none was forthcoming. The political atmosphere of the time resembled that described by C. W. C. Oman in his book, *The Seven Roman Statesmen*, first published by Edward Arnold & Co., London, 1902. In Rome, the politicians from Tiberius Gracchus to Pompey, who paved the way for the Emperor Julius Caesar, bought the votes of the proletariat with money created by enterprising men and, while they gained fame for themselves, deprived the people of freedom.

The formal meeting took place in an ornate conference room on the fifth floor of the new Social Security Building. We manufacturers, after proving our identities, were shown the entrance to an escalator which we discovered went only as far as the fourth floor. That word "escalator" had been borrowed in war contracts as a means of partial protection against unforeseen wage hikes.

To a large gathering round the council table, Sidney Hillman pointed out that, since collective bargaining in Southern California had broken down, Washington had been forced to settle wages, working conditions, and similar matters—for the entire industry. The decision, it appeared, had already been taken at a high level and we might just as well relax and enjoy it.

Our position was stated by a spokesman who pointed out that if labor would step up its output and reduce costs, the employer could meet the demands out of savings in cost. If, however, government increased labor rates without correspondingly modifying sales-prices, it would bankrupt manufacturers.

Sidney Hillman listened to our point of view with amused tolerance and then played his ace.

"Of course," he remarked, "you are protected by the escalator clause."

Reuben Fleet, of Consolidated, twisted in his chair and swallowed an aspirin tablet.

"When we came up to this fifth floor this morning," he said, "they showed us the escalator. But," he added, wagging a finger in Sidney Hillman's face, "the escalator stopped at the fourth floor."

At this pat retort the contractors gave vent to a whoop that broke up the meeting.

Shortly after President Roosevelt's announcement of his 50,000-airplane program, or the "numbers racket," newspaper headlines flared the story that government had called industry leaders to Washington to tell them off for their crime, "too little and too late." The call brought Phil Johnson from far-off Seattle, Donald Douglas, Bob Gross, and Dutch Kindleberger from Los Angeles, and others from farther or nearer. Phil Johnson, once driven out of air transport, had now been called back to Boeing to build heavy bombers.

But when we manufacturers foregathered together and proceeded to the assigned meeting places, we found the rooms so jammed with sound cameras, klieg lights, and heavy cable, there was room for but a few of the better-publicized culprits. The others watched through doors and windows while big politicos mugged cameras that would flicker their message to the hinterlands. Most of us had to see the newsreels to find out what message it was we had traveled so far to receive.

The problem of how to expand production, train licensees, and meet all Selective Service demands was always with us. For all United Aircraft divisions had accepted the responsibility for servicing in the field all equipment of our design whether manufactured by us or anyone else. This kept hundreds of trained service men in the field, including many in the front lines.

One day I received a visit from my old friend Joe Beach, former mayor of Hartford, once a good citizen but then a major assigned to the Army Personnel Procurement Branch. Joe, who knew our problems, regretfully advised me that he had received orders to recruit, from Pratt and Whitney, several hundred men conforming to a specification that described our best-trained field-service men, specialists who could be replaced only with the greatest difficulty. Joe tried to soften the blow by saying the men would be immediately commissioned captains or colonels or something. The Army would not take "no" for an answer; it was come across or else.

In this tough spot, I phoned for "Tiny" Flynn, our service manager, and with Joe listening asked him how many of his staff had been inducted into the Army and what the Army had done with them. The answers were "plenty" and "K.P." or "latrine duty." I then asked Tiny if he had their present addresses, and when Tiny answered in the affirmative, Joe grinned and walked out. Later he confessed to having never sprung one of these men out of "K.P."

After the Jap sneak attack on Pearl Harbor I called on my old friend Admiral Reeves in Washington to get his slant on what had happened. The admiral, now retired, had been recalled to active duty and assigned to the Navy Department in charge of Navy lend-lease. Always an Anglophobe, he there tried to keep our English cousins within reasonable bounds. Considerably older now, the admiral was said to require two traffic lights to get across the expanse of Constitution Avenue, but the old spirit flamed.

"The one thing the administration needed to bring the people into the war on the side of the British," he explained, with that sweeping gesture of his, "was Pearl Harbor. Who could have expected them to be so dumb as to play right into our own hand? Our big surprise wasn't Pearl Harbor; what defeated us was that the Japs could be so dumb."

After the attack, the admiral was ordered to Pearl Harbor as a member of the Roberts Board to investigate the efficacy of the Japanese assault under a strategic concept which the admiral had conceived but his contemporaries had not understood.

Following Pearl Harbor, aircraft production shifted to full throttle. Under Bill Knudsen's leadership, Ford, Buick, Chevrolet, and Nash created new facilities and shipped United products. Wright Aeronautical first built a huge plant near Cincinnati and then drew Studebaker and Chrysler into the complex. At United we stepped employment up to 75,000 and thought we had attained our peak production. Then we were called to Washington and told to build a new plant somewhere out west, one bigger than the Hartford establishment. This looked at first like the straw to break the camel's back, yet Jack Horner discovered an ideal plant site in Kansas City, Missouri.

In undertaking this job for BUAERO, we pointed out that we had no funds of our own with which to finance either construction or operation. We therefore suggested that we take the job on without profit to ourselves. The plant could be constructed by the Defense Plant Corporation under our plans and, when it came to operations, the Navy could put a disbursing officer at Kansas City who would pay the vouchers and invoices certified to him by our manager and approved by the Navy inspector. This was a procedure we had tested in Canada where James Young, president of our Canadian Pratt and Whitney, had been called on to build a propeller plant in Montreal.

Under that program His Majesty's Government had deposited funds in the local bank which were disbursed by His Majesty's disbursing officer in payment for services and materials approved by His Majesty's inspector. And if His Majesty's inspector elected to reject work in process, or exercise any other authority commonly assumed by government inspectors everywhere, then it was His Majesty's hard luck, not the manufacturer's. In other words, our nonprofit proposal was not entirely altruistic; we were also concerned with avoiding losses.

But now it developed that we must be allowed to earn some profit, in order to be able to absorb items of cost which one inspector or another might not allow. Thus when we made a contribution to the local Community Chest drive, and a cost inspector ruled it out as illegal, there must be some place for us to recover the expense. And so we finally accepted a nominal "profit" with the provision that any amount left over after all "illegal" fees had been paid would revert to His Majesty—or rather to Uncle Sam.

But the important fact developed by this transaction was that it was entirely possible for a reputable constructor in wartime to perform a public service without "profit" in the usual sense, and do an outstanding job at it. As a matter of fundamental equity, United Aircraft Corporation risked none of its funds in this effort and was not, therefore, entitled to receive profit for it, especially when its own resources were being fully employed and were earning a fair return. The principle here is that each enterprise engaged temporarily in the war effort has a distinctive problem of its own and no over-all legislation can be written to cover individual cases in an equitable manner. The place to reach decisions on these matters was the Price Adjustment Board.

As between United Aircraft and its licensees, the relationship was one of mutual respect and close cooperation. We spoke the same language and subscribed to the same principles. One could not say as much for relations between the airplane builders and the automotive industry. One day Dutch Kindleberger trumpeted a blast, pooh-poohing the automobile manufacturers as significant producers of airplanes, an outburst that threatened to revive the ancient feud between the mass production industry and the "carriage trade." This snort coincided with the mailing of a letter I had written to President Harlow Curtice of the Buick Division, complimenting him on the job Buick had turned in by constructing a new engine plant near Chicago, and getting it rolling. In reply to my letter Mr. Curtice later used a pat phrase which seemed appropriate to an address I was scheduled to deliver before the annual meeting of the Union League Club in Chicago.

I therefore suggested to the Union League dinner committee that they invite Mr. Curtice to sit at the speakers' table so that I might make acknowledgment of the Buick performance. The address was being broadcast over a nationwide hookup and I had taken for my title "The Fundamentals of Freedom." I reviewed the airplane story and took as my theme the idea that the magic of the aircraft performance lay in the creative power of individual freedom. And when the time came to quote the Curtice letter, I read it verbatim:

"I believe," read the letter, "that the people of this country will be happy to know that we manufacturers can cooperate in a crisis, as effectively as we are accustomed to compete in normal times."

In order to simplify the Pratt and Whitney problem, we had taken certain decisions with respect to standardizing our line of engines. First of all, we had definitely scrapped the abortive liquid-cooled program and had ceased to produce certain air-cooled models. With this behind us, we now faced a critical situation that threatened to negate some of our efforts along this line. Back in the late 'thirties, Bill Patterson, president of United Air Lines, had asked us to assist him by making a study of a completely new airplane, capable of coast-to-coast flight with two stops en route, and having such economic characteristics as would make it a great advance in air transportation.

We had studied the problem along the lines followed in developing the Pan American Clipper series, and had forced ourselves to conclude that we would need an engine somewhat larger than our popular 1830. The airplane would be a four-engined job carrying approximately forty passengers and would, at current rates for mail pay and passenger fares, be very attractive to all the airlines. We had recommended to "Pat" that he turn the study over to one of the established airplane companies with plenty of experience in producing transports. Pat had interested Don Douglas in the project, and Don had brought the other airlines into the picture with the idea of making the airplane a joint project. One ship had been built but when no production orders were forthcoming, and the armed forces had shown no interest, the project had lain idle.

Shortly after the outbreak of the war, the Army had issued orders to halt all production of transports, a mandate that was revoked only after a Congressional delegation had intervened. Later, in a quick turnabout, the Army tried to take over the airline transport system intact. Yet even after it had absorbed nearly half of the airplanes in service, along with a large number of key men, the commercial airlines stepped up their plane utilization to the point where they were carrying more passengers than ever before but with half the equipment. On January 19, 1942, the Navy organized the Naval Air Transport Service, or NATS, and on June 1, the Army followed with the Air Transport Command, or ATC. Out of the confusion as to the functions of air transport, these two military services emerged to become indispensable to the prosecution of the war.

After this, the Douglas four-engined transport project was revived and rushed into volume production. Almost overnight, Army and Navy C-54's, and the commercial version, DC-4's, began winging all over the world to carry important people and critical materials to meet desperate situations. Now as this service expanded, it hurdled the submarine blockade and became in fact the safest means of transport, as well as the most expeditious. Of all the various world services, that across the Himalayan Hump became the best known, but the over-all performance of the military air-transport services and the commercial operators was so outstanding as to lead to the conviction by many that economic air transport had arrived.

In United Aircraft, we lived in mortal terror of a sudden cessation of hostilities which, like that following the Armistice, would lead to disorderly reconversion, and the extinction of the private aircraft-manufacturing industry. For by now we were blown up so far beyond any size warranted by our own resources or possible for postwar production that we could not possibly survive the deflation. As a hedge against this debacle, we decided our only recourse was to build new engines as the basis for new and more economical commercial aircraft which would replace the war-surplus DC-4's and put the airlines in position to make money under peacetime conditions. In face of the feeling of certainty among our engineers that they just could not undertake any further developments with their current war load, management took responsibility for the decision and we set up the project.

With a view to strengthening our research division we made a number of changes. Frank Caldwell moved over from Hamilton-Standard. My old friend Dr. Lucke, now retired from active teaching but very much alive to new developments, joined John Lee on a consulting basis. To utilize the experience and facilities of scientific institutions, we farmed out numerous research projects pertaining to jet propulsion. As a final accomplishment, we enlisted the help of Charles A. Lindbergh.

After President Roosevelt had refused Lindbergh's offer to serve in the Army, rugged old Henry Ford had taken him on as research assistant in Detroit. Here Lindbergh, now fortyish, carried out some very high altitude research under conditions that would have tried the skill of the ablest young pilot. I wanted him in United as a personal aide to help resolve some of the conflicts in the latest revolution in aviation, jet propulsion. Aside from his unexcelled knowledge of aviation and his proved pilot's skill, Lindbergh had the clear incisive mind which we needed so badly in appraising some of the implications of jet power.

For jet propulsion was not quite so simple as the art of building piston engines; such problems as air-cooled versus liquid-cooled or in-line engines versus radials belonged in the kindergarten compared with the complexities of turbo-jet versus turbo-prop. And whereas our air-cooled radials had promised improvement in every factor pertaining to aircraft propulsion, these jets suffered the serious handicap of profligate fuel consumption at the moment when maximum range was a fundamental requirement for air tactics and commercial air transport.

While Lindbergh's sound judgment proved valuable in this role, it was back in his natural character as the Lone Eagle that he went to town for me. On a trip to the Pacific, made at my suggestion with a view to helping the Vought Corsair play its lawful part in carrier operations, Lindbergh flew with a squadron of Army Lightnings on a long-range over-water mission. During this period of island hopping, advances were restricted to the operating radii of escorting fighters. Charles Lindbergh, utilizing some of the savvy that had shown the way from New York to Paris, was able to stretch his own range some five hundred miles. Following his quiet example, the remaining squadrons were soon able to go and do likewise.

He dropped in unobtrusively one day on some marine fighter squadrons left behind to harass by-passed Jap installations on adjacent islands. The marines were accustomed to strafing Jap positions with the guns and light bombs of their Corsairs. Lindbergh quietly constructed a bomb rack for heavy bombs and progressively increased his load from 1000 to 2000 pounds and finally to 3000-pound bombs. When the marines discovered that the Corsair was truly a heavy dive bomber, they demanded a chance to participate in carrier-based close-support operations for amphibious forces. On receipt of this news, the Navy "discovered" the Corsair—so much so in fact that Adm. J. S. McCain, who had earlier confirmed current opinion that Corsairs were too big for carriers, now charged me with losing the war because Vought deliveries were inadequate to his needs over the Japanese island of Honshu.

At home a new threat appeared. A rumor ran like wildfire through the shop that Senator Truman's War Investigating Committee had discovered evidence of fraud in the inspection department of the Wright Aeronautical plant at Cincinnati, and was on the way to investigate. Almost immediately, the news headlines confirmed the story and the fat was in the fire. The reaction on Wright was practically to halt production; at Pratt and Whitney it threatened serious reductions in output, just at the time when demand was at its highest.

The matter of the inspection on a production line is one of its most delicate factors. No specifications or instructions can be written without leaving an element of judgment to an inspection department. All that is needed to freeze up the whole process is the threat of Congressional inquiry, especially when accompanied, as was this case, by jail threats for the guilty parties.

The investigation ran its customary course in the newspapers. The Committee had its innings. No crime was discovered that had warranted such a complete shutdown on deliveries of vital war materials. And after it was over, the manufacturers all over the country picked themselves up out of the gutter and went on with their production.

In light of the production miracles performed by private industry in spite of a militantly unfriendly administration, it is interesting, even though futile, to speculate what might have been done under an inspired leadership that had faith in the cooperative process, understood the technique of the voluntary method, and was determined to give it a friendly opportunity to perform. From the point of view of costs alone, results would have been startling. The impact on the human spirit would have been far-reaching. Too many of us functioned under little more inspiration than that associated with pride in craftsmanship. I had witnessed the magic that can be worked by inspiring leadership while under Admiral Beatty's command in the Grand Fleet. As World War I dragged to a close, two facts had become clear. Despite all the bloody trench warfare along the Western Front, victory would again rest with the nation which held command of the sea. In the existing stalemate, with the Hun unwilling to risk action, ultimate victory would crown the head of the fleet commander who displayed the best leadership; it was all a matter of morale.

It is now part of history that Beatty, himself a hard-riding fox hunter, succeeded in bringing his command to the peak of its fighting efficiency at the precise moment German sailors selected to mutiny. I had got an insight into Beatty's mind one day just prior to the Armistice when he had called me aboard the *Queen Elizabeth* to compliment me on some verses I had published in *The Arklight*, our ship's paper, under the title, "When the Grand Fleet Goes to Sea." On the settle before the open coal fire in his cabin, Admiral Beatty summed up a discourse on leadership.

"I appreciate the tribute in your verses," he had said, "because morale is the first responsibility of the leader and my every conscious and subconscious act has been directed toward maintaining high morale here in the fleet."

As United Aircraft spilled over into every vacant loft in the Hartford area and then expanded into huge satellite plants in Connecticut, Rhode Island, and Massachusetts, morale became my first responsibility. In order to indoctrinate our many new supervisors in our underlying philosophies, we organized seminars and conducted classes in leadership. In these I personally made it clear that United management had no faith in "shovership"; we would stand or fall on leadership.

CHAPTER TWENTY-NINE
FOR SURVIVAL

In the anteroom to the office of the Secretary of the Navy, Fred Rentschler and I waited our turn. A stream of visitors, mostly naval officers of high rank, swept in and out of the sanctum. The men who were furnishing the leadership for this war were contemporaries of mine back in those brave days at the turn of the century when Pax Britannica still reigned and when the chances for professional advancement or even a career looked slim indeed. Now as they moved in and out, many paused to greet us and say a word of congratulation on our industry's production miracle. Meanwhile, we wondered what the secretary might have in store for us.

Jim Forrestal sat behind his desk, taking a telephone call. As we took chairs in front of him, I glanced around at the flag-draped room and its collection of trophies. Jim had made a bid to refurnish the long room, decorating the walls with blow-up photos and seagoing mementos but even a powerhouse like Jim could not dispel the musty odor of the temporary structure or paint out its shabbiness. By 1945 that collection of shacks had served twenty-five years and seen two world wars, and it bid fair to go on indefinitely. Jim hung up the telephone, flicked a switch to his "intercom-squawker," barked a sharp order at the answering voice, and then turned to us.

James Forrestal, like Fred Rentschler, was a Princeton man. Curious how you can spot the stamps of Yale, Harvard, Princeton, Dartmouth, and other Ivy League colleges. Schools like this leave as much of an imprint upon their alumni as do West Point and Annapolis. Jim was a close-knit, clean-cut, youngish fellow, dark-complexioned, with the muscles of an intercollegiate boxer bulging around his shoulders and upper arms. A man of few words, he packed almost as much meaning in them as did Fred Rentschler.

"I am going to tell you fellows something, now," he began, "and if you repeat it, I'll deny I ever said it." He paused to pull open the upper left-hand drawer of the desk and remove a packet of gum. After offering us some, he wadded the wrapper of his own piece, flicked it into the wastebasket, and went on.

"You fellows are swamping us with your production," he said. "Engines, propellers, and airplanes are running out of our ears. The time has come to slow down."

I couldn't resist a crack. "So it's now 'too much and too soon.'"

Fred Rentschler looked serious.

"Jim," he began, "that remark of yours gives us the opening we have been waiting for. We have been worried about the same thing for some time, but with the criticism that has been leveled at us, we just didn't think it was time to bring the matter to you." He lighted a cigarette.

"Of course you know," he said, "that the aircraft industry has been blown up like a balloon. Our present output is all out of proportion to our own meager resources. If there should be a sudden cessation of hostilities, as in World War I, and that seems highly probable, and if no more preparation has been made for such an event than now exists, the whole aircraft industry will be wiped out in a matter of days. If any company could survive such a catastrophe, it would be United Aircraft, for we have been ultraconservative and taken every possible precaution against just this contingency, but I promise you even United would go out like a light." Jim Forrestal sat silent, watching Fred as he went on.

"We have made a quick study of our own situation," he said, "and concluded that, upon the sudden termination of existing war contracts, which under the law occurs immediately upon the cessation of hostilities, we could not complete the mechanics of paying off our employees in time to prevent liquidating our resources. The pay roll is so big," he added, "and the job of paying off is so complex, that the outgo would break us before we could finish the task." He paused.

"To sum up our position," he concluded, "the disorderly reconversion that seems sure to follow this war will wipe us out even more completely than it did after the Armistice. In our opinion," he added, "it's up to you military fellows to do something about it."

Jim Forrestal nodded. "I go along with you," he said, "up to the last statement. There is nothing the Army and Navy can do about this. We are public servants and, even under Franklin D. Roosevelt, subject to the people's will. The only people that can do anything about it," he added, "are you men. Your industry has got to carry its story to the public." Again his telephone rang; again Jim handled the call. He turned back to us.

"Your industry," he went on, dead-pan, "is the choicest collection of cutthroat competitors in the country. Maybe it's because pioneers still manage it. But if you pioneers expect to survive," Jim went on, "the industry must unite and do battle for its existence. Frankly, I doubt if anyone can unite the aircraft industry, but someone has got to try it." He glanced my way.

"If anyone can do it," he added, putting a finger on my knee, "you can."

He might as well have landed a fist on my chin. What he meant was that having come out of the Navy, and escaped the early personal rivalries, I was freed of a handicap.

Even as Jim had talked, orderlies had entered the room and begun shifting chairs, lining them up in an arc around the secretary's desk. Through the open door I caught glimpses of the uniforms and gray thatches of ranking department heads, standing by for a council meeting. As Fred and I stood up to leave, Jim walked us to the door.

"Why not stay for the council meeting?" he asked me, as we shook hands. "You'll see a lot of old shipmates."

"Thanks," I replied, "I guess we'd better go home and digest what you've just told us."

Back in Hartford, the four members of United's war council gathered around the long table in the board room where Fred Rentschler had his office. On the walls hung the portraits of men who had helped make the company—men like Chance Vought, George Wheat, George Mead, and Don Brown.

After discussing the problem Jim Forrestal had put up to us, we agreed that this new responsibility would require rearrangement of our own topside organization. An effort to organize the aircraft industry for a public relations effort just didn't fit in with the detailed administration of any single company. I would have to relinquish my job as chief executive.

And so I came face to face with the decision that I had known to be inevitable the moment Jim Forrestal put the finger on me. I had been in at the inception of Pratt and Whitney and United Aircraft. I had managed three of its four divisions and participated in vital decisions as to the other. I had helped hold it together in the trying days following the Black and Nye investigations, and had been its chief executive through the critical phases of the war expansion. Now that we were over the hump, I would have to give up my cherished title of president in order to try to help the company to survive.

As a matter of fact, we had long discussed the possibilities of a reorganization following the war. We well knew that the reconversion job would try the nervous and physical capacity of a man younger than any of us four seniors, and that our duty to the company demanded that we start bringing juniors along. We four would graduate into the category of elder statesman while my successor took over the reins. The logical man was Jack Horner, of Pratt and Whitney. Ray Walsh and I would fleet up to vice-chairmen and Jack in due course would become president. Meanwhile I would assume responsibility for "general-industry" matters and retain supervision of research. Jack would take over operations, and Fred would continue to exercise authority over the business affairs of the company. Ray Walsh, who had a unique capacity for handling policy, personnel, and legal matters, would continue on his course.

With these decisions reached, we began a discussion of the course to be followed in getting our story before the public. Had there been some independent aviation organization capable of doing the job, we should have looked to them, but under the circumstances, it seemed clear that we must depend upon our trade association, the Aeronautical Chamber of Commerce, in Washington. The war production councils, then functioning effectively, would automatically disband upon cessation of hostilities; the Aeronautical Chamber must be rejuvenated.

Discussion of the course to be followed brought out a key suggestion by Raycroft Walsh. Ray had been in the Air Corps in Washington during the Moffett-Mitchell dogfight and had participated in the hearings before the Morrow Board. Having in mind the constructive influence of the Board, he now suggested that we campaign for a new public air policy commission.

Fred Rentschler rather pooh-poohed the suggestion but, when I supported it, finally agreed wholeheartedly. Here was a little indicator of how difficult it might prove to sell the idea to the company presidents; if Fred Rentschler needed selling, how about the others less profound in their mental processes than he? We now decided that I should make a swing around the circuit to appraise the states of mind and try to plant the idea before we committed ourselves irrevocably to changes in our own organization that our directors might not approve. On our board, aside from the principal officers of the company, we had enlisted the help of several distinguished "outside directors." Joseph P. Ripley, president of the New York investment house of Harriman Ripley, had been active in the original incorporation of United Aircraft and Transport. Harry G. Stoddard, president of Wyman Gordon, had long served on our executive committee. Morgan B. Brainard, president of Aetna Life and Affiliated Companies, was a man of broad wisdom and wide business experience. Francis W. Cole, a prominent Hartford lawyer and later board chairman of the great Traveller's Insurance Company, brought us mature counsel. Mr. Peter M. Fraser, later president of the Connecticut Mutual Life Insurance Company, completed our coterie of able men. And if at times the technicalities of our business confused them somewhat, nonetheless, their unexcelled fundamental business knowledge was a priceless asset to the company. We outlined the plan to them but decided to defer final decision until I could check industry sentiment and determine if the Forrestal suggestion could command its support.

This check took me westward to Los Angeles, the center of the airframe section of aircraft production. As our representative in that territory, Russell R. Vought, younger brother of Chance Vought, had long maintained an office in Beverly Hills. Russ had gone west while still a young man, and founded his own business in San Francisco. Then back in 1928, when we had equipped the *Langley* with the new Corsairs, and especially the single-float amphibians, he had agreed to represent Chance Vought Aircraft on the West Coast on a part-time basis. Now he made his home in Beverly Hills and had a bungalow in Palm Springs. Arrived in Beverly Hills, I called up John G. Lee, the manager of the West Coast War Production Council, and asked him over to the office with a view to getting his appraisal of the problem.

John Lee, through his close association with the presidents of the West Coast companies, was able to give me an authoritative estimate of the sentiment out there. The presidents, he thought, were too much engrossed with their own immediate problems to become interested in the long-term difficulties. They were aware of the threat to survival but not as yet concerned with it. Like many other business chief executives, they were groggy and punch-drunk, and you couldn't blame them. As a reward for their pains they had found themselves characterized as munitions racketeers, war profiteers, and merchants of death. Now, through production miracles, they had given the lie to their detractors. The profit motive no longer provided an incentive to creative endeavor.

"Take Mr. Douglas, for instance," John summed up. "He is the key to the West Coast situation. If you could enlist his support, you could also get the help of the others; without it you'd be licked before you started. *Time* magazine recently quoted him as saying he had the perfect postwar plan: 'lock the door and throw away the key.' Of course Mr. Douglas didn't say that, even though he may have thought it, but the quote is significant."

Ever since that day in Jim Forrestal's office, I had been mulling over an idea evolved one evening at Admiralty House, Bermuda, where my wife and I had been the dinner guests of Vice Adm. Sir Charles E. Kennedy-Purvis, RN, K.C.B., Commander in Chief of British Forces in the Western Atlantic. As Comdr. Charles E. Kennedy-Purvis, Executive Officer of the light cruiser *Southampton*, I had known him well in the old Grand Fleet days. "K-P," as we called him, had recently been advised of his pending assignment as First Deputy Sea Lord, at the Admiralty, London, where he would be charged with responsibility for recreating the British carrier force after the decline suffered under the Air Ministry. He had asked us down for a visit in order to get my slants on the principles involved.

My idea had first come to me the evening following the German surrender in World War I when several of us wardroom officers had gone ashore to pay a social call on K-P and his wife in their tiny apartment over a cottage in the village of Limekilns. Upon my referring to Beatty's congratulatory signal to the Grand Fleet, K-P had taken pains to remind me that the message had been addressed to the British Empire.

"Beatty," he had said, "was not talking to the fleet but reminding the people that it had been the nine-knot tramps, the rusty colliers, the huge transports, the drifters and trawlers, all the 'Merchant Men' which had kept the Empire lifeline open. These," he had added, "are the backbone of our sea power."

K-P, who like most English officers was much better schooled in public affairs than were we, had gone on to give us a discourse on transportation. From the days of the aborigines' pursuit of game herds, the progress of civilization was marked by the milestones of the development of transport. In America, the railroads had sparked reconstruction after the Civil War by opening up the resources of the West. Following the World War, the automobile would likely perform the same function. Improved transportation had always increased the number of persons who could subsist on a given area and had always increased the wealth and living standards of lands in which it had been exploited.

When I had inquired what future K-P foresaw for the airplane he had shaken his head.

"The economics of the thing are all against it," he had replied. "The cost and complication of the airplane are out of all proportion to its limited useful load."

Subsequently, with the coming of age of air transport, I had begun to visualize an analogy between sea power and air power, a line of thinking that had led naturally to Pax Britannica and Pax Aeronautica. About this same time John W. Donaldson published a paper on the same subject. This would become the keynote of the aircraft manufacturing industry's struggle for survival, but first we must establish a wholly new definition of air power. Instead of its being synonymous with air force, the term must incorporate such other elements as aircraft production, airline transport, private flying, finance, public support, in fact everything that helps make a nation strong in the air. While advocating the preservation of our industry, we must predicate the need upon the public interest.

When I outlined this idea to John Lee, his eyes lighted up.

"It will take an idea like that to interest Don Douglas," he said. "Remember," he advised, "Mr. Douglas responds to the eye rather than to the ear."

In order that we might concentrate on this job, the Voughts now suggested that my wife and I join them at their cottage on the desert. Here at Palm Springs, the task was to do a sort of Mahan analysis of air power in history, and boil it all down to the simplest terms. After a lot of head-scratching, pencil-pushing, and earnest discussion, I finally got it in form.

Feeling now the need for the best possible counsel on this important matter, I wangled an invitation from Rear Adm. John H. Towers, then on duty at Pearl Harbor, and hopped out to Honolulu in a Pan American Boeing Clipper that left San Francisco before supper and arrived at Pearl before breakfast next morning.

Curiously enough, Jack had as his guest a young English lieutenant commander of the Royal Naval Flying Service, who had been sent out by my friend K-P to observe American carrier operations. After two decades, he was doing the Godfrey de Chevalier act in reverse.

During my two-day visit at Pearl Harbor, Chester Nimitz, Commander in Chief, entertained at a luncheon for his top commanders who had been called in by air for briefing on the next operation, and he invited me to join the party. As I sat down, the single civilian in a galaxy of top brass, I estimated that the average number of gilt stars among thirty-odd officers must be about two and a half per man. These fellows, all either contemporaries at Annapolis or men with whom I had been shipmates prior to leaving the Navy, had fought through two world wars and participated in world events none had even remotely foreseen.

After a review of my program with Jack Towers and Forrest Sherman, the latter now Nimitz's planning chief, I caught the Clipper back to San Francisco. We had a full load, top brass returning to Washington and young bluejackets returning home on top priority because of illness in their families or other personal difficulties. Arrived back at Beverly Hills in time for lunch, I called Don Douglas on the telephone, and made a date with him for the morrow.

As our company car pulled up at the entrance to Don's plant in Santa Monica, the California sun shown on the camouflaged village, which so completely concealed the sprawling plant that it was hard to find the gate.

Don sat behind the desk in the shadow of his lightproof and soundproofed ground-floor office, and stood up to greet me as I came in. After a few words to state my business, I handed him his copy of the air-power statement and as Don sat down to read it, I opened my copy with a view to pacing his reading. Don Douglas read carefully, noting every word.

"I'll go for this," he said simply, speaking in the soft voice that made it difficult to hear him at times. Then after a moment he added, "What do you want me to do?"

I explained the need for a meeting of our Aeronautical Chamber of Commerce at which the board of governors should adopt the program. We must reorganize the Chamber and give it a set of officers who could direct the program; I suggested that he become chairman of the board of governors. He countered with the statement that this job should be mine, but agreed to accept the vice-chairmanship of the board. I suggested that we borrow John G. Lee from the West Coast Aircraft War Production Council to head up the reorganization of the chamber and, after some consideration, he agreed. We would bring in Clyde Vandenburgh, of the East Coast Council, and Frank Russell, of the National Council, to assist. A meeting of the National Council was scheduled to take place in Los Angeles late in April, 1944, which would be attended by all the company presidents. We would call a simultaneous meeting of the Chamber and put the air-power program before the Board for consideration at that time.

On April 26, 1944, the board of governors of the Aeronautical Chamber of Commerce met in Los Angeles. In presenting the program, still in its tentative typewritten form, I pointed out that this was a preliminary statement and subject to revision by the members. After all, the Constitution of the United States had been no one-man job but the painstaking effort of many men of different minds; we needed the thoughts of everyone on what would prove an important action by the board. A number of constructive suggestions were offered and voted, after which the revision was adopted unanimously. The preamble to the resolution ran as follows:

> The Board of Governors of the Aeronautical Chamber of Commerce of America, in order to "provide for the common defense, promote the general welfare and secure the blessings of Liberty to ourselves and our posterity," and in order to ensure that the airplane which America created shall be used to maintain peace and secure the blessings of peace to mankind, does unanimously recommend the early formulation of an American Air Power Policy under the following guiding principles:

And the essence of these principles was summarized toward the end of the pamphlet in this paragraph.

The public character of aviation imposes upon it a dual role. Commercial companies, to advance their private interests and stimulate technical progress, must compete in the realm of operations. At the same time, they must collaborate in the realm of policy to promote the public interest.

We had naturally expected that when this document was released to the aviation press it would create something of a stir, but in this we were disappointed. After this warning that the idea would need to be sold, even to aviation writers, we began to appreciate the fact that we had a job on our hands. Through Deac Lyman, an old *New York Times* reporter, we were invited to lunch with Arthur Sulzberger and his editors in the executive dining room of the Times Building, where we briefed our situation. The *Times*, always alert to aviation matters, subsequently covered aviation news and handled aviation editorials against the background of the policy. The magazine *Aviation*, whose editor, Leslie Neville, was author of numerous books on aviation, caught the new spirit and developed the theme. Soon all the members of the Aviation Writers' Association took a hand in developing the broad background of air power as a trinity of commerce, industry, and security.

Subsequent events proved that we had acted none too early. Within a matter of weeks, we were haled before a Congressional investigating committee, the War Contracts Subcommittee of the Senate Committee on Military Affairs.

CHAPTER THIRTY
TOWARD PUBLIC INQUIRY

Having developed a certain gun shyness before such Congressional inquiries as the Nye inquisition and the air-mail investigation conducted by Senator Hugo Black, now Mr. Justice Black of the United States Supreme Court, we air craftsmen might have shied away from Senator Murray save for a bit of sage advice given me by Mr. Sam Rayburn, then Speaker of the House. When I called on him for counsel as to how we should proceed with our air-power program, the Speaker offered it as his opinion that we should avoid lobbying as we would a plague. All trade associations were suspect; they usually devoted their energies to the search for special advantage for their clients. And the munitions business was condemned out of hand. Besides, that was the wrong way under any circumstances. Congressmen, the Speaker assured me, were just average people, no wiser, no dumber than anyone else. But there was one thing a Congressman had to understand if he wanted to stay in politics, and that was the will of the people. He thought we had a good case for public approval in our air policy, and he advised following Jim Forrestal's advice and taking it direct to them.

He thought one of the best ways to get our story to the public was to appear at the public hearings held by Congressional committees. These, according to the Speaker, were good sounding boards from which to beam your point of view. Besides, you might actually influence a committee if you had an especially strong case. But it was a mistake to send lawyers or staff members of an association to these hearings. The company presidents should appear themselves; they were more convincing, and Congressmen liked to look them over. They respected men who had won their spurs in competition, especially if they also knew how to stand up and speak their pieces.

"Don't send a boy," the Speaker concluded, "to do a man's work."

By the middle of 1944, with the outcome of the war no longer in doubt, men began worrying about postwar and the inevitable letdown of peace. Nation-wide unemployment was taken for granted, and what to do about it became a live political issue. The aircraft industry, now one of the largest industries in the history of the world and one wholly dependent upon an inflated demand for war materials, seemed headed for the biggest bust imaginable.

And while this was a problem of national interest, it had its focus in Southern California. Thousands of people had left their homes and jobs and migrated toward the setting sun there to do their several bits and incidentally enjoy the climate. Almost immediately, public officials sensitive to the reactions of the working class began proposing legislation to meet the problem; a ticket back home for the dispossessed worker and six months' unemployment compensation were widely advocated. The fact that high wages had been paid them and that the thrifty could probably take care of themselves seemed to have been lost in the shuffle.

Looking back on this situation now, we can see how completely wrong the forecasts were. Most of those workers, having basked in the California sunshine, had already determined to settle there and could not have been driven out by an air raid. Their newly acquired mechanical skills would find ready employment in new industries. The war demand and the "total war" policy had drained all the pipe lines of consumer goods while the cold fear of the 'thirties had frozen the investment market and stopped the normal expansion of housing, plant construction, and so on. What the country really faced was a pent-up demand that would lead to a postwar boom, and a dearth of labor. The automotive industry, for instance, could expect to reconvert to a demand of unprecedented proportions; the aircraft industry, on the other hand, would face an overwhelming war surplus. The problem that faced the country was not that of unemployment; the real job was to keep alive a remnant of vital defense industry.

But this was not the problem before the War Contracts Subcommittee of the Senate Committee on Military Affairs and its chairman, Senator James E. Murray, of Montana. "Full employment" was the war cry of that era, and the C.I.O. echoed it through the halls of Congress. Full employment, it appeared, was the right of every citizen, and the government must guarantee it to him whether he wanted to work or not. Some industrialists applied similar thinking to their corporations; the idea of government-guaranteed corporate social security had prompted the creation of the NRA and the formulation of its monopolistic codes. Now labor unions on the one hand and trade associations on the other vied with each other in bringing pressure to bear on Congress to relieve them from the necessity for struggling to survive.

And so when Senator Murray extended us an invitation to appear at a hearing to be held on July 10, 1944, we decided to conform with the

Speaker's advice. The C.I.O. had tipped its hand in a circular distributed in advance, castigating aircraft manufacturers as profiteers who had averaged as high as 3,000 per cent on war contracts. Since we manufacturers were scheduled to make the first appearance and be followed by the C.I.O., it was a fair guess that we had been selected as whipping boys.

And so our association, using the air policy as its bible, prepared its case with a special slant at this matter of war profits. We divided our presentation into four parts, with a separate witness for each. I was to make the general introduction of the industry viewpoint, and submit our statement of air-power policy. J. C. Ward, president of Fairchild Aviation Corporation and a convincing witness, was to cover postwar national defense and the aircraft industry. Harry Woodhead, president of Consolidated-Vultee Aircraft Corporation, was to discuss the George-Murray bill, manpower demobilization, contract termination, disposal of war surplus, and reconversion. Joseph T. Geuting, chairman of the Personal Aircraft Council of the Chamber, was to discuss the role of personal aircraft in postwar readjustment.

When the hearing opened in one of the large committee rooms of the Senate Office Building, the place was crowded and the press table filled by Washington correspondents attracted by the C.I.O. handout. Senator Murray sat on the dais while the witnesses were called to testify from a table at his feet. This layout put the witness at something of a disadvantage and news photographers sometimes used it to get worm's-eye shots of bigshots looking anything else but. I recalled one taken of a friend of mine in the Black investigation, and widely used by the press, in which my friend, who was really a good egg, looked like nothing so much as a praying mantis.

This inquiry, however, appeared friendly. It wasn't important enough to warrant klieg lights or a radio hookup, but attracted the usual barrage of flash bulbs touched off at the instant best calculated to catch the witness with his mouth open or his guard down.

In my extemporaneous introduction, I pointed out to the Committee that we welcomed this inquiry and especially the Committee's interest in postwar unemployment. We had taken the position early in the war that the government should permit us to earn enough money on war contracts so that we might discharge our responsibilities to employees terminated by the cessation of hostilities. We had had in mind that, by adjusting each case on its merits, and out of funds set aside from earnings for that purpose, the employer could handle the problem with fairness to the employee as well as to the public which, after all, was the customer in this case.

However, Congress had disapproved that procedure and, through the excess profits tax, the Price Adjustment Act, the cost inspection service, and all other controls, had so limited our earnings that we now had no funds available for the purpose. As a matter of fact, our companies had been so blown up by war demands that a sudden cessation of hostilities must inevitably wipe out all our resources before we could reduce our working forces in any orderly manner. In short, our problem was not one of war profits; it was rather a question of how to survive.

But while on the subject of profits, it might be noted that only recently the National City Bank of New York had printed in its *Bulletin* an analysis of profits as a percentage of sales of the several groups of industries doing war work. This report had shown that the aircraft industry ranked lowest of all industries, with a record of approximately 1½ per cent. The same table had revealed that the automotive industry, now busy manufacturing products designed and developed by the aircraft companies, had earned nearly twice as much. This fact had resulted from the automotive industry's better tax base.

Meanwhile, I pointed out, my own company, United Aircraft, had from the beginning voluntarily stabilized its earnings at a figure based on the use of its own facilities and resources prior to the commencement of the United States aircraft production program. All these figures were, however, quite academic; they were simply estimated results of current operations based on an assumption that the war contracts might be terminated in an orderly manner. In the last war, no such thing had taken place; contracts had been closed out so brutally that, according to another National City Bank *Bulletin,* many companies had gone through the wringer and even the strongest, in the number of some sixty-six representative suppliers, had been forced to write down their apparent net worth by approximately one billion dollars, or 50 per cent. Our present "profit" was therefore but a temporary bookkeeping entry; no company could even guess where it would come out unless Congress proceeded with all speed to write new legislation that would facilitate orderly reconversion.

While I developed this testimony, our staff circulated a summary of the figures among the men and women at the press table, some of whom had, no doubt, read the C.I.O. pamphlet charging us with having made 3,000 per cent. C.I.O. figures showed gross profit before taxes as a percentage of net worth and, while accurate enough, manifestly emphasized what wide variations can result from the mere definition of the naughty word "profit."

In continuing my testimony, I went on to point out that the aircraft industry, now the biggest industry, was a vital factor in our domestic economy and that the public interest as well as the worker's interest demanded that we not upset the whole national picture through disorderly or even punitive procedure. By this we did not mean for a moment that our industry should be subsidized in any way; we hated subsidy because it tended to throttle technological progress. We had made rapid strides only because we had had rough going; in our struggle to exist at all we had been forced to conceive and create devices that would otherwise have never seen the light of day. What we asked of the government was that it make up its mind as to what it needed and then let us go back to cutting each other's throats in that exciting way which had kept United States technology in the forefront of world progress.

At this remark, I noted a stir among the newsmen and women; long accustomed to hearing special pleaders demand special privilege, they were taken aback by the aircraft industry's expressed preference for competition. Such unheard-of conduct was news of the "man-bites-dog" variety.

From this beachhead I went on to urge the appointment of a presidential advisory commission on aviation, one like the Morrow Board of 1925. After reviewing some of the background, I pointed out the rapid advances in technology since the day of that report, especially in the key element of air transport. This alone would seem to warrant a reappraisal of air policy, one based on the new concept that air power was not a military striking force but a trinity composed of air commerce, aircraft industry, and the armed service as well as all the other factors that went to make a country powerful in the air. All these factors were mutually interdependent and must be closely integrated if we were to employ our air power to keep the peace. The need for thinking through a new policy based on these ideas was obvious; it concerned government, labor, management—all the elements of the community.

In summing up, I pointed out again that our problem had never been a matter of profits but one of survival and that survival was our immediate concern. However, we were confident that, given an orderly reconversion and the necessary constructive air policy, air power could become the new reagent for keeping the peace of the world and better still, through the medium of improved transport, lead to the era of prosperity so vital to keeping the peace.

Following me, Harry Woodhead gave specific answers to eight questions propounded by the Committee and concerned with the industrial and human aspects of demobilization. Speaking in his clear, strong voice he made a convincing impression. Following Harry Woodhead, Joseph T. Geuting, Jr., submitted a comprehensive summary of things necessary to the orderly development of personal airplanes during the postwar adjustment period. Both Joe Geuting and Carl Ward, who now followed with his presentation, had been selected because of their knowledge of their subjects but even more important because both were good extemporaneous speakers and both had strong convictions as to the soundness of the industry policy. Carl Ward especially handled a complex subject with a knack rare in professional men; he reduced technical jargon to popular language.

At the close of the day, Senator Murray thanked us warmly for our constructive approach to the problem. During the sessions of the following days, Artemus L. Gates, Assistant Secretary of the Navy for Air, endorsed the industry stand. Robert P. Patterson, Undersecretary of War; Charles E. Wilson, executive vice-chairman of the War Production Board; and representatives of the U.A.W.-C.I.O. and I.A.M.-A.F. of L. made recommendations generally in accord with the suggestions of the industry representatives. The C.I.O. barrage on profits broke down against the record established by the industry, and Senator Murray himself later introduced a bill in Congress calling for the appointment of a new presidential advisory commission, like the Morrow Board. However, many critical months must pass before such a board would see the light of day.

Meanwhile, press comment on the hearing was favorable and David Lawrence dug the meat out of the cocoanut in an article in which he said that the aircraft industry had revealed its postwar plan to a startled Congressional committee. The industry, he said, had thought its problem through. And to the surprise of all, it had not asked for subsidy. It had asked only that the government make up its mind what it wanted and leave the rest to competition within the industry.

We drew encouragement from all these events. We knew that Senator Murray was close to the White House and that his introduction of the bill implied at least that the President was not unfavorably disposed to it. For prior to the hearing, Fred Rentschler and I had taken pains to cover this angle, by making a call on John W. Snyder. Mr. Snyder had recently come to Washington at President Truman's request and was destined to do a statesmanlike job in many fields for the Truman administration. We found him well informed on the whole air-power problem and fully prepared to advise the President on the industry's plans to bring the matter before the public. Early in the program we even hoped that the President might appoint the committee himself, even as President Coolidge had done, but now to our surprise we found active opposition in two quarters.

The Assistant Secretary of Commerce for Air, William A. M. Burden, developed no enthusiasm for the idea, and when Don Douglas, Bob Gross, and I called on him one day, he explained why. He felt that the existing legislation on the subject of air commerce was adequate and feared that a protracted public inquiry might hamper things already in the works and thus retard progress. But the big complication we faced came from the Army Air Forces.

The ancient Army-Navy rivalry had not died down under the impact of war but had flared anew and on many fronts. At heart it was the same old dogfight that had engaged Billy Mitchell and Billy Moffett twenty years earlier. The Army Air Force still battled for control of all military aviation, and the Navy scratched gravel to hang onto its own. Within the industry itself, whatever might be our private views, we took no position on the matter. After all it was a private grudge fight between two customers. We had hoped that the Air Force, now that it had won its battle for autonomy and demonstrated its decisive character, would welcome an opportunity to plead its case before a public tribunal. Instead, it resorted to the same tactics Billy Mitchell had used and thus confused the whole matter of air-power policy. The fact was that the Army Air Force, for all the miracles performed by the military air-transport services—managed as it was by personnel from the commercial air-transport lines—still remained blind to the significance of air transport.

In an effort to overcome this resistance we now asked the National Planning Association to study air power, hoping that this distinguished organization might support us with a recommendation for a national air policy board. For the National Planning Association, a private organization comprising men in all walks of life and of all shades of opinion had been organized to study just such problems as ours, namely those of vital import to national policy. Before a matter could be studied at all it must first be passed upon by a tough board of trustees who carefully screened out all subjects not included in its charter. Then after a problem had been accepted for study, it had to be debated by a selected panel in an open forum before which the burden of proof lay upon the proponents. The association finally accepted our request for study and numerous meetings were held under the supervision of competent moderators. Some of the labor representatives on the panel were especially keen, and since the industry's position safeguarded the working man and the public as well as the industry, we found ourselves on the strongest possible grounds.

Our problem lay with some of the many government agencies on the panel, for aviation concerned a whole flock of such agencies, many of whom were naturally more concerned with protecting their vested interests than with advancing the art of aviation as a whole. Debates before the panel helped us to crystallize our own ideas and to adjust them to practical circumstances. When, for instance, the representative of the Director of the Bureau of the Budget questioned the soundness of our view as to the fundamental economics of air power, he started me off on an expedition the results of which startled even our research group.

Having in mind, from my youth in the Northwest, the story of the land-grant railroads, I had begun a search for a factual basis with which to support the air-power theme. I knew that, following the Civil War, the whole force of the United States government had been placed behind the expansion of the railroads as a means of opening up the great West, providing jobs for discharged war veterans, and developing a vast area of rich territory. To encourage this expansion the government had given some 180,000,000 acres of undeveloped land to certain roads and in return had passed legislation requiring the railroads to rebate to the government a percentage of the charge for hauling government freight and passengers. The balance sheet on this project, if one could be found, might prove interesting to the air-transport situation.

Inquiry among railroad operators disclosed no record of the transaction and little interest in it, but research in the government records produced the surprising information that the roads had repaid their debt to the government however one might figure the original land values. If the figure selected was $1.00 per acre, the estimate at the time of the gift, the roads, having at the time of inquiry rebated some $640,000,000, had paid the debt back threefold. If the figure selected was $3.00 per acre, a fair average of the selling price the roads had received for the land, then they had still broken even. In other words, the government had not subsidized the roads with this grant; it had made instead a profitable investment. A short while after this inquiry was made, Congress revoked the land-grant rebates.

Similar inquiry into the air-mail situation now revealed an even more startling figure. At the time of the inquiry, the airlines were still making money. Having lost half of their equipment to the military air-transport services, and having supplied a large part of the operating leadership, they had stepped up their utilization of equipment, and reduced their costs, to the point where they were earning satisfactory profits from mail and passengers without yet having exploited the possibilities of air cargo. Had they been "reasonably regulated" as required by law, they might have continued their record instead of running into serious losses as they have since done. But at the moment of the inquiry, the Post Office Department could make the proud boast that receipts by the government from the sale of air-mail stamps alone had already exceeded payments made to the operators for carrying the mails, even after a heavy loading of Post Office Department overhead. The United States government was not subsidizing the airlines with mail pay; it was taking a nice profit from that operation. Post Office subsidies were granted for several different classes of mail by palpably low rates but the special air-mail stamp carried its own freight.

And so, out of the need for justifying our theory of air power, we discovered the greatest possible justification of it, namely, its economic soundness. The Post Office Department, like all government departments subjected to the handicaps of political patronage, was notoriously uneconomical, yet the air-mail operation could support a large slice of this excessive overhead and still show the department a profit on the operation. The railroads argued that the hidden subsidy of government airports and airways nullified the arguments, yet there was a long history of similar government support for highways and waterways. Meanwhile the Post Office subsidized directly the carriage of periodicals, and took serious losses on rural delivery and other classes of service. Here was a fact of profound importance to our air-power program: air mail was already self-sustaining and if subsequently the situation changed, losses could not be charged to air mail as such, but must be credited directly to inept management; that is, government regulation.

This raised the whole question not alone of the reasonableness of the "reasonable regulation" but also of the principle itself. There is nothing in the history of the railroads to support the principle; cutthroat competition could hardly have been more disastrous than the present regulation. When, earlier, the railroads had found themselves face to face with the penalties of their own mistakes, they had sought to lean on government; they had asked for regulation and they had got it. Of course they had sacrificed their birthright for a mess of pottage because, having eased the economic pressure of the struggle to survive, they had removed the chief incentive to technological development.

This point was admitted by Fred Williamson, then president of the New York Central, when he and I discussed the matter on a salmon-fishing trip to Anticosti Island. It had started as a bantering argument at a time when the New York Central was giving consideration to a suggestion that the railroad start its own airline. After I had set forth the case for air transport, Fred Williamson looked off down the Jupiter River and remarked in all earnestness:

"You know, if the railroads had invested in engineering all the money they have spent seeking to gain legislative advantage over motor and air transport, we'd be in a far better competitive position today."

This whole matter of "reasonable regulation," so critical with respect to a healthy air-transport industry, the key to air power, was one we had hoped to have studied by our air policy board, but in that hope we were disappointed. The National Planning Association issued a fine report on air-power policy, but certain government agencies blocked its support of our recommendation for the appointment of a presidential aviation commission. Under the circumstances we were not surprised when the President withheld action.

Now since one of the most important questions to come before a new board must be that of the long-term programs of procurement for air-force naval and commercial needs, we suggested that a study of this should be inaugurated. Meanwhile, in order to bring the many government agencies now concerned with aviation into some semblance of accord, the President had appointed an informal group called the "Air Coordinating Committee," an organization which included the Assistant Secretaries for Air of the War, Navy, and Commerce Departments. This committee now initiated a study by the Harvard School of Business Administration, to determine the absolute minimum of aircraft production of all types under which an aircraft industry might exist. Such an industry must, of course, keep in the forefront of world technological progress and be capable of rapid expansion in times of emergency. As the keystone of air commerce and air forces, the public interest seemed to require at least a minimum industry. The report, when finally issued, clearly indicated the vital need for a long-term, continuing program that would correlate all needs, public and private, and it specified the size of a minimum program in pounds of air frames to be built each year.

In order to remove any misunderstanding as to the character of our association we had earlier changed our name to the Aircraft Industries Association of America, and to help direct our public-opinion work, we employed skilled public relations counsel. From them we learned that one of the first steps in creating public opinion is to bring your case before writers and speakers everywhere whose comments and opinions command public respect. One method of accomplishing this is for industry speakers to address public gatherings, where writers and speakers are in attendance, and to bring a message that will command sufficient attention to warrant comment by the public press. Our air-policy program contained such a message and it now devolved upon me to carry the message to Garcia.

Time was, in this land of ours, when public speakers were few and far between; today they are many and underfoot. When any organization decides to hold an annual dinner, it must first recruit a speaker whose name may attract enough customers to help the dinner committee break even. And since the audience are themselves all public speakers, they will be less interested in what the speaker has to say, and more in how he says it; a new technique or a new story is of unusual interest. Having had no other training in public speaking than that which goes along with standing in front of a squad of bluejackets and selling them on hitting the target, my technique was informal, conversational, and flowing. I might have memorized and carefully prepared my extemporaneous address, but I tried not to reveal the fact. And when, after giving my air-power theme the particular twist that belonged with the particular audience, some of them came up to congratulate me, I soon discovered that few ever remembered the words, though some recalled the music. With this in mind, it is often more effective to slant the speech at the newsmen or the newsreaders; the listening audience is only waiting to get it over with anyway—even as you and I.

Meanwhile our several companies used their own resources to carry our story to their own localities where workers and businessmen were interested in the survival of the enterprise. Some of this, as Speaker Rayburn had foreseen, percolated back to Washington whether in the form of resolutions by various farm, labor, or business organizations, or just by letter or word of mouth. And so, with the hand of some government aviation agencies against us, we were encouraged by the reception given us by a group of senators and representatives who had come to dinner.

At an informal affair arranged to introduce our company presidents to some of the leaders in Congress on aeronautical matters, men who had previously known each other by name only, we divided our guests among small tables at each of which one of our presidents acted as host. Afterward, we called on our guests to speak to us and to our surprise found the burden of their discourse to be something like this: "You fellows have sold the public on air power, what do you think we ought to do about it?" In reply we pointed out that the whole problem was too complex for us; neither we nor anyone else could have the answers. We thought the matter deserved an airing before a public commission like the presidential advisory committee of twenty years ago.

Concrete action along these lines was forthcoming at the instigation of an able senator, Mr. Hugh B. Mitchell, from my native state of Washington. As chairman of a subcommittee of the Senate Military Affairs Committee, one that contained a number of outstanding men, the senator began conducting hearings on the subject. Our company presidents who appeared before this committee to present our case were much impressed by the fact that committee members attended the hearings and took an active interest in the problem. Before going back home to stand for reelection, Senator Mitchell introduced a bill calling for the appointment of a board to be constituted along the lines of the old Morrow Board. When the senator failed of reelection in the Republican year of 1947, a Democratic colleague, able Senator Brian MacMahon of my own state of Connecticut, reintroduced the Mitchell bill. Not to be outdone in courtesy, Republican Senator Brewster of Maine introduced the Brewster bill, one that differed from the MacMahon bill in that it provided for a purely Congressional committee.

From this point forward, matters dragged interminably. Most of us manufacturers, sold on our own doctrine, had now moved into the design and production of new transport aircraft intended to replace the war-weary war surplus. In United Aircraft, for instance, we had undertaken to expand the power output and increase the dependability of our current commercial engines and had at the same time inaugurated a wholly new engine, a twenty-eight-cylinder Wasp Major with a capacity of 4,360 cubic inches and an initial rating of 3,000 horsepower. This was over three times the cylinder displacement of the original Wasp but over seven times the power output, with possibilities of reaching ten times that output. It was expected to cost ten million dollars for development alone, or some ten times the original investment in Pratt and Whitney at the inception of the Wasp production.

Around these new models and the competitive engines under development by our rivals, Wright Aeronautical, the airplane manufacturers had gone overboard on new transports designed to carry increased loads at greatly reduced costs, and at much higher speed. All these companies appreciated the risks involved, but faith in the future of air transport justified to them the investment of their war earnings in the expansion of American air power. And this faith might have been justified had we been able to bring about the formulation of a dynamic national air policy, for the designs were sound in conception and well executed.

But now as time passed without concrete action, both air-transport and aircraft production drifted into severe difficulties. Save for a curious chain of circumstances, it is unlikely that the aircraft industry could have survived the long wait for an air policy board. Following the resignation of Charles E. Wilson, the great president of General Electric, from the War Production Board where he had been a bulwark of strength, and the subsequent departure of Donald Nelson, Julius Krug became chairman. By that time reconversion had become a live subject and a young lawyer on Cap Krug's staff, Mort Wilner by name, had become much exercised over the threatened extinction of the aircraft industry. While, under existing law, cessation of hostilities would automatically cancel all aircraft-production contracts, a provision in Section 102 of the Reconversion Act authorized the President to continue such contracts as could be shown to be clearly in the public interest. At Mort Wilner's suggestion I took John E. P. Morgan, able manager of the association, and called on Cap Krug to suggest that he obtain in advance a list from the War and Navy Departments of such contracts as could be shown to be in that category, and hold it in readiness against an emergency.

Thus it happened that when President Truman returned from Potsdam, Cap Krug gave John Snyder a letter for the President's signature, which John Snyder carried to Norfolk with him. In this letter addressed to the Secretaries of War and Navy, the President directed that the specific contracts primarily connected with research and development be continued in effect. On this slender thread the aircraft industry subsisted until Congress could make appropriations for a temporary program.

Meanwhile with both the aircraft manufacturers and the transport operators hanging on the ropes, a fortunate break occurred. Maj. Gen. Oliver P. Echols, United States Air Force, returned from duty with the military government in Germany and asked for retirement. Oliver had been to the Air Force Matériel Command what Admiral Moffett had been to BUAERO. Having lacked any interest in personal publicity, his name was not widely known, but his achievements had long been recognized by all those in a position to appreciate them. In a way he was reminiscent of the old aviation story about Charlie Lawrance, designer of Lindbergh's Wright Whirlwind engine. When asked why he had received so little recognition, Charlie is reported to have asked, "Whoever heard of Paul Revere's horse?" Now Oliver Echols had the qualities required of the president of the Aircraft Industries Association. He had the respect of the industry, the Air Force, and the Navy; he knew aviation; he was familiar with the routine of Washington; he had the respect of legislators; he was in sympathy with the principles of the association; and finally, because he had zeal for air power, he was willing to accept the appointment, though tired by arduous service.

Meanwhile, in an effort to crystallize opinion as to air policy, I had published a book called *Air Power for Peace*, which was issued early in 1945. Patterned on Mahan's method, this little book reviewed the history of aviation and appraised the impact of air power upon the war. And though history was still in the making and available only in censored headlines, the conclusions drawn in the book were later supported by the reports of the postwar Strategic Bombing Surveys. In light of the extravagant claims that had been made for aviation, it was necessary to keep the book wholly objective and, therefore, like Mahan, hard reading.

The outstanding conclusion drawn from this study was the important place air transport had held in the war. When the sea had been blockaded by enemy submarines, air transport had retained freedom of movement. With the Japanese in control of sea communications to China, air transport had hurdled the Himalayan Hump. With access by sea to Europe and Africa denied by German submarines, air transport, even though hastily improvised, had not only surmounted the barrier, but had become in fact the safest, cheapest, and often the only means of communication. Important persons and critical materials were delivered at critical points often just in time to exercise decisive influence on the outcome.

This fact was the result of the mobility of the airplane. On the ground, where movement can take place in but two dimensions and is often restricted by physical obstacles, blockade is relatively simple. At sea, where movement is still in two dimensions, obstructions are fewer and blockade is more difficult. In the air, where movement is three dimensional, and fixed obstructions few, effective blockade becomes almost impossible. And since freedom of communication is vital to security, the basic strategy in both war and peace is to guarantee freedom of communication to one's self and to deny it to an enemy. This must be the beginning and end of foreign policy and the basis of strategy in both war and peace. The actual performance of air transport in World War II therefore becomes one of the most vital factors of modern times. By comparison, the atom bomb is a dangerous explosive; air transport is a new key to economic, social, and military security.

While writing *Air Power for Peace*, I had been impressed by the need for presenting this point of view in another manner. In the case of sea power, Mahan, the historian, had deduced the lessons of history. But Hakluyt, the author, had helped create the history that Mahan recorded three hundred years later. Born in England, somewhere around 1553, Hakluyt had been depressed by the backwardness of his people. While on a visit to the Temple, his uncle had shown him a map of the world and had given him "a lesson in geography," which had inspired him to "prosecute that knowledge and kind of literature." After studying languages so as to be able to read whatsoever printed or written discoveries and voyages he found extant in many lands, he made himself acquainted with the chiefest captains at sea, the greatest merchants, and the best mariners. Hearing other nations extolled for their discoveries and notable enterprises, and depressed by the sluggishness of the English and their neglect of the opportunities afforded them, he undertook to edit the original journals and narratives with a view to showing that in sea power lay the means for abolishing squalor and poverty in England. Today Richard Hakluyt's *The English Voyages* is one of the English classics.

Having in mind the possibility of utilizing his method for the air-power story, I looked around for material. However, Americans seldom pause to record their observations, as did the explorers and merchants of the pre-Elizabethan era, and I was forced to fall back on my own experience.

Fortunately, this had been varied and I had played in the backfield of a number of Bowl games. The air-power story might be told from my own point of view.

Decision to undertake this, plus a number of other circumstances, including a visit to a hospital, prompted me to resign from business. In order to approach the task objectively, I found it necessary to detach myself from active operations. Since we had long ago laid the groundwork for bringing a younger generation into the picture, nothing seemed to stand in the way.

With the passage of time, the situation in aviation became more critical. Then at the moment when both air transport and aircraft production showed staggering losses, we got an unexpected assist from the Bear That Walks Like A Man. When he began showing his claws, a great public clamor arose in the United States and was quickly heard by sensitive Washington ears. Whatever the politicians may have missed about air power, the American people knew the answer. On July 22, 1947, the United States Congress passed an act to provide for the establishment of a temporary Congressional Aviation Policy Board. Four days earlier, on the eighteenth of July, the President appointed his temporary Air Policy Commission. The Congressional Aviation Policy Board, under the chairmanship of Senator Owen Brewster, of Maine, was made up of senators and representatives. The President's Air Policy Commission, under the chairmanship of Mr. Thomas K. Finletter, consisted of the chairman and four civilians. Now where we had asked for one investigation, we got two.

CHAPTER THIRTY-ONE
BEFORE THE BAR OF PUBLIC OPINION

The Finletter Board, convened by the President under date of July 18, 1947, held extensive hearings and on December 30, 1947, submitted its report, "Survival in the Air Age." Like the Morrow Board before it, the Board comprised able and distinguished men, including besides its chairman, Mr. Finletter, its vice-chairman, George P. Baker, and members, Palmer Hoyt, John A. McCone, and Arthur D. Whiteside. Prior to the Board's being convened, a step of far-reaching importance had been taken—the reorganization of the armed forces and the establishment of the Department of Defense, under the able leadership of James V. Forrestal.

Prior to this step, the Aircraft Industries Association had inaugurated an annual conference of its board of governors held in Williamsburg, Virginia, to provide a forum for the interchange of ideas among the representatives of industry and those of government and military services concerned with aeronautics, with a view to acquainting industry and government with each other's problems and responsibilities and to aid in finding solutions to these problems. At the first conference in 1946, it developed that the Army and Navy had become concerned over their faulty public relations and wanted advice and assistance.

Of course their unfavorable press had resulted from the ancient feud still being carried on in the press by Army and Navy over the problem of "integration" and "unification." Behind its façade, the battle was still the same jurisdictional dispute that had agitated Admiral Moffett and General Mitchell back in the early 'twenties. From the industry point of view, the dogfight tended to neutralize our efforts to develop a public understanding of air power in its broad aspects, and the board of governors now asked me to confer with Army, Navy, and Air Force with a view to relieving the situation.

Since the industry had always refrained from participation in the old feud, this mission posed a problem. To me, the arguments against the organization of a separate air force had always outweighed those for it, but I now realized that I had been influenced against the project by the Army's insistence on trying to grab off naval aviation. The record of what had happened in England under the Air Ministry had always stood out in my mind. But now, with commercial air transport coming of age, and with the brilliant record of military and naval air transport in the war, I began to see the problem in a different light. Air transport had opened up a new frontier. If the mission of the ground forces was the defense of the land frontier, and the mission of the seaborne forces was the defense of the sea frontier, then, logically, the mission of the air force must be the defense of the air frontier. The key to the problem was the advent of commercial air transport.

Pursuing this idea further, I came to the conclusion that our thinking had been confused by two unsound concepts. First, we had tended to organize the military on the basis of types of weapons or vehicles, and second, we had looked at the airplane as a weapon instead of a vehicle. Clearly, if the ground, sea, and air forces were to be held responsible for the defense of their frontiers, then each must have the implements essential to the discharge of that responsibility, and must have full authority over their design, development, and use. The ground, sea, and air forces must each have the aircraft necessary to the discharge of their responsibilities. The air is an ocean that gives uninterrupted access to every corner of the land and every reach of the sea. The air force is charged with responsibility for keeping the airlanes open to aerial commerce and should be provided with the ground or sea transport necessary to that job, but by the same token the ground and sea forces must develop and control all the instruments they require to perform their functions. And aside from the sound basis for this concept that lies in logic, the record is clear that it is equally sound in practice.

With this idea clarified in my own mind, I called on Vice Adm. de Witt C. Ramsey, Vice Chief of Naval Operations, and later on Gen. Carl Spaatz, Commander, United States Army Air Force, to sound them out on this concept as a solution to the conflict. In the Navy, Vice Adm. Forrest Sherman, when called in by Admiral Ramsey, pointed out that this was the traditional position of the Navy but that they had been forced to fight to retain their own aviation. However, Vice Adm. Arthur Radford, the Deputy Chief of Naval Operations for Air, looked at the matter somewhat differently. He saw the Naval Air Force as a mobile air force, one, to quote Admiral Moffett, "able to go anywhere on the backs of the fleet." The Army Air Force, anchored as it was, to the ground, was less mobile. From the Army's point of view, the vulnerability of the carrier to submarine attack compromised its usefulness. And here, I found, lay the nubbin of a great conflict of opinion. For my part, this difference of opinion was not one to be resolved on theoretical grounds alone. Our whole experience showed how dangerous it was to take decisions, especially those involving the national security, on the basis of prejudice or partisanship. The only safe course was to pursue both developments with an open mind and be ready to adapt either or both in support of national policy.

General Spaatz, after our interesting discussion, suggested that I call on Mr. Stuart Symington, Assistant Secretary of War for Air, and lay these ideas before him, in the hope of contributing something to the solution of the ancient dispute. I did so, but was disappointed. Mr. Symington, recalling my old Navy background, apparently recognized in me a trojan horse, a partisan bent on dividing the Army and its Air Force so that the Navy might defeat both in detail. Wholly unprepared for this novel reception, I was forced to retire in disorder. As time passed, however, it became clear that my one-man foray in the role of interservice peacemaking had not been without result. After my visit with "Duke" Ramsey, Secretary Forrestal abandoned his opposition to autonomy for the Air Force and supported reorganization along lines recommended to him by Ferdinand Eberstadt. That my visit may have helped tilt the scales in favor of unification is indicated in a letter to me from Jim Forrestal dated August 4, 1947, in which he said, "Your thinking and mine has had an evolution which has been more or less in phase."

A few months later, prior to the publication of the report of the Finletter Board, I discussed with the secretary some of the problems he faced in his effort to get agreement among the military with respect to a long-term program for aircraft procurement, development, and research. He expressed deep concern over the implications of the many major decisions he was called on to make in areas where no precedent or experience existed and asked me if I were in a position to help him.

To men like Jim Forrestal who understood the principles of war, catch phrases like "strategic bombing" and "unification" aroused deep concern. The first phrase overemphasized that doubtful tactic of indiscriminate bombing of nonmilitary objectives, and obscured the decisive character of such real strategic bombing as the assault on the Ploesti oil fields which brought German transport to a clanking halt. The second phrase screened a dangerous drift toward such a national general staff as had cost Germany two wars. Earnest students, fearing a dominant Air Force, leaned toward the opposite idea that the Ground Forces, like the Navy, must control its own air arm. Civilians like myself hoped to see such fundamental questions of national policy resolved by an informed public opinion through an air policy commission, but such was not to be. What might have been a decisive moment in history proved but another victory for the Douhet doctrine.

Even though Congress had supposedly integrated the armed forces by the time the Finletter Commission convened, the interservice feud raged worse than ever. The Board was unable to draw from Defense Secretary Forrestal any concrete program for aircraft procurement; the Chiefs of Staff had not been able to agree on one. Thus died the first objective of the manufacturing industry's air-power program.

However, when the Air Force took the stand before the Board, Stuart Symington, now its secretary, moved swiftly and decisively to the attack with a concrete recommendation for a "seventy group" air force. Out of his forceful presentation came ultimately appropriations by Congress which proved to be the salvation of the aircraft manufacturing industry. Congress, fully alive to the role of the aircraft industry in national security, was largely motivated by considerations of preservation of the establishment.

The air-transport people, shoved into the background by superior showmanship, made a sorry presentation. It had fine leadership in Adm. Jerry Land, its president, and in two vice-presidents, Bob Ramspeck and Milton Arnold. But its membership was torn by dissension over that time-worn conflict, the "chosen instrument." President Juan Trippe, whose creation of the great Pan American Airways system is one of the shining examples of inspired leadership in private enterprise, favored the policy of a single overseas American-flag airline, as the only means of competing with foreign, government-owned, or subsidized air lines. Other operators strongly opposed this concept as constituting a monopoly, and favored the system of "reasonable regulation" as practiced with domestic airlines.

This fundamental issue, long bitterly fought behind the scenes, had previously burst into the open at Chicago during the first meeting of the International Civil Aviation Conference. The United States State Department, ably represented by Adolphe Berle, had fought hard for the "five freedoms," a modern counterpart of the old doctrine of freedom of the seas. Against the powerful opposition of certain foreign governments, notably that of Great Britain, the United States, weakened by the inner controversy, had been forced to settle for three of its five freedoms. This same issue now confused the Air Transport Association's presentation before the Finletter Board. On this rock, a second great objective of the inquiry, an investigation of the reasonableness of regulation, was scuttled.

After exhaustive inquiry, the Finletter Board recommended numerous improvements as to policy in its report "Survival in the Air Age." The Congressional Aviation Policy Board, after waiting for this report, issued its findings on March 1, 1948, in a joint-committee print entitled "National Aviation Policy." But with echoes of Hiroshima still ringing in the ears of the investigators, air force displaced air commerce in top billing. The Congressional Board held frankly that a strong, stable, and modern civil aviation component is essential to air power for national security and that domestic and foreign commerce of the United States should be promoted by whatever means appear most practical until it reaches such stature in passenger and cargo capacity as to constitute in a crisis an adequate logistical arm of the national defense establishment. In other words, air commerce exists to support the armed forces. We in the aircraft industry had naïvely insisted that it must be the other way around. With the Congressional Committee's profound observation on the place of civil air transport in air power, and its denial of the first premise of the aircraft industry's air-power policy, we lost our third great objective.

While appropriations for military aircraft served momentarily to preserve the manufacturing industry and keep the military establishment from further deterioration, funds were forthcoming only on a hand-to-mouth basis. So long as Stalin continued pressure on Europe, Congress would appropriate; the moment he eased up, Congress would revoke. The essential long-term continuing program so necessary to technological progress went by the board. Even Representative Carl Vinson, whose vision had built the Navy of World War II and whose leadership had implemented the aviation programs, seemed unable to formalize a program to put into effect this generally accepted principle. Adding up the results of five years' effort, the Aircraft Industries Association had to admit failure to reach its goal. To me the reason was abundantly clear. We had failed to enlist the cooperation of the armed forces and airline transport operators under the basic precept of cooperation in public policy and competition in operations.

CHAPTER THIRTY-TWO
THE HAND ON THE STICK

Early in 1949 the Interstate and Foreign Commerce Committee of the Senate, under the chairmanship of Senator Edwin C. Johnson of Colorado, began inquiring into the ills of the airline transport industry. Senator Johnson had sat at my table at the dinner given by the aircraft manufacturers to Congressional leaders in aviation in Washington some five years earlier. A man well informed on the whole subject, he now began directing an inquiry that promised to initiate an important forward step in the formulation of American air policy. Unlike the Finletter Commission and the Congressional Aviation Policy Board, both of which had been held under the overcast produced by the cold front of fear incident to the Berlin crisis, the Johnson inquiry, following close on the brilliant success of the Berlin Airlift, focused attention solely on airline transport.

Curiously enough, the underlying significance of the Berlin Airlift was seldom touched upon in the flood of commentary that accompanied the lifting of the blockade. While it was generally recognized as a defeat for the Soviet, and served to ease the tensions and allay the fears of war, the epochal character of the operation went almost unrecognized. Paul Fisher, in the *Bee Hive*, house organ for United Aircraft Corporation, in a brilliant article written on the spot, hailed the victory of air freight. For the first time in world history, commercial air transports—not combat aircraft—had spearheaded United States foreign policy in a victorious action against the swashbuckling Soviet. The very forces which had once reduced Berlin to rubble with bombs had now saved the population from starvation with air cargo.

Meanwhile, rapid progress in the development of guided missiles had raised the question of the future of the airplane as a major weapon carrier. Some strictly military manufacturers had already begun giving serious consideration to the problem of whether to continue to specialize in aircraft or to shift over to the development of guided missiles. And once experimental aircraft had exceeded the speed of sound, some began to wonder if that velocity might not one day mark the division between combat aircraft and those designed for commercial purposes. In other words the Johnson Committee began its hearings against the background of a changing weather map.

Airline testimony before the Committee revealed some wide divisions within the transport industry itself. Captain Eddie Rickenbacker for example blamed the ills of the airlines on "too much coddling and wet nursing," while Carleton Putnam ascribed them to "slow starvation." The individual outlook reflected the color of the financial statement. And the airline operators, in making their "policy" recommendations, seldom came to grips with fundamentals but focused their attentions on revisions of administrative procedure. In this respect they reflected their long association with government agencies to whom policy so often means the detailed management of public affairs rather than a course of conduct. If the airline operators' recommendations seemed slanted toward measures calculated to advance the special interests of their individual companies, the fact was entirely understandable.

To us aircraft manufacturers who, five years earlier, had covenanted to cooperate in the public interest where policy was concerned, while continuing to compete with each other in operations to our own—and likewise—the public interest, it appeared that a precarious existence under government economic regulation had blinded the operators to the broad public interest, and hence, to their own enlightened self-interest. Leaning on government for a guarantee of their economic security, they competed with each other for legislative or administrative advantage, and primarily before Congressional committees or government agencies. And if some of them made forays into politics and acted more like rusty railroad executives than like jet-propelled pioneers, it was in keeping with the principles under which they operated.

Yet out of the confusion of conflicting testimony it was possible, by keeping in mind certain fundamentals learned from the history of aviation, to arrive at certain conclusions. The airline operators for all their controversies were unanimous on at least two points: they endorsed the principle of "reasonable regulation" upon which the Civil Aeronautics Act had been founded, and they condemned the administration of the Act by the Civil Aeronautics Board.

Yet in the face of the airlines' unanimous approval of the Act, an objective study of the testimony raises a serious question as to its soundness. Sifting out the wheat from the chaff, one could not help wondering whether Solomon himself, with the aid of all of his wives, could have administered such a document. Providing as it does for economic regulation of privately owned industries by political appointees, the Act flies in the face of the fundamental fact that politics and economics function under different basic precepts; in the one the ballot box calls the turn, in the other the cold arithmetic of an inescapable financial statement. But if the airlines' endorsement of "reasonable regulation" proved open to question, the testimony before the Committee left no doubt that recent regulation had been, in fact, wholly unreasonable.

It developed that the Civil Aeronautics Board had cut the mail rates in 1945 to a point well below the actual cost of transporting the mail. Furthermore it had authorized widespread duplication of existing services and had subsidized these duplicating services in competition with those already established. And when this action resulted in crippling losses, the Board compounded its blunder by making retroactive increases in mail which had the effect of putting the whole rate structure on a cost-plus basis. Captain Eddie Rickenbacker, of Eastern Airlines, voiced the position of the "Big Four" when he said, "The confused state of mail rates destroys all incentive for economy and efficiency—it discourages good management and high performance. It puts a penalty on accomplishment, and rewards the wasteful and inefficient."

Another diagnosis of the airline ills was offered by Harold A. Jones, a member of the Civil Aeronautics Board itself, when speaking before the San Francisco Advertising Club. The airlines, he thought, were ill from a "mysterious disease known as 'subsiditis,'" which disease he ranked "somewhere between bubonic plague and leprosy." However his shotgun diagnosis lacked clinical confirmation before the Senate Committee by his boss, Joseph J. O'Connell, Jr., chairman of the Civil Aeronautics Board.

"We are not in a position," testified Mr. O'Connell, "to give an accurate estimate as to the amount of the total air-mail pay bill which represents fair compensation for the carriage of the mail, and that portion that represents subsidy."

Postmaster General Donaldson agreed with the Board chairman and stated that the Post Office had long held the opinion that the mail rate, if shorn of its subsidy elements, should not in any case be greater than the passenger rate. On this basis the Post Office Department would have been credited with approximately one-half its present transportation expenditures inasmuch as passengers were paying approximately 50 cents per ton mile, while the Post Office was paying more than double that amount. This over-all figure, of course, obscured the wide variations between the compensations paid airlines thought to be self-sufficient and the much larger payments to those known to be heavily subsidized.

In the absence of even the most elementary data it is difficult to see how any regulation could be called reasonable or how the government could support any subsidy charge either against the industry as a whole or against any segment of it. The situation was further obscured by the Postmaster General's estimate of the total domestic and foreign air-mail subsidy for this year.

Using the excess of the cost of the service to the Post Office Department over the department's air-mail revenues, he arrived at the figure of $35,000,000. The cost to the department included of course all expenses allocated to air mail including department overhead, but it did not substantiate the reasonableness of any allocation. Under questioning by one of the senators of the Committee, this all inclusive definition of "subsidy" was discounted. Under business accounting principles the figure might have been labeled "deficit" and would have been charged against the Post Office rather than pinned on the airlines as a "subsidy." After all, the Post Office Department overhead, an item perhaps more political than economic in character, was not subject to airline control and was therefore the responsibility of the department. A subsidy is a public grant or subvention to aid an enterprise for the public convenience and not the deficit of a government department.

In the face of such fuzzy accounting the figure is interesting chiefly because of its small size. The Postmaster General, after referring to statistical exhibits, reported the total deficit incurred from the inauguration of the first air-mail service in 1918 up to 1948 as a little over three and one-half million dollars per year for the thirty-year period and added, "Probably no investment made by this government ever returned greater national benefits in commercial and cultural progress, and national security. The over-all value of air transportation system to the nation, particularly as an arm of defense, has been incalculable."

It is interesting in passing to compare the air-mail deficit with others submitted by the Postmaster General: penny postcards, $57,000,000; fourth-class mail, $82,000,000; third-class mail, $139,000,000; and second-class mail, $237,000,000—a total of $515,000,000. And so the air-mail deficit is but one of many and the least of them all. On the basis of such approximations as have been presented by government agencies, the airlines might have argued that by absorbing a portion of the vast overhead of the Post Office Department they were actually "subsidizing" other types of mail service.

In light of the dearth of figures that would indicate an approximation to the true air-mail subsidy, if any, Carleton Putnam, of Chicago and Southern, made an exhaustive analysis of government cost records, during which he checked his assumptions with responsible persons in the government. This indicated that from the inception of the air mail down to the year 1948, the postal revenues had exceeded the added costs of air mail to the Post Office by some $54,000,000. Summing up for the Committee, in a statement which was not challenged by the government, he testified, "Hence the American taxpayer has not only gained the greatest air transportation system on earth ... plus an adjunct to the national defense which would otherwise have cost him untold millions to provide—he is $54,000,000 ahead in cash as well."

And after charging the airlines for their share of the cost of building and maintaining the nation's airways and airports, an expenditure which would in any case have had to be made for the Army and Navy, the airlines would still owe the taxpayer but $61,000,000, all of which relates to maintaining the national airways system. Furthermore this clear demonstration that the air mail has not been subsidized comes in the face of grievous blunders by the Civil Aeronautics Board in certifying uneconomic competing services at extravagant mail rates.

One of the most extreme cases of this kind was reported by Captain Eddie Rickenbacker. The Civil Aeronautics Board had in the past two years certified twenty-one "feeder lines," some of which had been authorized to divert mail poundage from some stations which Eastern had served for twenty years without subsidy, and to charge ten times as much to transport the same mail between the same points. In other words, the Civil Aeronautics Board, impelled by some sense of political necessity to provide competition for the major airlines, had in effect forced them to subsidize competition for themselves. Meanwhile the government had paid such niggardly rates to others that the stockholders of the enterprises had been forced to subsidize the United States.

Such "reasonable" regulation had reduced the airlines from their once proud state of self-sufficiency to a critical status, and at the very moment when their futures should have looked the brightest.

"There can be little doubt," stated the chairman of the Civil Aeronautics Board, "that if our airline system were today the same size as it was in 1941 in terms of routes, points served, and service provided, it would be completely independent of government support." It was certain additions to the service, he further pointed out, and the fixing of certain "fair" compensations by the Board that slowed all airlines save Eastern down to stalling speed and all but put them into a flat spin. He shared his responsibility with the appropriation committees of Congress and thought that if funds were provided for an adequate staff the Board might do a competent job. However the fact that the Civil Aeronautics Authority and Civil Aeronautics Board already had

18,000 employees as compared with approximately 80,000 employees for all domestic and overseas scheduled airlines rather discounted this opinion.

That the damage did not end with heavy losses imposed by arbitrary rates but was multiplied by the award of retroactive payments is evidenced in the testimony of Roger F. Murray, vice-president of the Bankers Trust Company of New York.

"The Board's thinking," he said, "has apparently been that rates should be set so that *each* carrier will break even and perhaps earn some so-called 'fair' rate of return on it's 'used and useful investment.' Under these circumstances, enlarged payments have been made to rescue some airlines in difficulties or keep others going on a subsistence basis. While this may be reassuring to creditors of the airlines, it is the poorest kind of an appeal to potential purchasers of equity securities."

Translating this into lay language, the private investor or his agents just cannot be interested in buying stock in enterprises which are suffering economic regulation by political agencies. And once an enterprise is denied access to the highly competitive markets for risk capital, it is indeed on the verge of bankruptcy or about to crash into the abyss of nationalization. And if the government, after having reduced the market value of the airlines by its own mismanagement, then takes possession of them, it becomes guilty of expropriating the capital of private investors, some of whom had risked their savings in an enterprise they deemed secure because it was government regulated.

Now mismanagement of the airlines was not necessarily the fault of wicked or even stupid men. As Speaker Sam Rayburn had pointed out to me in the case of Congressmen, government administrators are no smarter nor more stupid than the average. But they hold their jobs by knowing which side their bread is buttered on and making the correct estimate of what action will produce the most votes.

The Civil Aeronautics Board, in light of current public opinion with respect to the profit motive, could hardly be expected to accept public responsibility for such economic regulation as would permit any airline to make a profit, especially one such as might be subject to political attack. Nor could it be expected to muster courage to defend such an apparent monopoly as its own route pattern had created, even though the law authorized it. Although the Board was directed to so administer the Act as to prevent "unfair or destructive practices," it must permit "competition to the extent necessary to insure sound development of an air transportation system properly adapted to the needs of the foreign and domestic commerce of the United States, of the Postal Service, and the national defense." Its decisions, predicated on an attempt to administer such complex mandates and still keep out of hot water, brought the airlines into jeopardy at the very moment when they had established their economic self-sufficiency and faced the brightest futures of their turbulent careers. In other words, economic regulation by political agency is an anachronism.

Meanwhile, with the real solution to the Board's competition problem ready at hand, the Board even messed that up. This drama was unfolded before the Committee by a group of enterprising young veterans who, having participated in such wartime miracles as the transportation of air cargo over the Himalayan Hump, had concluded that this and other services as yet unexploited by the certificated passenger carriers offered unique opportunities for their postwar reconversion. Perhaps the gist of their testimony can be extracted from the statement of Amos E. Heacock, executive committee chairman of the National Independent Carriers, and president of Air Transport Associates.

"Let me review briefly," he said, "the near miracles that have been wrought in the development of air transportation by United States veterans.... In the international contract air carrier field, Transocean Airlines, Seaboard and Western, Pacific Overseas Airlines, etc., have found an entirely new market for air transportation, formerly practically untouched by the scheduled airlines.... I want to point out to you an additional and perhaps the greatest air transportation feat performed by the veterans of World War II. I am referring to the amazing record of the Pacific Northwest-Alaska nonscheduled carriers.... The scheduled carriers that were subsidized to do the job of developing air transportation to Alaska were a miserable failure. The bulk of the cargo, 73.6 per cent of the northbound and 83.5 per cent of the southbound, was transported by the much maligned nonscheduled air carriers.... The records show that the non-skeds pioneered a wealth of new business."

After referring to Section 2(d) of the Act, which provides for competition, the witness stated, "With an unprecedented opportunity to preserve competition to develop the air transportation system and so provide adequate and economical service, the Board's actions have provided for just the reverse."

One explanation of the Board's action might be derived from the statement of C. R. Smith, chairman of American Airlines, one of the largest of the "Big Four."

"If the law of the land is to be enforced against the certificated air carriers," he said, "it should have similar enthusiasm of enforcement against the irregular carriers who compete directly for the same business of air transportation. We cannot live with economic health in an atmosphere half legal and half illegal. If this business is to be regulated, all should be regulated." It would be interesting to know just what significance attaches to the use of the word "against" in this statement.

"If the Civil Aeronautics Act is to mean but little," continued "C.R.," "then let us return to the rules of the road which obtained before the Act was passed, when competition was direct and unregulated." Had "C.R." gone on to urge this course, he might have given a demonstration of the rugged individualism for which he is credited; instead he summed up, "We were in favor of the Act, we are in favor of the continuation of the Act, but if we are to abide by the terms of the Act, we ask that our competitors be bound by the same rules of public conduct."

Juan Trippe, president of the Pan American Airways System, stated the issue in similarly clear terms:

"The fundamental problem, both domestically and internationally, is that although Congress intended to place the airline industry in the category of regulated public utilities, the airlines, while treated on one hand as public utilities, have, at the same time, been made subject to all of the competitive pressures proper and appropriate only in an unregulated industry. There is no precedent in American industry that I know of for such a Dr. Jekyll and Mr. Hyde arrangement."

After developing the principles under which public utilities are regulated and financed and suggesting that Congress should make up its mind as to whether or not they want to return the airline industry to its intended status as a regulated airline industry, Juan, like "C.R.," mentioned the alternative of eliminating the relative provisions of the Civil Aeronautics Act and exposing the airlines to the full competitive force which exists and should exist in ordinary commerce.

"There will be no real progress in the solution of the airline problems," he summed up, "until this issue is met squarely. An airline can't be a regulated public utility and a free enterprise at the same time."

However, the witness did not waste further time on this alternative but, acting on the assumption that the doctrine of regulating the airlines as a public utility would be preserved, went on to develop his own case with all the unique persuasiveness that had helped him pioneer Pan American in one of the most impressive displays of self-reliance, individual initiative, and private enterprise of modern times. His discussion led up naturally to the merger of Pan American with American Overseas Airlines which he and "C.R." had earlier submitted to the Civil Aeronautics Board. In justifying this, Juan expounded his well-known thesis of the "chosen instrument" advocating a government policy of maintaining one American-flag system—Pan American Airways—in the international field, supported with frank outright subsidies such as those paid under the Merchant Marine Act of 1936. He justified his position by citing its benefits to the stockholders of the company and argued that the higher wages thus made available to American workmen employed in international aviation would constitute a subsidy to them.

With the major certificated airlines mobilized solidly in support of the "chosen instrument" policy, the Committee received a clear statement of the opposing point of view from Raymond A. Norden, president of Seaboard and Western Airlines, Inc. One of the independents who had been characterized by Captain Eddie Rickenbacker as "irregulars," "latecomers," "interlopers," "pretenders," and so forth, Mr. Norden undertook to support Eddie's contention that the airlines were suffering from too much coddling. In perhaps the outstanding statement to be made to the Committee, he put his finger on the crux of the airline controversy.

"The Civil Aeronautics Act of 1938," he said, "is unusual among regulatory statutes in one very important respect. Other forms of transportation have not customarily been subjected to comprehensive regulation until the pattern of growth has been assured and until the industry has become so highly developed competitively that there is need for rigid controls and restraints in order to prevent destructive practices." Out of the background of the airplane story to date, one might argue the other way around, namely that once the rigid controls and restraints are imposed, the growth pattern becomes stabilized. Mr. Norden went on to argue with persuasion:

"Aviation is relatively a new business. Air freight, as distinguished from other forms of aviation business, is in its infancy. Yet the entire aviation industry is hedged about with red tape, the like of which has never been encountered in any other form of American industry. One has merely to look at legal payments made by some of the certificated carriers. TWA, for example, in 1948 alone, paid a single law firm the sum of $340,000. My own small company spent in excess of $50,000 in legal expense. Sometimes I feel as though I had more lawyers than pilots."

When the Russians blockaded Berlin in June, 1948, according to the witness, the Air Force, lacking reserve planes, called upon three certificated, subsidized North Atlantic carriers, Pan American, TWA, and American Overseas Airlines, to lift essential material between this country and Germany. Those carriers failed miserably; of the three irregular international carriers called upon to assist, Seaboard and Western lifted more than twice as much tonnage over the North Atlantic in the next six months as Pan American, TWA, and American Overseas combined. Yet under pressure from the certificated carriers, the Civil Aeronautics Board revoked Seaboard's authority to fly under its Letter of Registration, as of May 20, 1949, along with all other large irregular airlines in this country. In his indictment of the certificated carriers the witness said, "In their zeal to keep the air transportation field to themselves and to obviate the chance that a measurement will be set up against their operational efficiency, the North Atlantic carriers are doing a great disservice to the country. To put it bluntly, they are sabotaging the development of airlift which is vital to national security."

Mr. Norden then went on to quote from an article by J. A. Durham and M. J. Feldstein in the *Virginia Law Review* entitled "Regulation as a Tool in the Development of the Air Freight Industry":

"But where an agency is charged with creating new national wealth by developing an infant industry, the consequence of permitting established interests to employ the forms of justice to obstruct the attainment of statutory objectives may well destroy the value of the administrative process."

A less reasoned but even more revealing statement was that of Charles F. Willis, Jr., president of Willis Air Service, Inc., one of the "irregulars":

"Consequently it is with great bitterness that we have seen ourselves singled out by the Civil Aeronautics Board for denial of a certificate of public convenience and necessity.... It is even harder to accept the decision because the only reason we are given for it is that we don't have a million dollars. We never had a million dollars and we never needed a million dollars to perform our operations, but we do have almost all the dollars we started with. We feel that we have successfully demonstrated that an airline can be kept going, at a profit, if hard work, ingenuity, and a desire to make a profit are substituted for lavish spending of other people's money."

In such a sketchy review of the reams of testimony submitted to the Committee it is quite impossible to do more than attempt to summarize the major points of view and try to pan out the nuggets that reveal the vital issues. After sluicing away the rubble and uncovering bed rock, my own impression is largely one of intense sympathy for the Civil Aeronautics Board. Charged with an almost impossible task, it has been subjected to terrific forces by organizations skilled in the art of influencing public opinion. I also come away with a feeling of regret that airline management could not have approached the problem under the precepts adopted by the Aircraft Industries Association.

Most American early birds will recall with a nostalgic smile a cartoon that once adorned the walls of many a pioneer flight school. Entitled "His First Solo," it depicted a forlorn fledgling perched out on the end of a bare limb. Near its root poised an impatient mother bird from whose beak floated the command, "Come on, kid! Give 'er the gun!"

One day, while studying the conflicting testimony of airline operators in an endeavor to predict the next twist of the slipstream, I recalled this early masterpiece of contemporary art. The fledgling on the end of the limb seemed now to have feathered out; he appeared, in fact, almost overgrown. The mother bird cocked her head questioningly, "I wonder if he's got what it takes?"

From the days of Wilbur and Orville Wright on down to the present, aviators have groped for an understanding of the airplane's destiny. Charles A. Lindbergh, in his book *Of Flight and Life*, has stated the problem:

> The tragedy of scientific man is that he has found no way to guide his own discoveries to a constructive end. He has guarded none so carefully that his enemies have not eventually obtained it and turned it against him. He has developed a system in which his security today and tomorrow seems to depend on building weapons which will destroy him the day after. He has become so hypnotized by his search for knowledge that he must go on discovering and experimenting even though it leads to his own annihilation. With the key to science he has turned loose forces which he cannot re-imprison.

In the closing paragraph of his book Lindbergh states, "Our salvation, and our only salvation, lies in controlling the arm of western science by the eternal truths of God."

Igor I. Sikorsky, in *The Invisible Encounter*, goes back two thousand years for his solution. In a chapter called "Kingdoms of the World," he quotes from the Gospel according to Matthew: "Again the devil taketh Him up into an exceeding high mountain, and sheweth Him all the kingdoms of the world, and the glory of them and saith unto Him. All these things will I give Thee, if thou wilt fall down and worship me."

Mr. Sikorsky then goes on to say:

> The crown and recognition as Messiah the king were offered to Christ. But He refused to accept them. However, He offered his spiritual leadership to the whole Jewish nation but his offer was disregarded.... The real cause of the tragedy was the irreconcilable conflict between the Divine ideology

of Christ and the supremely evil spirit of the impending revolution.

After drawing an apt parallel in current history, Mr. Sikorsky remarks, "If the world is to be controlled by spiritually dead men, it is as if an unconscious crew were placed at the controls of an airliner."

Civilization stands today at the same crossroad. It need but accept the proffered leadership to commence an era of spiritual and material progress such as it has not yet known.

A single characteristic differentiates America from all other lands. Ours is a nation created by God-fearing men and women in search of liberty. Liberty is a force more explosive than atomic bombs. It created America. America stands today both as God's living proof of the power of human freedom and as the negation of conflicting human doctrine.

As we have seen from the record, the airplane is one of the miraculous creations of liberty. No result of human foresight or planning, it is a Divine revelation. And though, as yet, largely prostituted to the folly of war, it embodies in itself the potential of world peace and freedom.

For always the hand on the stick has been the Hand of God. The Berlin Airlift, hastily improvised amid the rubble of war, contrived out of dire necessity, uncertainty, and fear, gave the world an American answer to that eternal question, "Am I my brother's keeper?" The unequivocal answer came, not in a rain of destruction but on a flood of life-giving necessities.

"Yes, I am his keeper. I am the keeper of the peace!"

The triumph of the airlift was not one of men and machines but of the Christian spirit.

INDEX

report of,

Congressional committees, public hearings before,

Congressional investigations,

Connecticut State War Finance Committee,

Consolidated Aircraft,

army trainers,

Catalinas,

NY's,

ConsolidatedVultee Aircraft Corporation,

Cook, Capt. Arthur B.,

Coolidge, Calvin,

Cowlflaps,

Coyle, Mr.,

Coyne, Bob,

Crane, Henry,

Curtice, Harlow,

Curtiss, Glenn,

Curtiss Airplane and Motor Company,

Hawks,

TS's,

(*See also* CurtissWright)

Curtiss engines, D's,

R's,

CurtissWright,

(*See also* Wright Aeronautical Corporation; Wright Martin)

CurtissWright Flying Service,

D

Davis, Art,

Davis, Bill,

Davison, F. Trubee,

DC's,

Douhet, General Jiulio,

Douhet doctrine,

DuBose, Lieutenant Commander,

Duralumin,

Durant, William F.,

Durham, J. A.,

E

East Asia Coprosperity Sphere,

East Coast Aircraft War Production Council,

East Haddam Fish and Game Club,

East Hartford, Connecticut,

Eastern Airlines,

Eberstadt, Ferdinand,

Echols, Gen. Oliver P.,

Eclipse Machine Company,

Edgar, Graham,

Egtvedt, Claire,

Engineering,

intuitive,

and politics,

Engineering Thermodynamics,

Engineers, professional,

Engines (*see* Airplane engines)

England (*see* Great Britain)

English Voyages, The,

Ethyl Corporation,

Ethylene glycol,

Export permits,

F

Fagan, Tom,

Fairchild Aviation Corporation,

Farley, James,

Farmington, Long Island,

Fechet, Jim,

Feldstein, M. J.,

Fighter bombers,

longrange,

Fighter planes,

single seat,

twoseated,

Finland,

Finletter, Thomas K.,

Finletter Board,

Finletter Board, report of,

Fireside chat, on airplane production program,

Fisher, Paul,

Five freedoms,

Fleet, Reuben,

FLEET AIR (*see* Aircraft Squadrons, Battle Fleet)

Fletcher, Adm. Frank J.,

Flight Manual,

Flying boats,

Flynn, "Tiny,"

Fokker Anthony,

Fokker Universal,

Ford, Edsel,

Ford, Henry,

Ford Motor Company,

Ford Trimotor,

I

J

K

Kahn, Albert,

Kaiser, Henry J.,

Kansas City, Missouri,

Kartveli, Mr.,

Kauffman, Freddie,

KennedyPurvis, Vice Adm. Sir Charles E.,

Ketcham, "Dixie,"

Kettering, "Boss,"

Keyes, C. M.,

Keyes, Roy,

Keyport, New Jersey,

Kimball, Dr.,

Kindleberger, Dutch,

King, Adm. E. J.,

Kinney Manufacturing Company,

KLM,

Knerr, Hugh,

KNILM,

Knudsen, Bill,

Kraeling, Harry,

Kraus, Comdr. Sidney M.,

Krug, Julius,

L

Labor,

Labor unions,

Lakehurst Naval Air Station,

Lampert, Congressman,

Land, Capt. Emory S.,

Land, Adm. Jerry,

SC's,

TM's,

UO's,

(*See also* Kinds of aircraft, as Bombers)

Nazis,

NC boats,

Nelson, Arvid,

Nelson, Donald,

Neutrality proclamation,

Neville, Leslie,

New Deal,

New Knowledge, The,

New York, New York,

New York Central,

New York Times, The,

Niles Tool Company,

Nimitz, Chester,

Noble, Warren,

Norden, Raymond A.,

Norfolk Naval Air Station,

North American,

North American Mustangs,

North Island Naval Air Station,

Northrup, Jack,

Northrup Company,

NorthrupVought fighter plane,

sold to Japan,

Norway,

NRA,

Nulton, Adm. Louis M.,

Nutt, Arthur,